CIVIL SOCIETY AND TRANSITIONAL JUSTICE IN ASIA AND THE PACIFIC

CIVIL SOCIETY AND TRANSITIONAL JUSTICE IN ASIA AND THE PACIFIC

EDITED BY LIA KENT,
JOANNE WALLIS
AND CLAIRE CRONIN

Australian
National
University

PRESS

PACIFIC SERIES

ANU PRESS

Published by ANU Press
The Australian National University
Acton ACT 2601, Australia
Email: anupress@anu.edu.au

Available to download for free at press.anu.edu.au

ISBN (print): 9781760463281
ISBN (online): 9781760463298

WorldCat (print): 1128153764
WorldCat (online): 1128153731

DOI: 10.22459/CSTJAP.2019

Cover design and layout by ANU Press
Cover photograph by Martine Perret

Contents

Part 1 – Timor-Leste and Indonesia

Part 2 – Cambodia and Myanmar

Part 3 – The Pacific Islands

Abbreviations

ABG	Autonomous Bougainville Government
ACbit	*Associacaon Chega! Ba Ita*
ADHOC	Cambodian Association for Human Rights and Development
AJAR	Asia Justice and Rights
ALFela	*Asistensia Legal Ba Feto no Labarik*
ANTI	National Alliance for an International Tribunal
ASF	Avocats Sans Frontiers
ASSEPOL	Association of Ex-Political Prisoners
BCC	Bougainville Constitutional Commission
BCL	Bougainville Copper Limited
BPA	Bougainville Peace Agreement
BRA	Bougainville Revolutionary Army
CAVR	Commission for Reception, Truth and Reconciliation
CBO	community-based organisation
CDP	Cambodian Defenders Project
CEDAW	Convention on the Elimination of All Forms of Discrimination Against Women
CHRAC	Cambodian Human Rights Action Committee
CJR	Center for Justice and Reconciliation
CNC	*Centro Nasional Chega!*
CPD-RDTL	*Conselho Popular pela Defesa da República Democrática de Timor-Leste*; Popular Council for the Defence of the Democratic Republic of Timor-Leste
CPR	civil party representative

CRA	Conzinc Riotinto of Australia
CRM	*Conselho Revolucionário Maubere;* Maubere Revolutionary Council
CSD	Center for Social Development
CSO	civil society organisation
CTF	Commission for Truth and Friendship
DC-Cam	Documentation Center of Cambodia
DED	German Development Service (later merged into GIZ (German Agency for International Cooperation))
ECCC	Extraordinary Chambers in the Court of Cambodia
EXIM	Export-Import
FALINTIL	*Forças Armadas da Libertação Nacional de Timor-Leste*; Armed Forces for the National Liberation of East Timor
FBO	faith-based organisation
FRETILIN	*Frente Revolucionária de Timor-Leste Independente*; Revolutionary Front for an Independent East Timor
GNUR	Group for National Unity and Reconciliation
ICC	International Criminal Court
ICCPR	International Covenant of Civil and Political Rights
ICESCR	International Covenant on Economic, Social and Cultural Rights
ICRC	International Committee of the Red Cross
ICS	*Instituto de Ciências Sociais*
ICTJ	International Center for Transitional Justice
IFM	Isatabu Freedom Movement
ISMAIK	*Institutu Maun Alin Iha Kristu*; brothers and sisters in Christ
JSMP	Judicial System Monitoring Program
KBC	Kachin Baptist Convention
KIA	Kachin Independence Army
KID	Khmer Institute of Democracy
KIO	Kachin Independence Organisation

KKKHRA	Khmer Kampuchea Krom Human Rights Association
Komnas HAM	*Komisi Nasional Hak Asasi Manusia*; the National Human Rights Commission
LAC	Legal Aid of Cambodia
MEF	Malaitan Eagle Force
MNURP	Ministry for National Unity, Reconciliation and Peace
NGO	non-governmental organisation
NLD	National League for Democracy
OPMT	*Organização Popular de Mulher Timor*; Popular Organisation of Timorese Women
OSJI	Open Society Justice Initiative
PAS	Public Affairs Section
PKI	*Partai Komunis Indonesia*; Indonesian Communist Party
PMG	Peace Monitoring Group
PNG	Papua New Guinea
PNGDF	Papua New Guinea Defence Force
RAMSI	Regional Assistance Mission to Solomon Islands
RANHAM	National Action Plan on Human Rights
RENETIL	*Resistência Nacional dos Estudantes de Timor Leste*
SAP	Structural Adjustment Programme
SCIT	Serious Crimes Investigation Team
SCU	Serious Crimes Unit
SICA	Solomon Islands Christian Association
SSA-South	Shan State Army-South
TISI	Transparency International Solomon Islands
TPA	Townsville Peace Agreement
TPO	Transcultural Psychosocial Organization
TRC	Truth and Reconciliation Commission
UDHR	Universal Declaration of Human Rights
UDT	*União Democrática Timorense*; Timorese Democratic Union

UN	United Nations
UNCRC	United Nations Convention on the Rights of the Child
UNDP	United Nations Development Program
UNOMB	United Nations Observer Mission on Bougainville
UNOPS	United Nations Office for Project Services
UNTAC	United Nations Transitional Authority in Cambodia
UNTAET	United Nations Transitional Administration in East Timor
USDP	Union Solidarity and Development Party
USIS	United States Information Service
VSS	Victims Support Section

Introduction: Civil society and transitional justice in Asia and the Pacific

Lia Kent, Joanne Wallis and Claire Cronin

Over the last two decades, civil society in Asia and the Pacific has played an integral role in debates about transitional justice mechanisms for populations who have experienced violent conflicts or oppressive political regimes. As in other parts of the world, civil society organisations (CSOs) and actors have advocated for the establishment of criminal trials and truth commissions, monitored their operations once established, and pushed for take-up of their recommendations (Brahm 2007). CSOs have also been instrumental in developing community-based responses to address the legacies of mass violence (Hovil and Okello 2011). Many 'local' (national and grassroots) CSOs actively engage with regional and global transitional justice networks to support their work (Boesenecker and Vinjamuri 2011).

Despite these critical roles, there has been surprisingly little examination of the breadth and diversity of civil society transitional justice activity across Asia and the Pacific. This collection addresses this gap through an empirically grounded analysis of this activity in four Asian states—Timor-Leste, Indonesia, Cambodia and Myanmar—and three Pacific contexts—Bougainville (an autonomous region of Papua New Guinea), Solomon Islands and Fiji. It builds upon the rich discussions that took place during an interdisciplinary workshop on the theme of 'Civil Society and Transitional Justice in Asia and the Pacific' held at The Australian Nationanl University in September 2016, which brought together leading and emerging international and Australian scholars working in the field of transitional justice. Workshop discussions ranged across numerous themes, including the roles of faith-based organisations vis-à-vis secular

CSOs in transitional justice; the extent to which gender concerns shape civil society transitional justice efforts; the relationships (and tensions) between CSOs and the state; the influence of donor agendas on CSOs; and the significance of civil society–led transitional justice initiatives (including local reconciliation, art, memorialisation and community media initiatives).

Picking up on these themes, the chapters in this collection provide a nuanced picture of the *heterogeneity* of civil society in Asia and the Pacific. This picture challenges many assumptions about the nature of civil society and its role in transitional justice found in the literature. It illustrates that CSOs can have different – and sometimes competing – priorities, resources and approaches to transitional justice, and that their work may be underpinned by diverse understandings of what constitutes 'justice'. The aim of the collection is not to provide a comprehensive picture of civil society transitional justice activity in Asia and the Pacific (or to define its parameters); rather, it is to shed light on its diversity and on the factors that both enable and constrain certain forms of civil society activity in specific contexts.

In the remainder of this introductory chapter we grapple with the slippery concept of 'civil society'. We consider how the concept of civil society has evolved and its emerging prominence in the discourse and practice of transitional justice. We then highlight two key blind spots that are apparent in the current portrayal of civil society in the transitional justice literature: first, the tendency to view civil society as a homogenous and secular entity, which overlooks the diversity of civil society actors and the significance of institutions grounded in other forms of association, such as kin, ethnicity and faith; and second, the tendency to celebrate civil society as an unqualified good, which downplays the dynamics of power that shape and constrain it. Finally, we provide an overview of the chapters that comprise this collection.

'Civil society': An evolving concept

Civil society is a nebulous, slippery and ill-defined concept (Jeffrey 2013, 107). It is a concept that can potentially be applied to a bewildering range of non-state actors, including but not limited to: non-governmental organisations;[1] associations; church and faith-based groups; trade unions; sporting associations; youth groups; and issue-focused organisations. It can also be applied to actors with varying values, issues of concern, motivating philosophies, financial means and degrees of political, religious and/or ideological motivation. Nonetheless, in the contemporary period, civil society tends to operate as a kind of 'floating signifier' that carries connotations of 'civility and virtue' (Shepherd 2015, 893) and is perceived as operating in the interstices of the state and society.

To help contextualise current understandings of civil society it is useful to examine the historical origins of the concept, which are often said to lie in the late Enlightenment period, with the emergence of the 'secular state' (Jeffery, Kent and Wallis 2017, 381). The seventeenth-century philosophers Hobbes and Grotius emphasised the need for a 'civil' well-ordered society, and for Locke, 'civil' society was indistinguishable from the ideal 'civilised' state, which was set in contrast to primitive and savage societies. A shift occurred in the eighteenth century, when the term 'civil society' became popularised as a way of referring to a sphere of life that was distinctly separate from the state and from religious society (Jeffery, Kent and Wallis 2017, 382). Civil society came to be understood as a means of guarding individual rights against the overuse of power by the state (Glasius, Lewis and Seckinelgin 2004). Voluntary associations were seen to be essential in keeping in check the power of centralised institutions and protecting pluralism (Edwards 2004, 7).

The concept of civil society experienced a resurgence in the 1980s with the end of the Cold War and the collapse of socialism. Political parties and the mass media increasingly invoked the concept of civil society to refer to all forms of voluntary association that had previously been controlled by the state – from sports clubs to national groups (Hann 1996, 45). The concept came to signify 'utopian conditions, of democratic participation and tolerance, the antithesis of totalitarianism' (Hann 1996, 45). The so-called 'third wave' of transitions from authoritarian rule to democracy that took place in Eastern Europe and Latin America gave further force to these ideas (Huntington 1993; Jeffery, Kent and Wallis 2017, 382). The civil societies emerging in these regions

---

1   The terms 'non-governmental organisation' (NGO) and 'civil society organisation' (CSO) are often used interchangeably. However, as the chapters in this collection demonstrate, civil society is a broad concept, while NGOs generally work within an international development or human rights framework. Therefore, we view NGOs as constituting one element of a broader CSO base.

at that time have been 'credited with effective resistance to authoritarian regimes, democratizing society from below while pressuring authoritarians for change' (Foley and Edwards 1996, 38).

Many of the main protagonists of these civil society movements became key players in the debates that began to take place in the field of transitional justice that similarly emerged in the 1980s. In particular, these actors 'brought with them a set of agendas that emphasized, among other priorities, the pursuit of formal state-led responses to human rights violations' (Jeffery, Kent and Wallis 2017, 382). These agendas significantly influenced emerging understandings of 'transitional justice' and the roles of civil society in furthering a transitional justice agenda. The idea of transitional justice came to be equated with legal responses to past violence, including legal accountability for perpetrators of human rights violations, and with legal-institutional reforms that sought to entrench this approach. Civil society came to be conceived as supportive of this agenda, and separate from the state (Jeffery, Kent and Wallis 2017, 383).

While the relationship between transitional justice and civil society was forged in the 1980s, it has continued to evolve as the field of transitional justice has itself evolved. The concerns of transitional justice scholars and practitioners have expanded to encompass not only transitions from authoritarian rule to democracy but also transitions from conflict to peace (Jeffery and Kim 2014, 5). Since the 1990s, transitional justice mechanisms have been increasingly prescribed as part of the United Nations 'tool-kit' for successful post-conflict peacebuilding (Kent 2012, 5; Subotic 2009, 21). And while transitional justice continues to be underpinned by an emphasis on prosecutions, the field has broadened to encompass a much wider range of mechanisms, including truth commissions, institutional reform, vetting processes, customary reconciliation processes, memorialisation, and history curriculum reform. These developments have taken place alongside a growing interest in 'localising' transitional justice, in other words, adapting transitional justice to meet the context-specific needs of different post-conflict societies (Shaw and Waldorf 2010, 4).

These shifts have fostered a renewed interest in civil society actors and have generated new assumptions about what civil society can accomplish. While civil society continues to be understood as secular, as operating in a sphere that is separate from the state and as supportive of global accountability norms, it is also viewed as the repository of 'local knowledge' and as critical to fostering public debate about, and ensuring the public ownership of, transitional justice processes and norms (Kritz 2009, 18; Brahm 2007; Shaw and Waldorf 2010). In the context of peacebuilding and state-building interventions, civil society is often invoked to suggest ideas of 'autonomy, population participation and democratic validation' (Jeffrey 2013, 113). It is thought to 'carry the best hopes for a genuine democratic counterweight to the power-brokers, economic, exploiters and warlords' (Pouligny 2005, 496). These assumptions tend to be taken-for-granted rather than critically examined (Subotic 2012, 112; Hovil and Okello 2011).

Transitional justice and civil society: Rethinking secular assumptions

Prevailing accounts of civil society in the transitional justice literature tend to treat civil society as a 'unified, homogenous and secular entity' (Jeffery, Kent and Wallis 2017, 379). It is assumed that civil society operates in a sphere that is both separate to, and complementary of, the state and that CSOs are uniformly in favour of 'global accountability norms' that stress the importance of criminal accountability for perpetrators of mass atrocities (Jeffery, Kent and Wallis 2017, 379; Boesnecker and Vinjamuri 2011, 346). These assumptions, which are partly a reflection of the evolution of conceptions of civil society in 'the West' (Jeffery, Kent and Wallis 2017, 380; Boesnecker and Vinjamuri 2011), have led scholars and practitioners working in or on post-conflict societies to assume the existence of structures that are representative of 'the form that civil society has taken in modern western societies' (Pouligny 2005, 498).

This assumption has led to a significant blind spot in the transitional justice literature. Specifically, it has meant that the diversity of civil society actors and civil society practice has been overlooked, as have the historical and political contexts that have shaped the development of civil society in specific places (Jeffery, Kent and Wallis 2017, 388; see also Lewis 2002). For instance, current conceptions of civil society tend to overlook the degree to which institutions based on other forms of association, like kin, ethnicity or local 'tradition', may be significant in many societies (Lewis 2002). The importance of 'custom' in shaping local value systems in relation to transitional justice is highlighted in several chapters in this collection, in particular those focused on Timor-Leste and the Pacific Islands. For instance, Damian Grenfell's and Lia Kent's chapters draw out the significance of customary rituals and practices relating to the recovery and reburial of the dead in Timor-Leste. Joanne Wallis's and Volker Boege's chapters highlight the role of local sociopolitical practices in fostering reconciliation in Bougainville. These chapters underscore the continuing relevance of kinship networks, ties and governance structures, which they say retain 'a primary function in the organisation of social and political life' in these societies (Jeffery, Kent and Wallis 2017). They demonstrate, too, that in contexts where populations are largely rural-based, reliant on subsistence agriculture and have limited access to state services, these structures and ties play a critical role in ensuring the long-term survival of local communities. In some cases, customary actors or institutions may enjoy more legitimacy than 'elite' CSOs based in capital cities.

The tendency to conceive of civil society as a homogenous and secular entity has also led to a neglect of faith-based actors and organisations and of religious practices and rituals, which, in many societies, may be considered key in addressing the legacies of violent pasts. This is beginning to change (Inazu 2009; Abe 2004; Shore and Kline 2006; Brown 2004; Beu and Nokise 2009; Rožič 2014), and scholars such as Philpott have highlighted the significance of faith-based actors in promoting and spreading a paradigm of transitional justice based on the concept of 'reconciliation'. Philpott suggests that, unlike secular human rights organisations, faith-based actors tend to ground their work in faith doctrines rather than human rights discourses, emphasising 'apology, forgiveness, empathic acknowledgement of suffering and the transformation of enmity between both groups and individuals' (Philpott 2007, 97). Philpott (2009, 183) also argues that religious actors and organisations can influence the character of broader transitional justice processes by 'shaping the content of a society's political discourse – for instance, by injecting the language of reconciliation, apology and forgiveness into the media and political debate'.

With a similar focus on the contributions of faith-based actors to reconciliation, Kollontai (2013) and Brown (2004) emphasise religious actors' willingness and ability to work across religious and ethnic boundaries. Kollontai documents the work of the Jewish aid organisation La Benevolencia in Bosnia-Herzegovina, showing how, in an environment where religion had become synonymous with questions of ethnic identity, this organisation came to be thought of as representing neutrality and impartiality. Brown (2004) emphasises how the Melanesian Brothers in the Solomon Islands were regarded as neutral during the ethnic tensions that took place from 1998 to 2003. This was a context in which both sides of the conflict were Christian and religion did not play a significant role in fuelling animosities. Here, widespread beliefs in the *mana* (spiritual powers) of the Brothers meant that they were both respected and feared, and able to pass between both sides of the conflict, praying with militants and providing humanitarian relief and shelter.

Religious actors' willingness to enter dangerous environments, and their ability to negotiate between different sides of a conflict, can also place them in a unique position to provide humanitarian aid. For instance, Bouta et al.'s 2005 desk study, which analyses the role of 27 Christian, Muslim and multi-faith organisations working in peacebuilding, concludes that the unique strength of faith-based organisations lies in their ability and willingness to work both across religious boundaries and with secular actors. Their 'moral and spiritual authority' (Bouta, Kadayifci-Orelland and Abu-Nimer 2005, 8) is widely respected vis-à-vis the government, and they have stronger historical links to their communities than secular CSOs and the state (Shannahan and Payne 2016). This provides them with a unique niche to mobilise both the local community and international networks based on their affiliations.

This collection contributes to this emerging body of work by exploring the significance of faith-based organisations and approaches to transitional justice in Asia and the Pacific. A key theme that emerges from the chapters focusing on the Pacific Islands is that faith-based, primarily Christian, organisations have been among the most actively engaged CSOs on questions of transitional justice. These organisations have promoted globalised justice ideologies and institutions while simultaneously embracing more locally pertinent discourses of justice grounded in biblical theology. These themes are evident in Volker Boege's chapter, which identifies the influential role of church groups in facilitating reconciliation in Bougainville; David Oakeshott's chapter, which focuses on a Marist Brothers initiative in Bougainville and the Solomon Islands that sought to 'vernacularise' the child rights discourse to facilitate peacebuilding; and Claire Cronin's chapter, which highlights the role of the Solomon Islands Christian Association in promoting the Truth and Reconciliation Commission.

As these chapters and several others in this collection underscore, the distinction between 'global' and 'local' approaches to transitional justice is not always clear-cut: 'indigenous' and 'faith-based' actors and organisations may be influenced by global discourses (including liberal human rights discourse) and may attempt to 'vernacularise' or translate these discourses in ways that are locally resonant. As the chapters on the Pacific Islands highlight, however, these attempts are not always seamless. A key theme raised in both Cronin's and Oakeshott's chapters is that CSOs in the Pacific Islands have faced difficulties in their advocacy for formal transitional justice mechanisms because these mechanisms are grounded in liberal, individualistic understandings of human rights that are perceived as incompatible with local value systems grounded in Christianity and *kastom*.

Nonetheless, local CSOs may be successful in promoting creative responses that navigate between, and sometimes transform, international human rights norms and local value systems. Ken Setiawan's chapter, which examines how Indonesian civil society actors have made use of online platforms to promote the remembrance of stories about the 1965 anti-communist violence, illustrates the creative potential of civil society responses. Sperfeldt and Oeung also point to this creativity by examining the ways in which local CSOs in Cambodia have provided advocacy and outreach in a context where the political will of the state is lacking. In her analysis of another Cambodian CSO, the Bophana Centre, Rachel Hughes examines how it engages communities in public events and film screenings. She suggests that the creative arts–based programs organised by the Bophana Centre, which emphasise 'shared creative labour' that is 'cultural, material and relational', have reshaped the nature and scope of the outreach activities organised by the Extraordinary Chambers in the Court of Cambodia (ECCC).

Rethinking the dynamics of power: Donors and national political elites

A second blind spot in dominant accounts of civil society in the transitional justice literature relates to the eclipsing of power dynamics (including those between actors in the Global North and local CSOs in the South, and those between local CSOs and domestic political elites). This blind spot is partly due to the depiction of transitional justice as an arena of 'technical expertise' that involves the implementation of a 'standard menu' of offerings that includes trials, truth commissions, reparations initiatives and security sector reform (Nesiah 2016; Subotic 2012, 119–120) in diverse post-conflict contexts.

Writing against this depoliticised depiction, critical transitional justice scholars have argued that states in the Global North, donors and international NGOs can have a significant influence on the priorities and activities of 'local' civil society in conflict-affected societies. These power differentials, which can play out through decision-making about funding, as well as the exchange of technical expertise and capacity building (e.g. see Nesiah 2016; Pigou 2011), have become more pronounced as the field of transitional justice has become associated with externally sponsored state-building and peacebuilding programs. In such contexts, it is particularly likely that 'powerful countries of the global North' will play a role in 'advocating for a transitional justice mechanism in the global South' (Nesiah 2016, 14) and that states will be 'expected, encouraged and even coerced' to adopt such mechanisms (Subotic 2009, 5). As this can lead to legitimacy issues (Nesiah 2016, 14), the encouragement of civil society transitional justice activity may be viewed as a way to help counter these issues. Further exacerbating the power differentials is the increasing professionalisation of the transitional justice field, which is reflected in the mounting donor pressures upon local and international to demonstrate the effectiveness and impact of their work (Subotic 2012, 119).

The influence of donors on the activities and practices undertaken by local CSOs has been noted by Vasuki Nesiah (2016, 44), who argues that donors tend to gravitate towards, and fund, 'elite' civil society actors who are often of a secular orientation, and speak in 'an internationalised language of transitional justice' rather than those who 'may advance justice agendas and priorities that do not translate into that language because of indigenous (or other alternative) epistemologies'. Similarly, Piers Pigou (2011) observes how differences between elite CSOs who speak the international vernacular (and can tailor funding proposals to fit with donors' priorities and concerns) and grassroots, rural or more radical groups, can become more pronounced during times of transition. A lack of international funding may lead to some civil society groups becoming marginalised and sidelined by urban elites who claim to speak on their behalf. The funding of certain kinds of activities may, by creating incentives for CSOs to focus on certain issues, also detract from creative, community-based approaches to addressing the legacies of past violence, and marginalise 'local knowledges' (Nesiah 2016, 29; Subotic 2012, 121). It may also lead to a depoliticisation of civil society activities, as certain issues are prioritised (for instance, prosecutions) and others are left untouched (for instance, structural injustices that may be legacies of colonialism) (Nesiah 2016).

Many of these themes are explored in this collection. For instance, Sperfeldt and Oeung observe that while some Cambodian CSOs have benefited from the funding available for community outreach associated with the ECCC, other groups (including the nascent victims' association Ksen Ksan) have 'struggled to find a foothold in Cambodia's competitive society'. Wallis similarly notes that the international CSOs working in Bougainville have tended to 'engage with and fund elite, Bougainvillean CSOs that speak in an internationalised language of transitional justice and human rights'. Writing of the Timor-Leste context, Kent suggests that, while the alliances forged between local CSOs in Timor-Leste and international human rights NGOs have helped to augment the voice and impact of the former group, these links have not always been an advantage in a domestic political context. Local CSOs have been accused by domestic political elites of pushing a 'foreign' agenda that is of little relevance to the lives and priorities of ordinary people.

Further to the issue of power dynamics, several chapters in the collection highlight the ways in which civil society advocacy for transitional justice can become entangled with, and limited by, the political agendas of national political elites. Like the power dynamics between international actors and local CSOs, the conflicting political agendas that are at play in the process of 'dealing with the past' in specific contexts may be obscured by the professionalisation and institutionalisation of the transitional justice field, and its depiction as an apolitical and technical set of 'tools' (Nesiah 2016, 32). The diverse political stakes that are at play, and the concrete political struggles in which transitional justice debates and mechanisms are embedded are, however, very apparent to the contributors to this collection. In Timor-Leste, Kent describes how narratives of victimhood and suffering are downplayed by political elites who favour more 'heroic "imaginings"' of the Timor-Leste nation. Grenfell builds on this observation to describe how the Timor-Leste Government has used transitional justice 'framed in national terms' to reinforce the state. Grenfell's chapter offers caution about the dangers of CSOs being co-opted into transitional justice mechanisms that are part of state-building projects that might not be legitimate, or that might be exclusionary. The degree to which the transitional justice advocacy of civil society actors can become frustrated by the agendas of national political elites is also evident in Setiawan's chapter on Indonesia and Catherine Renshaw's chapter on Myanmar. Setiawan suggests that there has been a 'lack of political will to address past human rights violations' because many of the elites who were part of the repressive New Order regime remain influential. Setiawan observes that, while CSOs have advocated for transitional justice mechanisms, there is 'reluctance or even antipathy' among many Indonesians towards these mechanisms, perhaps demonstrating the difficulty of pursuing transitional justice in contexts where a so-called 'transition' to democracy has only partially occurred. In Myanmar, Renshaw describes how both the military and the National League for Democracy (NLD) have prioritised stability over strong accountability mechanisms, in part because, as in Indonesia, the military retains significant political power.

The challenge of pursuing transitional justice in contexts where previous elites remain influential is also evident in Wallis's and Boege's chapters on Bougainville, where elites have favoured customary reconciliation coupled with amnesties and pardons for human rights abuses, which has, according to Wallis, 'contributed to the emergence of a culture of impunity'. As in Indonesia, Wallis finds that 'proposals to establish a formal transitional justice mechanism have largely failed to gain traction among ordinary Bougainvilleans', perhaps again because of the difficulty of pursuing transitional justice in contexts where the political transition is ongoing or its outcome uncertain. In contrast, Sperfeldt and Oeung's chapter on Cambodia highlights how extensive transitional justice mechanisms, including an international criminal court, can be pursued in contexts where there has been a clear political transition, previous elites have been removed and where there is substantial international support.

Nonetheless, it is also important not to overestimate the power of states to shape transitional justice agendas. In the context of the Pacific Islands, for instance, Wallis argues that it is necessary to question 'liberal assumptions regarding the relevance and legitimacy of states as actors capable of facilitating or complying with formal transitional justice mechanisms'. As Wallis points out, these assumptions simply do not hold up in the Pacific Islands, where 'states themselves are only shallowly rooted in society and many people do not have a strong understanding of themselves as citizens of a state'. Similar observations are made by Oakeshott in respect of Solomon Islands, where he notes that churches have 'historically performed governance functions that a classical Weberian understanding of the state (as distinct from civil society) would view as state prerogatives', including 'governance in the absence of functioning states'.

Chapter overview

As the preceding discussion of blind spots suggests, rather than working with a pre-existing (Western, liberal) understanding of what civil society looks like or celebrating civil society as an unqualified good, it is necessary for transitional justice scholars to engage with what Mamdani refers to as 'actually existing civil society' (1996, 19). This means paying more attention to the historical and political contexts that have shaped the development of civil society in specific places (Jeffery, Kent and Wallis 2017, 388; see also Lewis 2002). It means attending to the ways in which local organisations define their moral and political agenda and critically engage with (or choose to disengage from) the 'inescapably normative' modern Western model of civil society prescribed and funded by international donors. It also requires widening the lens of what constitutes civil society to consider indigenous governance structures, which may help to challenge and problematise Western-centric norms (Hann 1996). At the same time, it requires sensitivity to the globalisation of ideas about civil society and transitional justice, and to the dynamics of power that imbue the relationships between donors, CSOs and national political elites. Responding to Mamdani's call for more attention to 'actually existing' civil society, the chapters in this collection engage in place-based analyses, exploring individual case studies that elucidate the diversity of civil society engagement with transitional justice processes across Asia and the Pacific.

Part 1: Timor-Leste and Indonesia

The first three chapters focus on Timor-Leste and Indonesia. Chapter 1, by Lia Kent, considers the limitations of the normative, liberal model of transitional justice endorsed by civil society in Timor-Leste. Kent instead advocates a broader approach based on a recognition of 'everyday practices'. Kent describes, for example, the importance of honouring the dead in Timorese *adat* (custom) and how 'the dead remain a very real presence in the lives of the living'. As such, for many who lost loved ones during the Indonesian occupation, locating the bodies of family members and affording them proper funeral rights is a pressing need. Despite this, Kent finds that these activities often occur 'with little or no connection to the work of CSO activists, including the victims' association'. Instead, much of this activity is undertaken by families and kinship groups with little external support, although some support is provided by faith-based actors.

Based on this analysis, Kent draws attention to potential shortcomings of the 'victim-centred' discourse promoted by Timorese CSOs. She argues that engaging with alternative subjectivities that are grounded in kinship structures may prove more useful in meeting the needs and priorities of East Timorese.

Chapter 2, by Damian Grenfell, documents how civil society actors in Timor-Leste have limited the effectiveness of both formal transitional justice initiatives and locally engaged forms of reconciliation and reparations by framing their efforts in terms of a 'national imaginary' closely linked to resistance to Indonesian occupation. Importantly, Grenfell defines civil society as 'forms of social collaboration grounded in a public virtue that do not challenge the state's claim to the monopoly over the legitimate use of violence within a given territory'. Grenfell argues that the nationalism that has shaped the transitional justice efforts has undermined their ability to respond to victims, as it has prioritised 'veterans over civilian survivors' and made a 'clear delineation in terms of gender'. As CSOs have reinforced a state-centric approach to transitional justice, this has also meant that cultural practices, particularly with regards to the burial of the dead, have been overlooked.

Chapter 3, by Ken Setiawan, considers the role of digital platforms in providing spaces for storytelling that challenge official narratives about past violence in Indonesia. Setiawan conceptualises civil society broadly to include these online spaces that fly under the radar of state control. She draws on Hirsch's (2008) theory of postmemory to describe how stories published through digital platforms can serve to connect those who did not directly experience violence with previous generations who did. In addition, such stories have an affiliative, horizontal effect, connecting people to contemporaries who lack a filial link to past violence. In the context of the Indonesian transitional justice process, which Setiawan describes as 'at best as "delayed" … at worst as "failed"', such stories 'generate factual knowledge about what has happened, to whom and who is responsible'. Importantly, these stories can also function as 'voices against silence, interpretation against incomprehension, empathy against indifference and remembrance against forgetting'.

Part 2: Cambodia and Myanmar

The next three chapters consider Cambodia and Myanmar. Chapter 4, by Christoph Sperfeldt and Jeudy Oeung, provides an in-depth case study of the evolution of civil society support to the Extraordinary Chambers in the Court of Cambodia from 2003 through to the present to demonstrate the many ways in which civil society can provide advocacy and outreach where government processes lack political will, and support and assistance where they lack resources. The authors document how CSOs took responsibility for advocating for increased victim participation in the process (phase one), to assisting victims in participating in the court (phases two and three), to assisting with collective reparations including remembrance and memorialisation, rehabilitation, documentation and education (phase four). While they argue that CSOs performed a valuable role, Sperfeldt and Oeung conclude that a more formalised, structured relationship would have streamlined the process to better meet the needs of victims.

Chapter 5, by Rachel Hughes, explores the work of Cambodian CSO the Bophana Centre. Bophana 'does not participate straightforwardly in the discursive field of "transitional justice"', as it eschews the normative approaches of humanitarian and human rights–focused initiatives. Instead, it focuses on educating the community, engaging them in active memory-work through film production and public screenings, organising conferences and providing the public with free access to its audiovisual archive. Bophana also works closely with the state-run Khmer Rouge Tribunal, providing its Public Affairs Section with resources and technical support to run 'Study Tour Memory Nights'. Hughes problematises the Centre's collaboration with the Khmer Rouge Tribunal, noting that concepts such as 'civil society' and 'transitional justice' can become 'rationales for the continued existence and salience' of CSOs, as while they are 'largely discursive' they are also 'economically consequential'.

Chapter 6, by Catherine Renshaw, examines the transition to democracy in Myanmar. Renshaw finds that 'there has been little justice' in this transition because it has occurred as the result of 'indigenous top-down change' and consequently the military, which would fear the consequences of a formal transitional justice process, particularly criminal trials, retains significant political power. The National League for Democracy, which was the most significant advocate of the transition, also prioritises stability over strong accountability mechanisms. In any event, many Burmese conceive justice broadly to include not only criminal accountability, but also broader political and economic reform. Such reform is unlikely to occur as long as the military and NLD are focused on maintaining the status quo. Burmese from Myanmar's ethnic states are also involved in ongoing conflict with the national government, highlighting that a transition to peace remains only aspirational for many Burmese. In this context, Renshaw argues that CSOs are 'critical actors in recording and articulating authentic expressions of what justice requires; and beginning the long process of recalibrating the political morality of post-transition society'.

Part 3: The Pacific Islands

The final four chapters focus on the Pacific Islands. In Chapter 7, Joanne Wallis examines the role played by reconciliation practices in social reconstruction after Bougainville's 1989 to 1997 conflict. Wallis juxtaposes reconciliation 'grounded in local sociopolitical practices' that is favoured by grassroots civil society, with the liberal, human rights–based mechanisms (namely, criminal trials and truth commissions) advocated by 'elite' CSOs. Wallis concludes that local sociopolitical reconciliation practices have helped to establish 'an environment in which Bougainvilleans have been able to negotiate and agree to the design of [effective governance] institutions, and in which they have been able to peacefully work through them to govern Bougainville'. However, she concludes that outcomes with respect to justice have been more mixed, as the pragmatic decision by Bougainvillean elites to favour reconciliation over a formal transitional justice mechanism has contributed to the emergence of a culture of impunity.

Chapter 8, by Volker Boege, also focuses on the role of reconciliation in peacebuilding in Bougainville, but takes a different approach by examining the ways in which reconciliation is practised. He observes that, while reconciliations are usually presented as the 'traditional' Bougainville approach to peacebuilding and (restorative) justice, today a broad spectrum of types of 'reconciliations' can be found, in different contexts and at different levels. However, he notes that there is growing concern about reconciliations losing their true 'traditional' meaning, becoming shallowly tokenistic and commercialised, and thus less effective and legitimate. He concludes by exploring the current state of reconciliations on Bougainville and their significance as an indigenous means of 'transitional justice', not least in the absence of more conventional transitional justice mechanisms such as a truth and reconciliation commission.

In Chapter 9, David Oakeshott considers the role that church organisations can play in post-conflict education systems, which Cole (2007) has claimed 'can function as the second phase' in transitional justice after official institutions such as truth commissions and trials. Based on a case study of the Child Rights Network – an initiative of the Marist Brothers of Melanesia – in two Catholic Church–run boarding schools in Mabiri (Bougainville) and Tenaru (Solomon Islands), Oakeshott analyses how human (specifically, child's) rights discourse can be vernacularised to facilitate peacebuilding. While Oakeshott finds that the child's rights discourse has been successfully interwoven with Marist teaching in the two schools to encourage students to see themselves as possessing rights equal to their teachers, and to shift teachers' emphasis from punishment to pastoral care, he concludes that it did little to change teachers' and students' attitudes to the authority structures that contributed to conflict in Solomon Islands and Bougainville. More broadly, Oakeshott cautions that, by stepping in to fill the void left by the state in the provision of education in a transitional environment, civil society (in this case, the church) may undermine one of the key goals of the transitional justice project – to build trust between the state and its citizens over the longer term.

Chapter 10, by Claire Cronin, looks at the role of faith-based organisation SICA (the Solomon Islands Christian Association) in promoting the Truth and Reconciliation Commission (TRC) in post-conflict Solomon Islands. Cronin argues that SICA was influenced by the perceived success of the South African Truth and Reconciliation Commission, which had interwoven Christian theological notions with internationally normative transitional justice discourses. Following the South African Commission, SICA believed that the TRC would provide a way for victims to talk about their experiences of suffering during the tensions, and be perceived as a morally legitimate institution, both by the international community and the Solomon Islands people. While Cronin finds that SICA's community advocacy around the TRC was largely successful because it emphasised the role that Christianity and the church might play, when the TRC submitted its Final Report to parliament in 2012, its analysis was overwhelmingly grounded in the international human rights discourse. Cronin concludes that the TRC is an example of superficial 'vernacularisation' of transitional justice discourses as there was no real attempt to amalgamate international and local understandings of (in)justice.

Conclusion

The chapters in this collection paint a picture of the heterogeneity of CSOs and actors in Asia and the Pacific and the breadth of their transitional justice activities. This is a picture that illustrates the need to broaden understandings of what constitutes civil society and civil society practice in relation to transitional justice, and poses a challenge to the globalised, standardised, primarily legalistic, model of transitional justice that tends to dominate much of the scholarly and policy literature. The CSO organisations and actors discussed in these chapters are engaged in a great deal of activity beyond advocating for short-term, formal mechanisms such as criminal prosecutions and truth commissions. The richness of this activity suggests that local populations have much deeper understandings and expectations of what transitional justice should involve and achieve.

Bibliography

Abe, Toshihiro. 2004. 'Christian Principles in Social Transition: The South African Search for Reconciliation'. *African Study Monographs* 25 (3): 149–165.

Beu, Charles Brown and Rosalyn Nokise, eds. 2009. *Mission in the Midst of Conflict: Stories from the Solomon Islands*. Suva: God's Pacific People, Pacific Theological College.

Boesenecker, Aaron P., and Leslie Vinjamuri. 2011. 'Lost in Translation? Civil Society, Faith-Based Organizations and the Negotiation of International Norms'. *The International Journal of Transitional Justice* 5 (3): 345–365. doi.org/10.1093/ijtj/ijr018.

Bouta, Tsjeard, S. Ayse Kadayifci-Orelland and Mohammed Abu-Nimer. 2005. *Faith-Based Peace-Building: Mapping and Analysis of Christian Muslim and Multi-Faith Actors*. Washington DC: Netherlands Institute for International Relations in cooperation with Salam Institute for Peace and Justice.

Brahm, Eric. 2007. 'Transitional Justice, Civil Society, and the Development of the Rule of Law in Post-Conflict Societies'. *International Journal of Not-for-Profit Law* 9 (4): 62–69.

Brown, Terry. 2004. 'The Role of Religious Communities in Peacemaking: The Solomon Islands'. *Anglican Religious Life Journal* 1: 8–18.

Cole, Elizabeth. 2007. 'Transitional justice and the reform of history education'. *The International Journal of Transitional Justice* 1 (1): 115–137. doi.org/10.1093/ijtj/ijm003.

Edwards, Michael. 2004. *Civil Society*. Cambridge: Polity Press.

Foley, Michael W. and Bob Edwards. 1996. 'The Paradox of Civil Society'. *Journal of Democracy* 7 (3): 38–52. doi.org/10.1353/jod.1996.0048.

Glasius, Marlies, David Lewis and Hakan Seckinelgin. 2004. *Exploring Civil Society: Political and Cultural Contexts*. Abingdon: Routledge. doi.org/10.4324/9780203358290.

Hann, Chris. 1996. 'Introduction: Political Society and Civil Anthropology'. In *Civil Society: Challenging Western Models*, edited by Chris Hann and Elizabeth Dunn, 1–26. London: Routledge.

Hirsch, Marianne. 2008. 'The Generation of Postmemory'. *Poetics Today* 29 (1): 103–128. doi.org/10.1215/03335372-2007-019.

Hovil, Lucy and Moses Chrispus Okello. 2011. 'Editorial Note'. *The International Journal of Transitional Justice* 5 (3): 333–344. doi.org/10.1093/ijtj/ijr028.

Huntington, Samuel P. 1993. *The Third Wave: Democratization in the Late 20th Century*. Norman: University of Oklahoma Press.

Inazu, John D. 2009. 'No Future Without (Personal) Forgiveness: Reexamining the Role of Forgiveness in Transitional Justice'. *Human Rights Review* 10: 309–326. doi.org/10.1007/s12142-009-0120-8.

Jeffery, Renée, Lia Kent and Joanne Wallis. 2017. 'Reconceiving the Roles of Religious Civil Society Organizations in Transitional Justice: Evidence from the Solomon Islands, Timor-Leste and Bougainville'. *The International Journal of Transitional Justice* 11 (3): 378–399. doi.org/10.1093/ijtj/ijx020.

Jeffery, Renée and Hun Joon Kim. 2014. 'Introduction: New Horizons: Transitional Justice in the Asia-Pacific'. In *Transitional Justice in the Asia-Pacific*, edited by Renée Jeffery and Hun Joon Kim, 1–32. New York: Cambridge University Press. doi.org/10.1017/CBO9781139628914.001.

Jeffrey, Alex. 2013. *The Improvised State: Sovereignty, Performance and Agency in Dayton Bosnia*. Oxford: Wiley Blackwell. doi.org/10.1002/9781118278789.

Kent, Lia. 2012. *The Dynamics of Transitional Justice: International Models and Local Realities in East Timor*. Abingdon: Routledge.

Kollontai, Pauline. 2013. 'Adopting a Peace-Education Approach in Religious Schools: Perspectives from Bosnia-Herzegovina'. In *Leadership and Religious Schools: International Perspectives and Challenges*, edited by Michael T. Buchanan, 69–87. New York: Bloomsbury.

Kritz, Neil. 2009. 'Policy Implications of Empirical Research on Transitional Justice'. In *Assessing the Impact of Transitional Justice: Challenges for Empirical Research*, edited by Hugo van der Merwe, Victoria Baxter and Audrey R. Chapman, 13–22. Washington, DC: US Institute of Peace Press.

Lewis, David. 2002. 'Civil Society in African Contexts: Reflections on the Usefulness of a Concept'. *Development and Change* 33 (4): 569–586. doi.org/10.1111/1467-7660.00270.

Mamdani, Mahmood. 1996. *Citizen and Subject: Contemporary Africa and the Legacy of Late Colonialism*. Kampala: Fountain Publishers.

Nesiah, Vasuki. 2016. *Transitional Justice Practice: Looking Back, Moving Forward*. Scoping Study Research Report. The Hague: Impunity Watch.

Philpott, Daniel, ed. 2006. *The Politics of Past Evil: Religion, Reconciliation, and the Dilemmas of Transitional Justice*. Notre Dame: University of Notre Dame Press.

Philpott, Daniel. 2007. 'What Religion Brings to the Politics of Transitional Justice'. *Journal of International Affairs* 61 (1): 93–110.

Philpott, Daniel. 2009. 'Has the Study of Global Politics Found Religion?'. *The Annual Review of Political Science* 12: 183–202. doi.org/10.1146/annurev.polisci.12.053006.125448.

Pigou, Piers. 2011. 'Special Feature: IJTJ Interviews, Interview with Piers Pigou'. *The International Journal of Transitional Justice* 5 (3): 504–518. doi.org/10.1093/ijtj/ijr024.

Pouligny, Beatrice. 2005. 'Civil Society and Post-Conflict Peacebuilding: Ambiguities of International Programmes Aimed at Building "New" Societies'. *Security Dialogue* 36 (4): 495–510. doi.org/10.1177/0967010605060448.

Rožič, Peter. 2014. 'Religion Matters, Quantifying the Impact of Religion Legacies on Post-Communist Transitional Justice'. *Journal for the Study of Religions and Ideologies* 13 (37): 3–34.

Shannahan, Chris and Laura Payne. 2016. *Faith-Based Interventions in Peace, Conflict and Violence: A Scoping Study*. Coventry: Centre for Trust, Peace and Social Relations, Coventry University.

Shaw, Rosalind and Lars Waldorf. 2010. 'Introduction: Localizing Transitional Justice'. In *Localizing Transitional Justice: Interventions and Priorities after Mass Violence*, edited by Rosalind Shaw and Lars Waldorf, 3–26. Stanford: Stanford University Press.

Shepherd, Laura J. 2015. 'Constructing Civil Society: Gender, Power and Legitimacy in United Nations Peacebuilding Discourse'. *European Journal of International Relations* 21 (4): 887–910. doi.org/10.1177/1354066115569319.

Shore, Megan and Scott Kline. 2006. 'The Ambiguous Role of Religion in the South African Truth and Reconciliation Commission'. *Peace and Change* 31 (3): 309–332. doi.org/10.1111/j.1468-0130.2006.00377.x.

Subotic, Jelena. 2009. 'The Paradox of International Justice Compliance'. *The International Journal of Transitional Justice* 3 (3): 362–383. doi.org/10.1093/ijtj/ijp011.

Subotic, Jelena. 2010. *Hijacked Justice: Dealing with the Past in the Balkans*. Ithaca: Cornell University Press.

Subotic, Jelena. 2012. 'The Transformation of International Transitional Justice Advocacy'. *The International Journal of Transitional Justice* 6 (1): 106–125. doi.org/10.1093/ijtj/ijr036.

Part 1 – Timor-Leste and Indonesia

1

Rethinking 'civil society' and 'victim-centred' transitional justice in Timor-Leste

Lia Kent

Over the course of conducting research in Timor-Leste over the past decade I have become increasingly aware of the limits of the globalised, standardised model of transitional justice. My research has revealed to me that local understandings and expectations of transitional justice exceed – perhaps inevitably – the justice possibilities available through formal, time-bound mechanisms such as criminal prosecutions and truth commissions. It has also highlighted that the process of 'dealing with the past' is not confined to the initial transitional period but is being shaped in an ongoing way through the practices of, and the interactions between, a wide range of actors who possess varying degrees of power. These observations have led me to argue that transitional justice needs to be thought about differently – as a dynamic and open-ended social and political process, rather than as a short-term project oriented around a set of formal mechanisms. In other words, I have come to the view that transitional justice scholars, practitioners and activists need to move beyond a preoccupation with official institutions and short-term outcomes and consider how best to support people's ongoing and locally grounded efforts to rebuild their lives after conflict.

With these insights in mind, I was initially optimistic about the decision by East Timorese civil society organisations (CSOs) around 10 years ago to establish a national victims' association. It seemed to me that a victims' association (comprised of civilians who directly experienced human rights violations during the 24-year Indonesian occupation) presented an opportunity to build a locally grounded and inclusive social movement for transitional justice that was responsive to ordinary people's needs and priorities. I also thought that this movement might help to challenge the forward-looking, heroic narrative of nation-building promoted by East Timorese political elites (which privileges the experiences and rights of elite former combatants) by encouraging new forms of solidarity and political agency grounded in common experiences of suffering.

Yet, over the past 10 years, I have observed the victims' association struggle to develop into a social movement. In this chapter, I draw on recent fieldwork in Timor-Leste to reflect on some of the reasons why this may be the case. I have concluded that the victims' rights agenda promoted by CSOs is grounded in a liberal, individualist human rights paradigm, which has limited mobilising power in a context where other, very different, subjectivities coexist. This agenda, I suggest, is unable to respond to people's immediate and everyday needs and priorities, including the imperative to restore relations of trust, sociality and reciprocity with their kin.

In the first part of this chapter, I describe the evolution of the victims' association and its connection to ideas of 'victim-centredness' that are now prominent in the field of transitional justice. I then draw on my observations of the 2015 Victims Congress to reflect on some of the challenges that arose in building the association, showing how many of these challenges reflect the degree to which victim-centred strategies have been interpreted narrowly, in accordance with a liberal transitional justice framework. In the second half of this chapter, I explore how ordinary East Timorese are seeking to address some of their important economic, social and spiritual needs in the aftermath of the conflict through strategies and practices embedded in the realm of the everyday. Some of these activities are being initiated by local communities with little or no external support, while others are being led by faith-based actors. I suggest that attending to these practices – which are often overlooked by the liberal, institutionally oriented transitional justice field – might foster a broader, more pluralistic understanding of civil society transitional justice activity.

Building the victims' association: Promoting 'victim-centredness'?

The establishment of Timor-Leste's victims' association needs to be understood against the backdrop of political leaders' ambivalent responses to the report of the Commission for Reception, Truth and Reconciliation (CAVR). Entitled *Chega!* (No More! Stop! Enough!), and tabled in the National Parliament in 2005, the report offers a disturbing account of the 'massive, widespread and systematic atrocities' that took place during the Indonesian occupation – including extrajudicial killings, torture, disappearances and sexual violence –and finds the Indonesian Government and security forces 'primarily responsible and accountable' for the deaths of between 100,000 and 180,000 civilians (CAVR 2005, ch. 8, 5–6). *Chega!* also contains 205 recommendations for policy reform in areas as diverse as prosecutions for serious crimes perpetrators; reparations; human rights training; education; reforms to the military, police and security forces; prisons; missing persons; commemoration and memorialisation; and the rights of women and youth.

Since the report's completion, East Timorese CSO activists and their international supporters have continued to advocate for the implementation of its recommendations, focusing their efforts on the need for a reparations program to support 'vulnerable victims' and for the establishment of an 'Institute for Memory' (to implement other agreed-to *Chega!* recommendations, including a commission for missing persons). This small group of elite, educated, Dili-based activists has also continued to lobby both the Timor-Leste Government and the international community for the establishment of an international tribunal to prosecute those who committed war crimes and crimes against humanity during the Indonesian occupation (among them senior members of the Indonesian military). More than 10 years later, progress towards many of these goals remains elusive. There was some renewed momentum around the time of *Chega!*'s 10-year anniversary, when civil society activists successfully lobbied Timor-Leste's president to host a workshop on the report's legacy and decided to bypass the parliament and appeal directly to the prime minister and president to establish an Institute for Memory. These efforts led, in 2016, to the passing of a presidential decree law to establish a *Centro Nasional Chega!* (National *Chega!* Centre) to implement some of the CAVR recommendations (as well as those of a second, bilateral truth commission, known as the

Commission for Truth and Friendship (CTF)).[1] Despite this promising development, the mandate of the new centre is limited. The focus is on the 'institutionalisation of memory' and the promotion of human rights through education and training; there is no reference to prosecutions, reparations or a missing persons' commission, and the term 'victim' is eschewed in favour of the more politically palatable term 'survivor'.[2]

The political elite's lukewarm responses to *Chega!* can be understood, in part, as a reflection of the pragmatic priority that has been placed on building bilateral relations with Indonesia, the nation's large neighbour and former occupier. This focus has led to the rejection of a prosecutorial path and the promotion of a 'reconciliatory agenda' that is perhaps best embodied in the bilateral institution of the CTF. Political leaders have argued that a reconciliatory path is more culturally appropriate to the Timor-Leste context than the pursuit of prosecutorial justice; in this vein, they have criticised local CSO activists – who have links to international non-governmental organisations (NGOs) such as Human Rights Watch, the International Center for Transitional Justice and Amnesty International – for pushing a 'foreign' agenda that is of little relevance to the lives and priorities of ordinary people (Kent 2015, 66–67). In addition to pragmatic, geopolitical considerations, however, there is something about the narrative of civilian suffering contained in *Chega!* that members of the political elite take issue with. This narrative undercuts current heroic 'imaginings' of the Timor-Leste nation that celebrate the capacity, forbearance and fortitude of the East Timorese people in overcoming successive national occupiers and achieving independence. The heroic narrative of the conflict is contained in the nation's Constitution, which underscores the importance of 'valorising' the nation's heroes. Valorisation is occurring in a very tangible sense, through an elaborate and graduated veterans' pension scheme that provides monthly pensions to those who can claim to have participated in the resistance struggle for the required number of years and to family members of deceased veterans (martyrs). Through the scheme, which provides monthly payments that are well

---

1   The CTF was established by the East Timorese and Indonesian governments in 2005 to seek the 'conclusive truth' in order to contribute to a 'definitive closure on issues of the past [that] would further promote bilateral relations' (Government of Indonesia and Democratic Republic of Indonesia 2005, para. 8).

2   Decree Law 48/2016, Establishing the *Chega!* National Public Institute: From Memory to Hope. It should be noted that since this chapter was written, the CNC has shown itself to be a creative institution that is pushing the boundaries of its mandate.

above the average East Timorese monthly income, a clear hierarchy of citizenship has been constructed, in which the status of elite (mostly male) former combatants is elevated over that of other citizens.

It is against this backdrop that CSOs have, since 2008, worked to establish and foster the national victims' association. The association – known as the National Association of Victims of the Political Conflict 1974–1999 – consists of district-based 'focal points' in each of Timor-Leste's 13 districts, plus a national coordinator, who is funded by a small consortium of Dili-based CSOs. The association holds annual meetings and a National Victims Congress every three years, during which members reflect on the progress made over the previous years and plan for the future. The activities of the association include, among other things, lobbying political leaders on the need for prosecutions and reparations, linking 'vulnerable victims' in each district into existing forms of social support and organising forms of commemoration of violent events of district significance.

The decision to build a national victims' association resonates with the priority that has been placed on 'victim-centred' transitional justice over the last decade by scholars, practitioners and civil society activists. While victim-centredness remains ill-defined, it is often construed as requiring 'institutionalised avenues' for victim participation in formal transitional justice mechanisms (Nesiah 2016, 24) and as suggesting that victims and/or victims' representatives need to be engaged in the planning and implementation of transitional justice measures (Robins 2011, 77). Simon Robins proposes a more radical formulation, suggesting that a victim-centred transitional justice process 'arises in response to the explicit needs of victims, as defined by victims themselves' (Robins 2011, 77). Yet, regardless of how it is defined, victim-centredness is understood both as a good in itself and as having a 'strategic' value (e.g. Magarrell 2007, 2). Its inherent good is said to lie in the fact that it reinforces victims' dignity by treating them not as passive recipients of transitional justice measures but as active agents with the ability to claim their rights (Nesiah 2016, 24). Its strategic value is thought to lie in the fact that victim-centredness increases the ground-level legitimacy of transitional justice processes and therefore enhances their long-term effectiveness. For East Timorese CSO activists working to establish the victims' association, then, an implicit objective of this work is to build legitimacy for the transitional justice agenda (both among the political elite and among the broader community) by ensuring that victims themselves have an opportunity to shape the national debate on questions of justice, reconciliation and reparations.

Despite these worthy goals, the very slipperiness of the concept of victim-centredness has led some scholars to express wariness about its promotion as a panacea for questions of transitional justice legitimacy. Vasuki Nesiah (2016, 24–25), for instance, suggests there is a need to be alert to the ways in which victim-centredness is constructed within a transitional justice field that has become increasingly standardised and normative. As transitional justice has come to revolve around a 'toolkit' of prescribed mechanisms, including trials, truth commissions and reparations programs, there is a danger that victim-centredness may amount to little more than requiring victims to channel their demands into a narrow, predetermined set of priorities 'that may not accord with the specifics of local context' (Nesiah 2016, 20). Current conceptualisations of victim-centredness have also been criticised for promoting a 'homogenising model' of victimhood that papers over the differences present within victimised populations (for instance, among victims of different socioeconomic, religious, ethnic, geographic and other backgrounds, and among victims with different political and ideological agendas) (Nesiah 2016, 25). It has also been argued that, because transitional justice has a close relationship to – and often intrinsically embodies the values of – ideological liberalism, victim-centred strategies tend to promote narrow, individualistic victim identities. This may not do justice to the ways in which people in different societies conceptualise their identities, or understand questions of harm or redress (Robins 2015, 182–88). As I will now discuss, many of these issues have been at play in the context of the victims' association in Timor-Leste.

Challenges of building the victims' association in Timor-Leste

As many East Timorese CSO activists concede, progress in building the victims' association has been slow. These difficulties were evident at the 2015 Victims Congress I attended and during interviews I conducted around it. The congress involved the district focal points from around Timor-Leste and was facilitated by a number of prominent human rights CSO activists from Dili. A key aim was to consider how the victims' association could reduce its reliance on the financial support of CSOs (which, in any case, is minimal).[3] The congress also reviewed progress made on resolutions since the last congress, in particular: strategies to support vulnerable women victims in the rural areas; collaborate with government, political parties and business; strengthen national and international cooperation; and lobby for a reparations law.

It soon became clear, however, that in some districts there was not a great deal happening at all. One very practical issue raised was that a lack of resources and transport made it difficult for district-based victims groups to organise themselves and plan activities. Compounding this was the fact that, 10 years after the winding up of Timor-Leste's truth commission, it was felt that donors were no longer interested in supporting transitional justice initiatives. The difficulty of garnering support from the Timor-Leste Government was also raised. While two members of the victims' association had recently been elected to the National Parliament as part of a deliberate strategy to build the association's profile and ensure victims' interests were directly represented in the formal political process, these parliamentarians had 'lost their spirit of voluntarism', according to several congress participants, and were no longer interested in victims' issues.[4] All of this has left the association reliant on Dili-based CSOs (who themselves struggle with declining levels of donor funding) for logistical and financial support. Very little progress was made at the congress on how to reduce this dependency.

Yet, even if victims could overcome some of the financial and other constraints to meeting regularly, it was clear that other factors were complicating attempts to build a strong victims' association. For instance, the difficulties of building common goals among a diverse group were evident. Aside from experiencing a violent event (for instance, the death of a family member, a rape, an experience of torture) at some point during the Indonesian occupation, the group of victims present at the congress seemed to have little in common. They were geographically dispersed, had very different socioeconomic circumstances and education levels and different political affiliations.

---

3   Only $30,000 is provided annually for the secretariat of the victims' association in any case, which covers the running costs of one car and the costs of organising several meetings.
4   Observations from 2015 Victims Congress.

Over the course of the congress, other confusions and anxieties also emerged. Several participants suggested that the population in their district remained confused about the purpose of the victims' association. It was said that some community members erroneously believed that joining the association might provide a means through which they could negotiate access to a veterans' pension. An undertone of anxiety also seemed to be present during the discussion of district-level memorials and commemorations; the subtext seemed to be that, in a context where political leaders were seeking to promote reconciliation with Indonesia, efforts by district-based victims' groups to organise large-scale commemorations of violent incidents would be provocative. Anxiety also seemed to be present among those who had been victims of violence committed by Timor-Leste's resistance movement. For instance, several participants who, during the early years of the Indonesian occupation had been detained and mistreated in makeshift FRETILIN-run rehabilitation prisons (*Rehabilitação Nacional* – RENAL) for 'reactionaries', raised questions about whether they could legitimately be part of the victims' association.

The challenges that emerged at the congress suggest, then, that the victims' association has struggled due to several overlapping obstacles. First is the general difficulty of building social movements in contexts of impoverishment and limited resources, where people are preoccupied with basic livelihoods concerns. Second is the extent to which, in accordance with the prescribed transitional justice toolkit, victim-centredness has been understood narrowly; it seems clear that CSOs have sought to deliberately create and shape the activities of victims' groups, rather than responding to and supporting organic, 'bottom-up' initiatives (e.g. see Robins 2013, 204). Third, and relatedly, there seems an anxiety – perhaps borne from recent conflict (both with Indonesia and internally, as in the conflict of 2006) – about antagonising the state by undercutting its reconciliation agenda. Yet, more than this, there is also a sense that CSOs have attempted to promote a certain kind of subjectivity among members of the victims' association – that of the individual, rights-holding victim who, through forms of active citizenship, is capable of exerting claims to rights (Jeffery and Jakala 2015, 44; Basok and Ilcan 2016, 314). In the Timor-Leste context, this form of subjectivity, and its related assumptions about political agency, associative life and citizenship, appears – now at least – to have limited resonance.

As the work of Sally Engle Merry underscores, individuals are 'the location of multiple and potentially contradictory subjectivities' that are influenced by dominant and subdominant discourses (Merry 2006, 184). This is no less the case in Timor-Leste, where victim subjectivities promoted by CSOs coexist with other, often more powerful, forms of identification. In a context where the national liberation struggle continues to exert a powerful influence on understandings of identity, discourses that highlight the need to recognise the suffering of victims of all political persuasions struggle to compete with heroic, nationalist discourses that promote the rights of, and reward for, those who sacrificed for the nation's liberation. The concerns raised at the victims' congress by former detainees in FRETILIN prisons speak to these difficulties, revealing the extent to which discussion of violence committed by the East Timorese resistance movement remains taboo.

As already noted, resistance-based identities have in fact been deliberately cultivated by government policies in recent years, which have seen the establishment of a veterans' scheme that provides substantial pensions to those who can successfully claim to have participated in the resistance struggle. In a context where many people struggle to meet their basic needs, the significant economic, social and political capital that is gained by successfully negotiating a veterans' pension is a key driver of this form of identification. By contrast, there is very little to be gained, either socially or materially, by identifying as a victim.

Coexisting with nationalist, resistance-based identities are strong locally embedded conceptions of identity. As in many other kinship-based societies, East Timorese strongly identify as part of extended families, as linked to clan and ancestors. Survival, both social and economic, is fundamentally dependent on the maintenance of relations of reciprocity. These relations are regulated by strong moral codes – referred to as *adat* (custom) – that provide the basis for both solidarity and social control. In such a context, conceptions of harm as the violation of the rights of an individual, autonomous agent do not encompass the degree to which harm is experienced as socially shared, as a fracturing of complex webs of kinship and social alliances (Robins 2015, 196; Sakti 2013, 441). The fact that the state has a limited capacity to uphold rights, particularly outside of the nation's capital, Dili, (and has shown little interest in recognising victim identities in any case) further reduces the power of the victims' rights agenda. All of this means that while this agenda may promise a great deal, it is currently unable to respond to some of the most important social, economic and spiritual needs of those who have been affected by the conflict. As I will now discuss, these needs are to some degree being addressed through everyday practices and strategies of social repair that are embedded in the realm of the extended family.

Beyond the victims' association: Everyday reconciliation and the work of faith-based actors

To illustrate what I mean by everyday practices, let me begin with an anecdote. In July 2016, I travelled to the district of Aileu to interview the district-level 'focal point' for the national victims' association about their activities. 'Mario', the young coordinator, who was also a teacher in the local school, explained to me that it was difficult to generate interest in the victims' association and that there was very little district-related activity taking place. When I asked about programs such as organising district-level commemorations or lobbying local leaders on issues of justice or reparations, he had little to report. Most of the time, said Mario, he waited for direction from the national coordinator of the victims' association. From time to time, he was called to participate in meetings or workshops in Dili. At other times, he was asked to provide the names of 'vulnerable women victims' so that they could be linked into forms of material support.

Feeling disappointed at the lack of interview data, I asked Mario if he would be willing to accompany me to some of the mass graves where, in 1974/75 (at the height of the internal political conflict between Timor-Leste's two key political parties, UDT (*União Democrática Timorense*) and FRETILIN (*Frente Revolucionária de Timor-Leste Independente*)), UDT prisoners had been buried after being killed by FRETILIN. While on our travels, Mario and I talked about many things, including his own family background. He told me that he was originally from Viqueque District and that his mother, who had been a key member of the women's resistance organisation OPMT (*Organização Popular da Mulher Timorense*), had been killed in the late 1970s. Mario then described how he had recently travelled as part of a group of 150 members of his extended family to collect his mother's remains. The family, he said, had used 'traditional methods' to locate the site of the remains (which had involved listening to one member of the family, for whom the location had appeared in a dream). Mario further explained that when they arrived in the vicinity of the remains they were able to identify the exact location because some blood suddenly appeared on the ground as a sign. Once recovered, Mario's mother's remains were reburied at her birthplace after elaborate rituals – both customary and Catholic – had been performed. It was clear that the whole process had taken many months of planning, had been a significant expense and had consumed several days. It had required all the members of Mario's extended family to be present.

Mario's story of recovering his mother's remains is by no means unusual. Much has now been written about the extensive activity that has been occurring since the end of the occupation as families work to identify, recover and rebury the remains of those who died or were killed during the conflict (e.g. McWilliam 2008, 224–225; Bovensiepen 2014, 103; Grenfell 2012, 97; Kent 2016, 43). The whereabouts of many of these bodies was often unknown during the occupation. Large numbers of civilians perished from aerial bombardment, starvation and disease as they sheltered in the mountains behind FRETILIN lines in the early years of the occupation, their bodies interred in shallow bush graves or left to decay. Others were never seen by family members following their arrest by the Indonesian military or police. Part of the significance of these practices and rituals lies in the ways in which they work to reinforce kinship relationships, webs of sociality and trust that, in the wake of the fracturing effects of the Indonesian occupation, are critically important to families' sense of wellbeing.

Reburial rituals such as those described by Mario also underscore the degree to which, for many East Timorese, the dead remain a very real presence in the lives of the living. It is well known that in contexts where burial rituals have been disrupted and where uncertainty surrounding the fate of disappeared persons persists victims' families experience acute anxiety. This anxiety is magnified in a context such as Timor-Leste where the dead are thought to have a continuing influence in the lives of the living, and where relations with the dead are paramount to the wellbeing of their descendants. Maintaining good relations with the dead requires responding to their demands for attention and compensation, and conducting 'proper' burials (Myrtinnen 2014, 97). In cases where people are thought to have died 'bad deaths' – that is, deaths due to sudden and violent circumstances – there is a particular urgency about the need to conduct mortuary rituals, because of the power of the dead to disrupt the lives of the living. In these cases, it is often suggested that the dead will continue to 'wander' as ghosts and torment the lives of their descendants (by causing illness and death among the living) unless rituals are performed to render them spiritually harmless (McWilliam 2008, 224–225; Sakti 2013, 438).

An appreciation of the importance of maintaining equilibrium between the world of the living and the dead helps to shed a different perspective on some of the motivating factors behind families' attempts to claim veterans' pensions on behalf of their deceased relatives (martyrs). These efforts should not be understood simply as attempts by families to elevate their social, economic and political status (in contexts of acute poverty), but perhaps first and foremost as a means of appeasing the spirits of the dead by giving due recognition to their contributions and providing them with a dignified secondary burial. Accessing a veteran's pension enables families to undertake expeditions to recover the remains of the dead, purchase cement to construct new graves and headstones, and conduct associated rituals, all of which are often extremely costly. As one informant explained to me, it is only after appropriately reburying the dead that money from veterans' pensions can be used for everyday necessities. 'The dead come first.'[5]

In addition to family-led practices of remembrance and reburial, which often take place with little external support, faith-based actors are also assisting Timorese communities to rebuild their lives after the violence of the occupation. For instance, alongside customary mortuary rituals, Catholic priests are often called upon by families to organise special masses to remember and bless the dead. Faith-based actors are also working to assist some of the hundreds of thousands of East Timorese who, after the 1999 referendum, were displaced across the border into neighbouring West Timor, to reconcile with their families and, in some cases, to return to East Timor.

One prominent faith-based actor is Maria Lourdes (or Mana Lou as she is popularly known) who, since 1989, has run a Secular Catholic Institute known as ISMAIK (*Institutu Maun Alin Iha Kristu*; brothers and sisters in Christ), based in Dare, in the hills behind Dili, that is dedicated to working with the poor and the marginalised.[6] Since the 1999 referendum,

---

5   Interview with Oldericho Coimbra, Los Palos, July 2017.
6   A Secular Catholic Institute is an Institute of Consecrated Life in which men and women live as lay people in the world and seek to provide an example of Christian living.

Mana Lou has been engaged in efforts aimed at reconciling East Timorese families living on different sides of the border, which she describes as spiritually informed. She intensified these efforts after 2012, when she had a vision of Christ on the cross during a mass at Timor-Leste's 10-year independence celebrations. Since then, she has been visiting West Timor every month to provide spiritual companionship to displaced East Timorese, working with the leaders of the refugees (many of them former militia leaders) to pray and reflect. She also offers support and encouragement to those seeking to return to Timor-Leste.[7]

Faith-based actors such as Mana Lou command enormous respect among the communities in which they work. This respect is a legacy, in part, of the Indonesian occupation, when Catholic leaders took on an increasingly activist role and churches became 'safe havens' for resistance fighters and those seeking sanctuary from persecution (McGreggor et al. 2012, 1134–1135). Catholic doctrines also provided a source of solace and strength to those who were suffering. Moreover, the church's decision to use Tetum as the language of the church and its preparedness to tolerate the coexistence of animist beliefs and practices allowed Catholicism to become interwoven, over time, with local cultural and spiritual beliefs and practices. Significant rituals – such as those surrounding burials of the dead – often incorporate both Catholic and animist components (Grenfell 2012).

But more than this, the respect commanded by faith-based actors such as Mana Lou is grounded in their long-term relationships with specific local communities. Indeed, Mana Lou is at pains to stress that ISMAIK is not an NGO, and that she never does 'proposals' for her activities because, regardless of whether funding is available, she is committed to ongoing accompaniment of the poor and marginalised. Perhaps most importantly, in comparison to the transitional justice activities promoted by CSOs, which are grounded in a liberal rights framework and are directed towards building a nationwide victim constituency capable of directing rights claims to the state, the activities undertaken by faith-based actors such as Mana Lou implicitly recognise that, for those for whom the state is often a remote presence, the ongoing rebuilding of highly localised community and family relationships (including with the dead) is essential to viable social life.

---

7   Interview with Mana Lou, July 2016.

Conclusion

What I have drawn out in this chapter is that a great deal of the activity taking place in Timor-Leste, as families and communities seek to negotiate the legacies of the Indonesian occupation, bears little resemblance to the liberal transitional justice strategies promoted by CSO activists. This activity often occurs with little or no connection to the work of CSO activists, including the victims' association. Much of this activity is being undertaken by families and kinship groups with little external support. All of this suggests that, while CSOs may be facing difficulties cultivating a certain *kind* of civil society transitional justice activity in Timor-Leste, there is a lot of this activity going on if both 'civil society' and 'transitional justice' are viewed through a wider lens.

To be clear, I do not wish to argue that the strategies pursued by CSOs are fundamentally flawed or misguided. Over the long term, it may prove attractive, or empowering, to some East Timorese to identify as victims of the conflict and to elevate aspects of their identity associated with liberal conceptions of human rights over others, such as resistance credentials or kinship. My argument is simply that, at this point in time, there is a need for careful and critical reflection on the form of 'victim-centredness' that is currently being promoted by CSOs in Timor-Leste, and the extent to which it accords with prevalent understandings of subjectivity and people's immediate and everyday needs. In a context where families, clan and ancestors are intricately linked through blood, spirit and ties to the land, the victims' rights agenda – with its assumptions about individual victimhood and rights that should be upheld by the state – cannot, for ordinary East Timorese, necessarily be taken for granted as natural or self-evident (Robins 2015, 188). Moreover, investing in the victims' rights agenda requires a considerable leap of faith (not to mention time and resources) in a context where the state's presence in most of the country is remote, intermittent or in name only, and where basic issues of survival are paramount. In this context, there is little evidence that the victims' rights agenda will be transformative.

At a broader level, the Timor-Leste experience provokes reflection on how conceptions of both 'civil society' and 'victim-centredness' are constructed within a transitional justice field that has become increasingly prescriptive. Specifically, it raises questions about the kinds of activities and practices that current imaginings of transitional justice render visible and invisible, and how these imaginings connect to broader relations of power.

That there are significant power differentials at work in Timor-Leste is evident in the fact that local CSOs are required to navigate declining levels of donor funding, a state that has little interest in a victims' rights agenda and an international transitional justice industry that demands increased professionalisation and standardisation. This context inevitably provides incentives for CSOs to focus on certain issues, and detracts from their efforts to incorporate 'local knowledges' and develop creative, community-based approaches (Nesiah 2016, 29). It also leads to the neglect of everyday practices and strategies of social repair, due to their foreignness to the liberal transitional justice template. Greater attention to these practices might help to imagine more pluralistic, locally resonant, ways of addressing legacies of mass harm.

Bibliography

Basok, Tanya and Suzan Ilcan. 2006. 'In the Name of Human Rights: Global Organisations and Participating Citizens'. *Citizenship Studies* 10 (3): 309–327. doi.org/10.1080/13621020600772099.

Bovensiepen, Judith. 2014. 'Paying for the Dead: On the Politics of Death in Independent Timor-Leste'. *The Asia Pacific Journal of Anthropology* 15 (12): 103–122. doi.org/10.1080/14442213.2014.892528.

CAVR (Commission for Reception, Truth and Reconciliation). 2005. *Chega!. Report of the Commission for Reception, Truth and Reconciliation.* Dili. Timor-Leste. CAVR.

Government of Indonesia and Democratic Republic of Timor-Leste. 2005. *Terms of Reference for the Commission of Truth and Friendship.* 10 March. Available at www.etan.org/et2005/march/06/10tor.htm (accessed 16 October 2017).

Grenfell, Damian. 2012. 'Remembering the Dead from the Customary to the Modern in Timor-Leste'. *Local Global: Identity, Security, Community* 11: 86–109.

Jeffrey, Alex and Michaelina Jakala. 2015. 'Using Courts to Build States: The Competing Spaces of Citizenship in Transitional Justice Programmes'. *Political Geography* 47: 43–52. doi.org/10.1016/j.polgeo.2015.02.001.

Kent, Lia. 2015. 'After the Truth Commission: Gender and Citizenship in Timor-Leste'. *Human Rights Review* 17: 51–70. doi.org/10.1007/s12142-015-0390-2.

Kent, Lia. 2016. 'Sounds of Silence: Everyday Strategies of Social Repair in Timor-Leste'. *Australian Feminist Law Journal* 42 (1): 31–50. doi.org/10.1080/13200968.2016.1175403.

Magarrell, Lisa. 2007. 'Reparations in Theory and Practice'. *Report for the International Center for Transitional Justice.* New York: ICTJ.

McWilliam, Andrew. 2008. 'Fataluku Healing and Cultural Resilience in East Timor'. *Ethnos: Journal of Anthropology* 73 (2): 217–240. doi.org/10.1080/00141840802180371.

Merry, Sally Engle. 2006. *Human Rights and Gender Violence: Translating International Law into Local Justice.* Chicago: University of Chicago Press. doi.org/10.7208/chicago/9780226520759.001.0001.

Myrttinen, Henri. 2014. 'Claiming the Dead, Defining the Nation: Contested Narratives of the Independence Struggle in Post-Conflict Timor-Leste'. In *Governing the Dead: Sovereignty and the Politics of Dead Bodies*, edited by Finn Stepputat, 95–113: Manchester and New York: Manchester University Press.

Nesiah, Vasuki. 2016. *Transitional Justice Practice: Looking Back, Moving Forward.* Scoping Study Research Report. The Hague: Impunity Watch.

Robins, Simon. 2011. 'Towards Victim-Centred Transitional Justice: Understanding the Needs of Families of the Disappeared in Postconflict Nepal'. *The International Journal of Transitional Justice* 5 (1): 75–98. doi.org/10.1093/ijtj/ijq027.

Robins, Simon. 2013. *Families of the Missing: A Test for Contemporary Approaches to Transitional Justice.* London: Routledge.

Robins, Simon. 2015. 'Mapping a Future for Transitional Justice by Learning from Its Past'. *The International Journal of Transitional Justice* 9: 181–190. doi.org/10.1093/ijtj/iju031.

Sakti, Victoria Kumala. 2013. 'Thinking Too Much: Tracing Local Patterns of Emotional Distress after Mass Violence in Timor-Leste'. *The Asia Pacific Journal of Anthropology* 14 (5): 438–454. doi.org/10.1080/14442213.2013.826733.

2

Justice within the National Imaginary: Civil society and societal transition in Timor-Leste

Damian Grenfell[1]

Since the end of the Indonesian occupation of Timor-Leste in 1999 there has been much energy expended by activists, international aid agencies, non-governmental organisations (NGOs) and United Nations (UN) agencies towards ensuring a sustainable civil society. Such an effort can be understood for a range of reasons: the necessity of responding to immense suffering following 24 years of occupation; the need for broad societal participation in the creation of a new state and nation; and as a reflection of the commonly held view that a liberal democracy requires an active civil society. Given the extraordinary material destruction, mass displacement and wide-ranging human rights abuses that occurred as a result of the Indonesian occupation, civil society actors working in the field of transitional justice have concentrated efforts in Timor-Leste since in two key ways: first, through attempts to support victims; and second, to ensure that those responsible for crimes are held to account.

---

1   I would like to thank my colleagues in the Centre for Global Research at RMIT University in Melbourne, Australia, and the Instituto de Ciências Sociais (ICS) at the Universidade de Lisboa where I was based while drafting this chapter.

While civil society very often plays an important role in transitional justice efforts, the experience of Timor-Leste demonstrates that any assumption of a *necessarily* positive impact should at least be met with caution. As the key contention for this chapter, it is argued that as long as civil society remains anchored within a 'national imaginary' it can, at certain points, relegate or even diminish forms of recognition important to victims. This is especially the case where patterns of mourning and remembrance do not sit in commensurate relation with the 'nation'. In the continuing need to identify the fate of the missing or advocate for justice for those accused of human rights violations, for example, civil society efforts have been drawn into a fraught relationship with the state. Moreover, the experiences of victims have often been embedded discursively in national terms rather than reflecting the localised sociocultural patterns of remembering the dead and missing.

To make this argument, the chapter opens with a conceptual discussion that distinguishes civil society from the state on the basis that each are founded in different forms of legitimacy and each have a different relationship to the use of violence. Even as the state and civil society remain distinct in key ways, the second section nevertheless argues that civil society actors in Timor-Leste have often imagined justice largely in national terms, reinforcing the same territorial dimensions that demarcate state sovereignty. The third section draws the first two together to demonstrate that the emphasis given to the nation by civil society actors has limited the effectiveness of transitional justice efforts to some extent. Justice framed in national terms has on the one hand been undermined by an antagonistic state, while on the other it has risked alienating survivors and families of those killed and missing. In terms of the latter, this occurs both discursively and in practice via attempts to 'draw together' a war-torn society in ways that may not always give adequate priority to victims, including in the forms of recognition given to the dead and missing.

The ideas in this chapter are based on interviews with civil society actors in Timor-Leste between 2003 and 2017, analysis of policy and programmatic documents, project-related work within civil society and donor organisations, and general observation. The arguments made here are not of absolutes but of important trajectories and do not seek to diminish the many social benefits generated by civil society actors. It is nevertheless important to identify points of possible tension between the contributions of transitional justice processes to nation-building on one the hand and the needs of those who have suffered on the other.

Civil society and transitional justice

Transitional justice refers to a multifaceted process that simultaneously accounts for the crimes of perpetrators while creating new systems of justice in societies that have experienced widespread violence (Brahm 2007; Grenfell 2009; Lambourne 2009, 34, 36). For Andrieu (2010, 540), transitional justice represents 'nothing less than the transformation, or regeneration, of a whole society' requiring a range of interventions. Civil society actors are typically central to this process, and in Timor-Leste transitional justice initiatives have included support for victims' material restoration, assisting displaced peoples, locating the missing, collecting the remains of the dead, recording the experience of survivors, commemorating and memorialising incidents from the occupation, holding reconciliation events, promoting human rights, campaigning for an international tribunal to bring Indonesian perpetrators to trial, as well as developing a formal justice system. Together such practices are often assumed by policy actors, donors and academics as pivotal to 'ending the cycles of violence' (Minow 2002; Kovras 2012) in post-conflict states, drawing the intimate experiences of violence into larger societal frameworks that achieve a 'transition' in society.

To explore the tensions between programmatic assumptions and the needs of victims, it is important that some definitional shape is given to the concept of civil society. While 'civil society' is frequently employed in justice and peacebuilding literature, its actual meaning is often left implicit. In some instances it is defined empirically, for example by a typology of organisations, while elsewhere it is described by negation, as Gray and co-authors acknowledge:

> civil society (of which NGOs are an element) is that which exists between other elements of our social world and hence, civil society is defined by what it is not. Definition is, as a result, difficult and contingent on definitions/descriptions of the other elements of society from which civil society emerges. Changes in these other elements will, likewise, affect the size and character of civil society (Gray, Bebbington and Collison 2006, 322).

What is meant by the other 'elements' tends to shift according to ideology and context, though they typically include government (or state), market (or capital) and the family (or private sphere), with the 'civil' broadly encompassing other associations and collaborations that comprise social life. Civil society is not, however, simply the sum of the 'rest' of society, but defined in this chapter rather as marked by two key traits: first, in terms of the legitimating claim to civic virtue; and second, via a particular kind of relationship to violence.

In terms of the first trait, in accounting for associations outside of the state the 'civil' in civil society refers to actions that in some way claim to be for the wider benefit of a particular community. Such claims will differ remarkably and, as such, do not suggest a homogeneity other than the activity is legitimated by the claim that it positively contributes to social needs, wellbeing or sustainability. The emphasis on both its associational nature and public virtue has meant that civil society is often strongly associated with either the creation or the maintenance of democratic society as discussed by Foley and Edwards (1996) in a response to Michael Walzer (1992).

> In the rough pastiche that has become the commonly accepted version, a 'dense network of civil associations' is said to promote the stability and effectiveness of the democratic polity through both the effects of association on citizens' 'habits of the heart' and the ability of associations to mobilize citizens on behalf of public causes. Emergent civil societies in Latin America and Eastern Europe are credited with effective resistance to authoritarian regimes, democratizing society from below while pressuring authoritarians for change. Thus, civil society, understood as the realm of private voluntary association, from neighborhood committees to interest groups to philanthropic enterprises of all sorts, has come to be seen as an essential ingredient in both democratization and the health of established democracies (Foley and Edwards 1996, 38).

While civil society actors may make this claim at all different levels of society – including at the most local community level – in the case of transitional justice in Timor-Leste public benefit or 'cause' has been largely framed in terms of the potential contribution to nation-building in the wake of conflict. Speaking more generally, Shils points to the importance of the connection between civil society and the state by arguing that 'nationality is a necessary ingredient, perhaps even precondition for civil society. It is the collective self-consciousness which sustains the civil society. Concern for one's nation reinforces the concern for the common good' (Shils 1995, 116). While perhaps overstating the case, Shils points to an important aspect that is common to civil society actors: namely that the nation frequently sets the methodological and operational parameters to how activities are organised and the terms on which a 'common good' are imagined. How this relates more specifically to transitional justice is discussed in the next section, though here the point is that the kind of 'civicness' displayed is very often done so in national terms.

A second defining trait is that civil society actors do not challenge the state's claim to the monopoly over the legitimate use of violence within a given territory. Such an approach clearly adapts Weber's famous definition of the state (Gerth and Mills 1946, 77), albeit by following Gray and others in forming definitions based on other 'contingent elements of society', namely the state. The key here is to delineate the purpose of the violence, as civil society actors frequently contest the state including to the point of violence – seen often for instance with civil rights groups, unions and as part of social movement protests.[2] The important difference to highlight here is that between violence that is used towards specific objectives or occurs incidentally compared to that which overtly challenges the central legitimating claims of the state. Armed social movements may be thoroughly coherent in their claims to act for a common good and be recognised as having widespread authority. Nevertheless, in challenging the foundational legitimacy of the state, such groups and movements transition out of the category of civil society actors.[3]

In the case of Timor-Leste, FALINTIL[4] – the armed force for East Timorese independence during the Indonesian occupation – was part of a larger movement that included civil society actors. However, given its own commitment to the violent overthrow of a state, FALINTIL itself is understood here as an actor located outside of civil society. Even as

---

2   For example, a key policy platform of government may be challenged in strident terms and via large-scale mobilisation of people – as was the case in Timor-Leste when the Catholic Church demonstrated against government changes to school curriculums in 2005 – but when it does not challenge the core legitimacy of the state then such groups remain as part of civil society.

3   This position is distinct to that of the work of authors such as Labigne and Nassauer who name three distinct forms of violence that occur within civil society: reformist violence, demarcation violence and non-political violence. Demarcation violence is defined as politically radical and often opposed to the state, and includes organisations such Obraz, a fascist Serbian group. Such a group is able to be included in their definition as they define civil society without any reference to its civic nature, namely as 'the arena – outside of the family, the state, and the market – which is created by individual and collective actions, organizations and institutions to advance shared interests' (Labigne and Nassauer 2012, 3). As such, in effect beyond the state, family and market, any form of association is deemed as civil society, even fascistic ones. See Labigne and Nassauer (2012).

4   *Forças Armadas da Libertação Nacional de Timor-Leste*; Armed Forces for the National Liberation of East Timor.

civil society actors contested Indonesia's unlawful claim to legitimate rule of Timor-Leste – and therefore ultimately shared the objectives of independence with FALINTIL – at an organisational level they did not engage directly in armed insurrection and thus remained distinct from the militarised responses to occupation.

In the post-independence period, groups such as *Conselho Popular pela Defesa da República Democrática de Timor-Leste* (CPD-RDTL) maintained a significant space in contesting the state (Escollano Brandão 2015) until they were disbanded by the combined efforts of the police and the military (Belun 2017). This was also the case with the *Conselho Revolucionário Maubere* (CRM) – a group led by a dissident commonly known as 'Mauk Moruk'[5] – which was targeted again by joint police-military operations with Moruk being killed (RDTL 2015).[6] Again, the approach here draws a connection between civil society and the form that the challenge to the state takes; once violence is used to challenge state legitimacy then such actors move beyond that realm (and are often named in terms of criminals, terrorists, extremists and so forth by the state they are contesting).

In short then, in this chapter civil society accounts for forms of social collaboration grounded in a public virtue that do not challenge the state's claim to the monopoly over the legitimate use of violence within a given territory. Such a relationship ebbs and flows as the state itself changes, as seen in Timor-Leste across the transition from pre- to post-independence. The Suharto regime that was in power in Indonesia for almost the full duration of the occupation of Timor-Leste permitted at times a narrow and highly prescribed civil society to counter international criticism and manage internal dissent. In comparison, the kind of liberal democratic state that has been advanced in Timor-Leste post-independence has seen a civil society that is interested in the consolidation and maintenance of democratic society, often emphasising a role in providing a 'check on government' (Bell and O'Rourke 2007; Cubitt 2013, 91). This is particularly evident through the development of local NGOs whose key

5   His actual name was Paulino Gama.
6   In 2014, civil rights monitoring group *Yayasan Hak* (HAK) provided an update of Parliamentary Resolution No. 5/2014 outlawing the CPD-RDTL and CRM, and initiating joint operations between the police and military targeting these groups (Asosiasaun HAK 2014).

purpose is the monitoring of the state justice sector (JSMP[7]), government spending and development projects (*Lao Hamutuk*), security (*Belun*), human rights (*Yayasan Hak*), as well as corruption.

In a development or post-conflict context, aid organisations and donors tend to focus on the most structured and institutionalised aspects of civil society. Local NGOs provide a point of mutual legibility that facilitate shifts in resources from international agencies into national and local contexts. In practice, this can often mean that NGOs and civil society are treated as synonymous, even though, as recognised by Holloway, civil society encompasses far greater diversity in Timor-Leste:

> [The] interpretation of what constitutes civil society in Timor-Leste is very limiting and very unfortunate since it puts forward only a partial selection of Timorese organisations to represent what is, in fact, a very rich and complex series of associations and organisations. The interpretation partly springs from the language of donors who have put a high priority on supporting NGOs with their funds, and who have not identified or engaged with the richer complex of CSOs that exist in East Timor (Holloway 2004, 3).

In Timor-Leste, civil society incorporates a range of social collaborations including local, national and foreign NGOs, as well as NGO networks and umbrella organisations. However, it also extends much further – encompassing religious groups, including church governance, orders, parishes, prayer groups; community groups, including women's, youth, veterans and sporting groups; a myriad of community-based organisations (CBOs); not-for-profit education providers; farmer cooperatives and collectives. While recognising the need to consider these groups as part of civil society, the focus in this chapter will largely be on NGOs and related networks given that they have been so central to transitional justice efforts in Timor-Leste.

Finally, it is important to be clear that in this chapter the nation and the state are taken as two distinct entities: the state is a set of political structures, practices and processes involved in a particular form of governance within a defined territory (and legitimated as per the above), whereas a nation – which typically encompasses a state – is comprised of people who identify with and are integrated into a particular territorial domain. For the latter, the term the 'national imaginary' is used in this

---

7   Judicial System Monitoring Program.

chapter in the tradition of Benedict Anderson (1983). It is shorthand for the 'patterned convocations of the social whole' as argued by Steger and James (2013, 23), meaning the dominant ways the basis or parameters on which social life and collective endeavour are imagined. The national imaginary is a powerful way of understanding the connection between people, not least where independence has recently been won. Where this first section has argued that a key point of differentiation between civil society and the state are in the claims to sovereign power and the use of violence, the following section discusses how the two share the national imaginary and in turn the consequences for transitional justice.

Transitional justice, the state and the national imaginary

Arguably the three most significant transitional justice initiatives for Timor-Leste have been the Commission for Reception, Truth and Reconciliation (CAVR), the Serious Crimes Unit (SCU) and the Commission for Truth and Friendship (CTF). The CAVR was initiated in 2001 during the United Nations interregnum (from October 1999 though to May 2002) and undertook nationwide truth-telling and community reconciliation programs for less serious crimes committed during 1999. The SCU ran from 2000 through to 2005 and examined human rights abuses deemed severe, making 391 indictments over a five-year period[8] (Kirk and da Costa Bobo 2010, 9). As a later initiative, the CTF began in 2005 as a joint Timor-Leste–Indonesia state-level effort mandated to establish the truth with regards to human rights abuses committed in 1999 (CTF 2008; Hirst 2008). Rather than being part of civil society, these three organisations are understood as para-institutions of state formed via different orders of legislated authority.[9] Nevertheless, they remain important for discussion of civil society in this chapter for two reasons.

---

8   According to the International Center for Transitional Justice (ICTJ), of the total SCU indictments made, 84 defendants were convicted, 3 were acquitted during trial while more than 300 avoided trial as they remained in Indonesia, which would not comply with the indictments (Kirk and da Costa Bobo 2010, 9).

9   CAVR was created under the United Nations Transitional Authority for East Timor (UNTAET) via UNTAET Regulation 2001/10. It was given significant autonomy under this regulation though remained the legal creation of a transitional authority that in effect was a surrogate state. The SCU was likewise created under UNTAET Regulation 2000/11, while the CTF was created directly by both the East Timorese and Indonesian governments.

First, the CAVR and the SCU generated significant resources that could in turn be used by civil society actors. This included the collection and publication of different kinds of information including testimonies, indictments and qualitative and statistical analysis, their efforts in organising events that linked actors and communities together, as well as giving public legitimacy to transitional justice agendas. Even though there was much criticism that the CTF was designed to absorb international critique rather than further claims for justice (Kent 2011, 449–450), its final report has also become an important resource, especially as it endorsed much of CAVR's work (Kent 2011, 450).

Second, all three institutions framed and reinforced discourses and the programmatic purpose of transitional justice as bound tightly to the new national form. The CTF was justified in terms of ensuring sustainable relations for Timor-Leste as a new nation with its former occupier Indonesia. The SCU – and a follow-up Serious Crimes Investigation Team (SCIT) – viewed prosecutions as pivotal to the sustainability of a new nation in the establishment of accountability and the rule of law, and the CAVR considered reconciliation rather than retributive forms of justice as an important step in preventing future cycles of violence. Whether moving outwards to discussions of an international tribunal, or inwards towards reconciliation at the level of local community, the national imaginary provided the cornerstone from which transitional justice agendas were formed.

This approach has appeared to be again reflected in the formation of the state-sanctioned *Centro Nasional Chega!* (CNC), created in late 2016 by the East Timorese Council of Ministers and inaugurated in 2017. Carrying on the tradition of CAVR and the work of the Post-CAVR Secretariat, CNC focuses on important transitional justice efforts that include memorialisation and human rights advocacy (Leach 2016, 214). Reflecting its name, CNC's remit is a national one, and thus it continues the work of threading justice and nation together in how it engages with survivors and communities. This connection has been a constant theme in academic literature over the last two decades in terms of the state (Fletcher, Weinstein and Rowen 2009; Hamber and Wilson 2002) as well as truth and reconciliation commissions (Babo-Soares 2004; McAuliffe 2008; Wilson 2003). However, here the focus is on civil society actors and the consequences of framing transitional justice within a national imaginary.

The principal endogenous civil society actors – namely, those that have originated within and remain organisationally based within Timor-Leste – whose work has included transitional justice initiatives are NGOs, church-related organisations, community level activism and, in turn, associations and networks that incorporate, represent or are in part resourced by the former. For instance, East Timorese NGOs such as *Yayasan Hak*, *Fokupers* and *Lao Hamutuk* took leading roles in the early years of independence[10] (Robie 2015, 218). Other groups joined these three as part of the Timor-Leste National Alliance for an International Tribunal (ANTI), a 'coalition of organisations representing local and international NGOs, churches, students and victims' who campaigned for international mechanisms that would bring particularly Indonesian perpetrators of abuse to justice (ETAN 2004). The JSMP emerged principally to promote judicial accountability with its support of female victims of violence leading to the formation of *Asistensia Legal ba Feto no Labarik* (ALFela).[11] Other associations and networks have included the Popular Organisation of Timorese Women (OPMT)[12] that, following independence, undertook various activities including a women's history project. The 12 November Committee is comprised of victims of the 1991 Santa Cruz massacre, and the National Association of Victims and Martyrs and the Association of Ex-Political Prisoners (ASSEPOL) have represented different survivor led efforts (See Kent 2012; Rothschild 2017). In addition, *Associacaon Chega! Ba Ita* (ACbit) has undertaken the task of continuing to promote the work and principles of the CAVR through research and publications, as well as through initiatives such as reforming school curriculums and supporting activities for survivors. Into the early years of independence, these organisations and networks very often imbued their actions with a similar nationalism to that which fuelled their pursuit of independence, particularly the conflation of 'nation' and 'struggle'. This kind of sentiment is reflected in an interview with a RENETIL (*Resistência Nacional dos Estudantes de Timor Leste*) leader in 2004 where themes of struggle and liberation connect through to the national 'whole':

---

10   *Fokupers* for instance developed a database on violence against women during 1999 as well as provided support to widows post-independence, while all three organisations were advocated strongly on human rights.

11   *Asistensia Legal Ba Feto no Labarik* is a local NGO which provides free legal assistance to women and children.

12   *Organização Popular de Mulher Timor*.

> We still maintain the vision of a national liberation. In two
> different ways. People liberation, and country liberation. Still
> country liberation is relevant because we still have problem of
> sea border with Australia, the government … And the second
> is people liberation, means liberating people from poverty, from
> illiteracy, from disease and so on. It's very ambitious, it's not
> organization vision, it's the country vision. But you take this as
> a kind of RENETIL vision as well, to motivate people to see the
> reality, not as a part but as a whole. That's why we still keep this
> vision as an organization vision (interview, Dili, 2004).

Here, the nation remains the motivating frame for practice. Even as
a civil society organisation, the task of securing the national territory
remained a priority, while the second objective was one that took 'the
people' as a generalised and homogenised entity. Of relevance here is that
this vision of post-independence liberation would be performed 'not as
part but as a whole', a comment that is analogous in terms of scale to
the quote from Andrieu (2010, 540) at the outset of this chapter where
transitional justice is described as the transformation of 'a whole society'.
In both instances the society in question is that of the nation.

Whether classified as endogenous or exogenous, CSOs in Timor-Leste
have tended to work in ways that are grounded in the national imaginary.
This is manifest in various ways: for instance, discursively in terms of
the justification for transitional justice measures being important to the
'sustainability of the nation' or, as discussed above, to prevent cycles of
violence that may put the new nation at risk. Participation of victims
in programs has often been justified as an individual's or a community's
role in founding the nation. It is also seen, more implicitly perhaps, in
the design of programs where representatives from different locations are
drawn into events, workshops and other programming efforts on the basis
of ensuring national representation. Stories of abuse are told by people
from an 'illustrative number' of districts in spaces supported by civil
society, drawing their narratives into a national framing in a way that
is repeated as compilations of testimony that are published in reports,
advocacy materials and academic literature.

Concentrically related to these endogenous actors are a host of what
will be categorised here as exogenous CSOs. These are organisations –
typified by NGOs that are globally networked such as the International
Committee of the Red Cross (ICRC), the Jesuit Refugee Service, Amnesty
International and the International Center for Transitional Justice (ICTJ)

– whose authority and resource base are located beyond Timor-Leste while they are working directly on programs 'in country' and/or by the further funding of local partner organisations for projects. For instance, the International Committee of the Red Cross (ICRC) has coordinated with the Jakarta-based Asia Justice and Rights (AJAR) and the Timor-Leste Red Cross to reunite families that fled Timor-Leste to Indonesia in 1999 and continues to assist with the identification of those killed during the independence struggle (ICRC 2016). Other initiatives have included the Living Memory Project driven by Australia-based activists and ASSEPOL to record the testimonies of former political prisoners, as well as teams of forensic experts from both Australia and Argentina who have worked with the 12 November Committee in searching for the remains of victims.[13]

In Timor-Leste, demands for justice in national terms have been reinforced, rather than negated, by these exogenous civil society actors. This might sound contradictory given that NGOs have often been seen as central to an emergent 'global civil society' (Glasius 2009, 497) that can contest or undermine national sovereignty. Yet even NGOs that are part of highly mobile networks remain bound into, and typically self-organise along the lines of, a nation-state system. Moreover, exogenous and highly globalised NGOs have often set their practice according to a 'methodological nationalism', namely a belief that the nation is the appropriate scale for political and social organisation. In other words, an aid worker may be born elsewhere but still be motivated by the task of building a sustainable 'Timor-Leste' as it is assumed that, as anywhere, the nation sets the basic parameters for political life. The following quote from an ICTJ report written by both foreigners and East Timorese typifies how human rights abuses, their effects and the need for intervention are often framed (at least discursively) in a way that takes the nation as the natural basis for justice:

> Valorising victims and responding to their material needs can assist Timor-Leste's nation-building project. Although not posing a significant political threat due to their lack of organisation, victims of the past conflict represent a large, angry and disenfranchised group with a legitimate claim to reparation

---

13   The Jesuit Refugee Service assisted with border visits and communication between refugee groups (and resumed working with refugees during the 2006–2008 political crisis), West Timorese organisations collected information on human rights abuses in refugee camps, and other organisations such as Catholic Relief Services that have run peacebuilding programs.

from the Timor-Leste state. By addressing victims' specific needs, Timor-Leste will combat one of the underlying causes of social disadvantage in Timor-Leste – the experience of a serious human rights violation. It will also promote an inclusive Timor-Leste society by supporting victims' ability to enjoy their rights as full citizens (Kinsella and Pereira 2010, 3).

As per the discussion above, here again the frame is the national. Where the first section of this chapter discussed key elements of civil society, the contention in this section has been that civil society actors working in the field of transitional justice have tended to take the nation as the natural platform from which discourse and practice is oriented. Civil society actors may move downwards into 'local' communities or upwards to the 'international', but these shifts are anchored in an assumption that the national is the starting point for activity. Even 'universal human rights' become embedded in national treaties. In this way, civil society often reinforces the territorial basis for states, albeit even when there is antagonism and contestation between different elements of the state. That civil society actors are geared to such a scale may not be surprising given the origin of the nationalist conflict that underpinned the creation of Timor-Leste as an independent nation-state, though as will be discussed in the following section, this has ramifications for how civil society has engaged on issues of transitional justice.

The limits of national justice

In many respects, framing transitional justice agendas in national terms might seem the most obvious way in which to secure positive outcomes for survivors. Linking the experiences of people who have suffered abuse and human rights violations with the interests of the state via a nationalist discourse could conceivably lead to broadly inclusive and empathetic forms of recognition. The careful founding of common narratives based on inclusion and difference, and the development of solidarity and compromise as a way to navigate community-wide claims for justice, could also be potential outcomes of approaching justice integrated into broader processes of nation-formation. However, this has largely not been the case in Timor-Leste, where working at the level of the nation has limited the possibilities for justice in some respects. This is explored in this final section by examining the ramifications of approaching transitional justice in close association with the state and also imagining justice on a macro-level. Here, and as reflected on in the following quote by McEvoy as he engages with the work James Scott, there is a continuous risk in generating interventions that are imagined at a scale that in practice may limit rather than fulfil justice:

> One of the reasons Scott suggests 'state-centric' grand schemes often fail spectacularly is that they oversimplify. They may fail to take sufficient account of local customs and practical knowledge and to engage properly with community and civil society structures. Such failures, often justified in the name of efficiency, professional expertise or simply 'getting the job done', may in turn lead to incompetence or maladministration and encourage grass-roots resistance to such state-led initiatives (McEvoy 2007, 424).

As suggested by McEvoy, while large-scale programs may be justified in terms of efficiency, they can fail by not being able to adapt to local intricacies. Beyond instrumental reasons of efficiency, programs may also be driven by actors that see a particular scale as appropriate, needed and justified in ideological terms, including that of nationalism. The concern here then is not that civil society is left out of consideration, but rather that civil society may take on some of the same characteristics as a state, in this instance in terms of imagining the nation as the appropriate scale by which justice is primarily located. This, it is argued, has at least two quite different ways of limiting the opportunities for transitional justice to gain traction.

In the first instance, by making a strong connection between the nation and justice, civil society actors draw debates into a framework that can be directly contested in cases of an antagonistic state. This is not to conflate the nation and the state, but rather to argue that when civil society actors frame transitional justice in national terms the topic is drawn into a domain where the state tends to be able to claim a very significant level of legitimacy. If the state takes a contrary position to civil society, the latter can become quickly outmanoeuvred and justice agendas delegitimated. In cases where a governing elite is antagonistic to particular strategies or programs, claims to know and act in the national interest can be used to contain and undermine advocacy for transitional justice measures. This is a position that can be consolidated even further in sites such as Timor-Leste where a state elite is comprised of former resistance leaders who have themselves paid heavily for their contribution to national independence.

In Timor-Leste, political leaders have shown considerable reluctance to engage in transitional justice measures, including those proposed or initiated by civil society actors (Kingston 2006). In fact, the response from the political elite has very often been one of antagonism, particularly to agendas that have called for different forms of international accountability for human rights abuses, especially those committed by Indonesia. State responses from the East Timorese state to such agendas and advocacy have included undermining the CAVR report when it was first released, continuously delaying the debate of the CAVR recommendations in parliament, opposing the issuing of indictments by the SCU, creating organisations such as the CTF to undermine claims that an international tribunal was required, and the granting of pardons (including in contravention of the law preventing the release of indicted Indonesians who have re-entered Timor-Leste). Further to this, a governing elite has sanctioned clear hierarchies in the commemoration, recognition and distribution of resources, not only giving priority to veterans over civilian survivors but also with a clear delineation in terms of gender (Kent and Kinsella 2014). The significance of these hierarchies is that it focuses forms of recognition on former combatants for its own ends, though this has also meant that any claims for justice by or for the broader population occur without the legitimating support of the state.

The state's undermining of transitional justice agendas has occurred for domestic political reasons (for instance, to ensure veterans are seen as a priority) and also as a reflection of the desire not to antagonise its former occupier. Indonesia geographically surrounds Timor-Leste, controls the western portion of the same island as well as vital air and sea routes, and is the key source of imported goods. To be seen to be supporting civil society agendas for prosecutions or an international tribunal could potentially antagonise elements within the Indonesian state, not least the military, and create any number of potential problems for Timor-Leste.

While the placation of Indonesia has led to much criticism of former president and prime minister Xanana Gusmão (Kingston 2006), antagonism by the state can in part be understood via the distinctions made earlier in this chapter between the state and civil society. The state claims sovereign authority and, as an enabler of that, a monopoly over the legitimate use of violence. While civil society plays a role in governance – for instance, the regulation of social relations via changes in norms and behaviours frequently referred to as 'socialisation' in Timor-Leste – civil society actors do not make a claim to a legitimate use of violence. As such, contestation over transitional justice in Timor-Leste, and what often appears as an inappropriate level of appeasement to the Indonesians, can be understood as born out of one of the key points of differentiation between civil society and the state. As such, civil society has often approached transitional justice (especially on questions of accountability for human rights abuses) within a national imaginary that has left it vulnerable to an antagonistic state that cannot risk the same 'civic virtue'. In Timor-Leste, no matter the nationalist credentials of civil society actors, state elites have often claimed a pre-eminent relationship to the nation as a way to undermine certain transitional justice initiatives in a bid to avert risking challenges from other states to capacity to govern, including a claim to the legitimate use of violence.

While working within a national imaginary has meant that certain civil society efforts have to date been countered by the state, the second limitation discussed here relates to the effect of giving preference to the national over other more localised forms of polity. This is particularly evident when addressing the issue of the dead of war and the burial of human remains in Timor-Leste. As a result of the struggle for independence, a large number of people remain missing. Statistically it is almost impossible to know how many, though the figure has been put at the 'tens of thousands' (Robins 2010, 5). Children were forced to work with the Indonesian military and thousands were abducted and taken to live in the homes of Indonesians across the archipelago (CAVR 2005, 26). Many thousands of other people died as combatants and civilians: buried in massacre sites and temporary graves, left where they were killed, or were 'disappeared'. Since 1999, remains have been recovered through the efforts of former East Timorese commanders, forensic investigations undertaken with support from countries such as Australia and Argentina, along with support from civil society actors and by the efforts of families themselves (Kinsella and Blau 2013, 4). Many remains have yet to be located and the state's approach to the missing thus far can be described as ad hoc and at times selective, where priority is given to retrieving the remains of the political elite.

It is difficult to overestimate the importance of recovering the remains of the deceased in any circumstance in Timor-Leste, even more so when the person has died or been killed through violent events (Bovensiepen 2014, 116). Of fundamental importance is ensuring that the spirits of the deceased are shown proper respect. Following funerary rituals is key in fulfilling this need. An unnatural or violent death, or one where the death incurs a sense of debt to those still alive, can mean a spirit is left in a restless state and can be a source of potential risk to the living. Poor health, misfortune and accidents are often understood as being caused by angry ancestors. This is not a secondary or residual element in Timorese culture, but is frequently expressed as foundational to understanding why and how things happen to people. Often scarce resources are deployed to ensure recognition. The need to recover the remains of the dead, or to undertake surrogate forms of recognition, is considered of paramount importance (Winch 2017).

The burying of former veterans in the 'national heroes' cemetery in Timor-Leste, or in one of the various ossuaries that have been built in regional centres around the country, ensures that these deaths are irrevocably tied to the formation of the nation (Viegas and Feijó 2017). And yet these bodies and their spirits, along with the thousands of non-combatants killed in the war, are very often connected into a different community comprised of the living and the ancestral domain, via association with an *uma lulik* (sacred house). This is a kind of 'customary polity' that exists across a different kind of space and time to that of the nation (Grenfell 2015) where there is a specific and exclusive affiliation to one sacred house.

On issues of transitional justice, civil society actors may reach into the local levels and gather the most intimate stories of abuse, but these stories are elevated and recalibrated via workshops, research, training, advocacy and campaigns as if part of a national 'whole'. Even as civil society has shifted its focus from an international tribunal to reconciliation, reparations and the rights of survivors (and has recognised the need to include more space for their voices) (Kent 2012, 194–195), the national imaginary still figures as the natural basis from which organising occurs: from how initial engagement with communities is framed and legitimated, to how programs are designed in terms of lifting discreet communities into common dialogue and, in turn, to how final presentation of facts are framed in national terms. This may have some benefits, but such an approach should also be met with some caution.

Drawing testimony from victims in order to advocate on their behalf for reparations, or to create a record of their struggle as a public good, presents risks when people are drawn into a domain where there are not the resources or political will to, in turn, ensure adequate recognition and action.[14] Testimony can lead to a sense of emptiness rather than fulfilment and, as Simon Robin's work attests, it can lead communities who do not receive hoped-for outcomes to disengage from the efforts of civil society:

> Like from the Red Cross, they came here last year and informed us that, for those who had lost their family and did not find their bones yet, you come together here so we can find ways or solutions to resolve this problem, and afterwards we never heard anything again from them and it seems they lost it [the bones] on the way. As we said before the Red Cross also came here, collected all our names, they brought the entire list but where are they now; they have probably thrown them away or thrown them in the garbage. That is why we as the family of the victims, we find it hard to meet or talk to you people, as if you came now. Because so many interviews on the same topics have been made with us as the victims' family but they never yield any result (Focus group participant, Bobonaro) (Robins 2010, 32).

Whether this is a common experience or otherwise is not the point. Rather, what is important are the dynamics that produce antagonism or indifference to efforts that are framed as assisting the community.[15] Either way, such a sentiment is indicative of the kind of dilemma where the experience of personal trauma and abuse is elevated into a national discourse without the necessary resources or political motivation at that level to respond adequately. Asking for people's participation raises expectations and when these remain unfulfilled then people may choose to withdraw. This is even more difficult when there is a failure to recognise the implications for customary practice. Giving testimony means to '*konta uluk*' – to talk about the past. Yet, to speak about the dead and then not respond with action is to risk the wrath of one's ancestors (Robins 2010); the ancestors are listening and their own heightened expectation of recognition and peace may lead to reprisal if left unmet.

---

14   This is not to say that there are not advantages for people in the way that testimony has been collected, as it may assist with the return of remains for instance, or with end results that assist with everyday needs including spiritual. There may also be therapeutic and social advantages in drawing victims together to share and be afforded some level of public recognition, even more so in instances where the state has not provided adequate levels of recognition.

15   See also Lia Kent's 'Sounds of Silence' (2016) for her analysis of silence, in this instance for reasons of pragmatism as well as civility.

Conclusion

The establishment of the *Centro Nasional Chega!* over 2016 and 2017 may give a new momentum to the transitional justice agenda in Timor-Leste. And it is not insignificant that this body was formed by the Council of Ministers, thus suggesting that both difference and space may exist at the upper levels of state for certain transitional justice agendas to be recognised. Given the above arguments, the CNC could also be an opportunity to explore different ways forward in terms of how discourses, activities and strategic objectives are formulated and enacted. It may mean that working locally, for instance, is given emphasis and in a way where what the nation means to people evolves as one part and one layer to how justice is approached. If this is to occur, however, it is important that consideration is given to how different actors – including civil society – interact with local communities and the way priorities and needs are expressed to emanate outwardly from that level. Again, this may mean that survivors will choose to speak in terms of the nation as part of that discourse. However, it may also give survivors the space necessary to forge a localised form of recognition that answers to customary sociality while also finding avenues for recognition and reconciliation at the national level in a way that is negotiated with and supported (rather than contested) by the state. This might enable a new and necessary space for justice to be imagined.

Bibliography

Anderson, Benedict. 1983. *Imagined Communities: Reflections on the Origin and Spread of Nationalism.* London: Verso Books.

Andrieu, Kora. 2010. 'Civilising Peacebuilding: Transitional Justice, Civil Society and the Liberal Paradigm'. *Security Dialogue* 41 (5): 537–558. doi.org/10.1177/0967010610382109.

Asosiasaun HAK. 2014. 'Relatoriu Monitorizasaun Direitus Umanus Periodu Fevreiru – Abril 2014'. Civil Society Monitoring Report, Centre for Global Research Timor-Leste Library, Melbourne.

Babo-Soares, Dionísio. 2004. '*Nahe Biti*: The Philosophy and Process of Grassroots Reconciliation (and Justice) in East Timor'. *The Asia Pacific Journal of Anthropology* 5 (1): 15–33. doi.org/10.1080/1444221042000201715.

Bell, Christine and Catherine O'Rourke. 2007. 'The People's Peace? Peace Agreements, Civil Society, and Participatory Democracy'. *International Political Science Review* 28 (3): 293–324. doi.org/10.1177/0192512107077094.

Belun. 2017. *'From Kindergarten to High School': Perceptions of Timor-Leste's Military and Police Ten Years after the 2006 Crisis*. Dili: Belun.

Bovensiepen, Judith. 2014. 'Paying for the Dead: On the Politics of Death in Independent Timor-Leste'. *The Asia Pacific Journal of Anthropology* 15 (2): 103–122. doi.org/10.1080/14442213.2014.892528.

Brahm, Eric. 2007. 'Transitional Justice, Civil Society, and the Development of the Rule of Law in Post-Conflict Societies'. *International Journal for Not-For-Profit Law* 9 (4): 62–69.

CAVR (Commission for Reception, Truth and Reconciliation). 2005. *Chega! The Final Report of the Timor-Leste Commission for Reception, Truth and Reconciliation (CAVR)*. Dili: Post-CAVR Technical Secretariat.

CTF (Commission for Truth and Friendship). 2008. *Per Memoriam Ad Spem: Final Report of The Commission for Truth & Friendship (CTF) Indonesia-Timor-Leste*. Denpasar: Commission for Truth & Friendship Indonesia-Timor-Leste.

Cubitt, Christine. 2013. 'Constructing Civil Society: An Intervention for Building Peace?' *Peacebuilding* 1 (1): 91–108. doi.org/10.1080/21647259.2013.756274.

Escollano Brandão, Constantino da Conçeição Costa Ximenes. 2015. *Istoria Ezistensia CPD-RDTL no Implikasaun sira ba Futuru Estadu Demokratiku*. Policy Brief No. 10, Dili: Early Warning Early Response (Belun).

ETAN (The East Timor National Alliance for an International Tribunal). 2004. 'Statement to the Technical Assessment Mission from United Nations Headquarters, New York'. ETAN, 15 January 2004. etan.org/news/2004/01alliance.htm.

Fletcher, Laurel E., Harvey M. Weinstein and Jamie Rowen. 2009. 'Context, Timing and the Dynamics of Transitional Justice: A Historical Perspective'. *Human Rights Quarterly* 31: 163–220. doi.org/10.1353/hrq.0.0058.

Foley, Michael W. and Bob Edwards. 1996. 'The Paradox of Civil Society'. *Journal of Democracy* 7 (3): 38–52. doi.org/10.1353/jod.1996.0048.

Gerth, Hans H. and Charles W. Mills. 1946. *From Max Weber: Essays in Sociology*. New York: Oxford University Press.

Glasius, Marlies. 2009. 'What is Global Justice and Who Decides? Civil Society and Victim Responses to the International Criminal Court's First Investigations'. *Human Rights Quarterly* 31 (2): 496–520. doi.org/10.1353/hrq.0.0075.

Gray, Rob, Jan Bebbington and David Collison. 2006. 'NGOs, Civil Society and Accountability: Making the People Accountable to Capital'. *Accounting, Auditing & Accountability Journal* 19 (3): 319–348. doi.org/10.1108/09513570610670325.

Grenfell, Damian. 2015. 'Of Time and History: The Dead of War, Memory and the National Imaginary in Timor-Leste'. *Communication, Politics & Culture* 48 (3): 16–28.

Grenfell, Laura. 2009. 'Promoting the Rule of Law in Timor-Leste'. *Conflict, Security & Development* 9 (2): 213–238. doi.org/10.1080/14678800902925143.

Hamber, Brandon and Richard A. Wilson. 2002. 'Symbolic Closure through Memory. Reparation and Revenge in Post-Conflict Societies'. *Journal of Human Rights* 1 (1): 35–53. doi.org/10.1080/14754830110111553.

Hirst, Megan. 2008. *Too Much Friendship, Too Little Truth: Monitoring Report on the Commission of Truth and Friendship in Indonesia and Timor-Leste*. New York: International Center for Transitional Justice.

Holloway, Richard. 2004. 'What is Civil Society in Timor-Leste?' Non-peer reviewed article, Centre for Global Research Timor-Leste Library, Dili.

ICRC (International Committee of the Red Cross). 2016. 'Indonesia and Timor-Leste: Facts & Figures, January-September 2016'. ICRC, 20 October. www.icrc.org/en/document/indonesia-timor-leste-facts-figures-january-september-2016.

Kent, Lia. 2011. 'Local Memory Practices in East Timor: Disrupting Transitional Justice Narratives'. *The International Journal of Transitional Justice* 5 (3): 434–455. doi.org/10.1093/ijtj/ijr016.

Kent, Lia. 2012. *The Dynamics of Transitional Justice: International Models and Local Realities in East Timor*. Abingdon: Routledge.

Kent, Lia. 2016. 'Sounds of Silence: Everyday Strategies of Social Repair in Timor-Leste'. *Australian Feminist Law Journal* 42 (1): 31–50. doi.org/10.1080/13200968.2016.1175403.

Kent, Lia and Naomi Kinsella. 2014. '*A Luta Kontinua* (The Struggle Continues)'. *International Feminist Journal of Politics* 17 (3): 473–494. doi.org/10.1080/14616742.2014.913383.

Kingston, Jeffrey. 2006. 'Balancing Justice and Reconciliation in East Timor'. *Critical Asian Studies* 38 (3): 271–302. doi.org/10.1080/14672710600871430.

Kinsella, Naomi and Soren Blau. 2013. 'Searching for Conflict Related Missing Persons in Timor-Leste: Technical, Political and Cultural Considerations'. *Stability* 2 (1): 1–14. doi.org/10.5334/sta.au.

Kinsella, Naomi and Manuela L. Pereira. 2010. *Unfulfilled Expectations: Victims' Perceptions of Justice and Reparations in Timor-Leste*. Brussels: International Center for Transitional Justice.

Kirk, James and Carlito da Costa Bobo. 2010. *Impunity in Timor-Leste: Can the Serious Crimes Investigation Team Make a difference?* New York: International Center for Transitional Justice.

Kovras, Iosif. 2012. 'Explaining Prolonged Silences in Transitional Justice: The Disappeared in Cyprus and Spain'. *Comparative Political Studies* 46 (6): 730–756. doi.org/10.1177/0010414012463879.

Labigne, Anaël and Anne Nassauer. 2012. 'Violence in Civil Society: Insights from the CSI Databases'. In *Conflict and Violence: Insights from the CIVICUS Civil Society Index Project*, edited by Wolfgang Dorner and Regina A. List, 127–143. London: Bloomsbury Academic.

Lambourne, Wendy. 2009. 'Transitional Justice and Peacebuilding after Mass Violence'. *The International Journal of Transitional Justice* 3 (1): 28–48. doi.org/10.1093/ijtj/ijn037.

Leach, Michael. 2016. *The Politics of Timor-Leste: Democratic Consolidation after Intervention*. Ithaca: Cornell University Press. doi.org/10.22459/NE.09.2015.04.

McAuliffe, Pádraig. 2008. 'East Timor's Community Reconciliation Process as a Model for Legal Pluralism in Criminal Justice'. *Law, Social Justice and Global Development* 12 (1): 1–21 (online journal).

McEvoy, Kieran. 2007. 'Beyond Legalism: Towards a Thicker Understanding of Transitional Justice'. *Journal of Law and Society* 34 (4): 411–440. doi.org/10.1111/j.1467-6478.2007.00399.x.

Minow, Martha. 2002. 'Breaking the Cycles of Hatred'. In *Breaking the Cycles of Hatred: Memory, Law and Repair*, edited by Martha Minow and Nancy L. Rosenblum, 14–76. New Jersey: Princeton University Press.

RDTL (República Democrática de Timor Leste). 2015. 'Regrettably, Mauk Moruk Killed in the Joint Operation'. Media Release, 8 August 2015. timor-leste.gov.tl/?p=13009&lang=en.

Robie, David. 2015. 'La'o Hamutuk and Timor-Leste's Development Challenges: A Case Study in Human Rights and Collaborative Journalism'. *Media Asia* 42 (3–4): 209–224. doi.org/10.1080/01296612.2016.1142247.

Robins, Simon. 2010. *An Assessment of the Needs of Families of the Missing in Timor-Leste*. York: Post-War Reconstruction and Development Unit (PRDU), University of York.

Rothschild, Amy. 2017. 'Victims Versus Veterans: Agency, Resistance and Legacies of Timor-Leste's Truth Commission'. *International Journal of Transitional Justice* 11 (3): 443–462. doi.org/10.1093/ijtj/ijx018.

Shils, Edward. 1995. 'Nation, Nationality, Nationalism and Civil Society'. *Nations and Nationalism* 1 (1): 93–118. doi.org/10.1111/j.1354-5078.1995.00093.x.

Steger, Manfred B. and Paul James. 2013. 'Levels of Subjective Globalization: Ideologies, Imaginaries, Ontologies'. *Perspectives on Global Development and Technology* 12 (1–2): 17–40. doi.org/10.1163/15691497-12341240.

Viegas, Susana de Matos and Rui Feijó. 2017. 'Territorialities of the Fallen Heroes'. In *Transformations in Independent Timor-Leste: Dynamics of Social and Cultural Cohabitations*, edited by Susana de Matos Viegas and Rui Graça Feijó. London and New York: Routledge. doi.org/10.4324/9781315535012.

Walzer, Michael. 1992. 'The Civil Society Argument'. In *Dimensions of Radical Democracy: Pluralism, Citizenship, Community*, edited by Chantal Mouffe, 89–107. London: Verso.

Wilson, Richard A. 2003. 'Anthropological Studies of National Reconciliation Processes'. *Anthropological Theory* 3 (3): 367–387. doi.org/10.1177/14634 996030033007.

Winch, Bronwyn. 2017. '"*La iha Fiar, la iha Seguransa*": The Spiritual Landscape and feeling secure in Timor-Leste'. *Third World Thematics: A TWQ Journal* 2 (2–3): 197–210. doi.org/10.1080/23802014.2017.1320200.

3

The omnipresent past: Rethinking transitional justice through digital storytelling on Indonesia's 1965 violence

Ken Setiawan

Almost 20 years since the fall of authoritarianism, Indonesia is yet to deliver justice on the human rights violations the country witnessed during the New Order (1966–1998). As such, the Indonesian transitional justice process can be described at best as 'delayed' (Suh 2016, 241) or at worst as 'failed' (Kimura 2015, 73). This raises the question of how Indonesian civil society actors have responded to this situation, particularly regarding arguably the most complex of past human rights violations in the country: the 1965–1966 violence (henceforth the 1965 violence) during which more than half a million were killed and hundreds of thousands were detained for long periods of time without trial. This chapter focuses on the recent emergence of digital activism on Indonesia's 1965 violence in which the non-witness generation, who were not physically present at the event (Jilovski 2015, 11), has taken a prominent role. I will discuss why these platforms have emerged and what the stories disseminated through them can tell about processes of transitional justice, taking a particular interest in the societal legacies of the violence.

This chapter starts with a historical background of the 1965 violence and the trajectory of transitional justice in Indonesia following the fall of the New Order regime in 1998. The 1965 violence is particularly significant in the context of transitional justice in Indonesia, both because of its large scale and because it marked the ascendancy of authoritarian rule. Moreover, the New Order regime successfully hijacked the memory of the violence, portraying communists as traitors and a threat to stability and security. In so doing, the regime justified the killings as necessary for the nation's survival and legitimised its political rule. As this chapter will show, this discourse has remained strong in the post-authoritarian period despite increased human rights protections in law and the development of transitional justice mechanisms. The salience of this discourse has once again become evident during the current presidency of Joko Widodo ('Jokowi'), where dominant political discourses remain largely unconducive towards transitional justice efforts.

The second part of this chapter addresses how civil society actors continue to challenge these narratives, representing a 'fragile, but persistent culture of contestation' (Kuddus 2017, 82). Focusing on the emergence of digital storytelling websites on the 1965 violence, in which I also have been personally involved, I discuss why civil society actors have turned to digital media. Through analysing two stories of grandchildren of those who were directly affected by the 1965 events, I will argue that these websites are not only relevant for transitional justice because they seek to connect young people with a largely unknown past, but also because stories of the non-witness generation convey how a dark chapter of history is experienced today. Using the concept of postmemory, or the strong connection of persons to an event that preceded their births (Hirsch 2008, 106–107), this chapter explores what the experiences of the non-witness generation may offer to the understanding of the transitional justice process in Indonesia, and in particular the societal legacies of state terror.

The 1965 violence

On the night of 30 September 1965, a group of conspirators in the Indonesian Army abducted and murdered six high-ranking generals and a lieutenant. Almost immediately Major General Suharto, the then commander of the Army Strategic Reserve, took action and crushed the '30th of September Movement' within a day. In the period that followed, the Army-controlled press labelled the movement as 'counter-revolutionary' and accused the PKI (*Partai Komunis Indonesia*; Indonesian Communist Party) of being its mastermind. In mid-October, Suharto was appointed commander of the Army, in which capacity he ordered troops to initiate operations against remnants of the movement. Between October 1965 and early 1966, approximately 500,000 party members and their sympathisers were killed, while another 600,000–750,000 were imprisoned, often for lengthy periods without trial (McGregor 2013, 138).

The massacres and mass imprisonments provided the stage for Suharto's ascendancy to power. He ruled the country until 1998, during which time Indonesia witnessed severe and systematic human rights violations. The Suharto regime, named the New Order, portrayed its role in crushing the 30th of September Movement as saving the country from the communist threat. In so doing, it legitimised the killings and mass detentions, which served to eliminate the Indonesian Left and created an authoritarian state friendly to western geopolitical objectives in the context of the Cold War.[1]

With anti-communism being the cornerstone of the new regime, the consequences were grim for members of leftist organisations or individuals who had an affiliation to them. This included family members, who became 'Indonesia's own version of the untouchables' (McGregor 2013, 139). The stigmatisation of 'communists', a label used not only to describe party members but also anyone regarded as subversive, was propagated by the government through mass media and at schools. Consequently, during the New Order public memories of the 1965 violence were surrounded by 'fearful silence and … collective amnesia' (Wahyuningroem 2013, 120). There was virtually no space for alternative discourses as political opposition was shut down violently by the Suharto regime. It was only after the fall of the New Order in 1998 that experiences of the violence could be shared in the public domain, and that human rights groups were able to demand openly that the government take responsibility for its crimes.

Seeking to end an inconvenient past: Transitional justice in Indonesia

In the immediate years following the fall of the New Order, human rights protections swiftly became incorporated into Indonesia's legal system because of international and domestic pressure. This included the enactment of the Human Rights Law (Law 39/1999), which provided

---

1   The elimination of the Left repositioned Indonesia into the Western bloc, and secured Western economic and military interests across maritime South-East Asia (McGregor 2013, 140–141).

guarantees of both civil and political, as well as economic, social and cultural, rights and strengthened the legal status and mandate of Komnas HAM (*Komisi Nasional Hak Asasi Manusia*; the National Human Rights Commission). Human rights norms were also included in the Constitution (2000), which saw the addition of a specific chapter on human rights, modelled on the Universal Declaration of Human Rights (UDHR). In addition, the Human Rights Courts Law (Law 26/2000) established permanent Human Rights Courts with the jurisdiction over gross human rights violations including crimes against humanity and the crime of genocide. This law also provided the possibility to establish Ad Hoc Courts for cases that occurred before 2000. Indonesia ratified all major international human rights treaties, established a number of state institutions charged with human rights protection and introduced the first five-year National Action Plan on Human Rights (RANHAM), setting out priorities and strategies with regard to human rights implementation. State capacity for responding to present and past human rights cases thus improved remarkably (Setiawan 2016a, 12–13).

Yet justice for past human rights violations remained an uphill battle, whether through judicial or non-judicial mechanisms. To date, only two Ad Hoc human rights courts have been established. These concerned gross human rights violations in East Timor in the lead up to, and following, the 1999 independence referendum[2] and the 1984 Tanjung Priok case.[3] These tribunals did not have the desired outcomes: in both cases, only lower-ranked military officers were tried, and all were acquitted at various stages of the judicial process (Sulistiyanto 2007; Cammack 2016). While Komnas HAM recommended that a number of cases of past violations be addressed in Ad Hoc Courts, these were rejected by the Attorney General's Office (Setiawan 2016a, 24–25) and contributed to ongoing impunity. In 2012, following a lengthy investigation, Komnas HAM recommended the establishment of an Ad Hoc Court for the 1965 violence,[4] which

---

2   This meant that violence perpetrated by the Indonesian military during the occupation of East Timor was excluded. The establishment of an Ad Hoc Court served to pre-empt the creation of an international tribunal (Cammack 2016, 191).

3   In the Tanjung Priok case, the Indonesian military opened fire on demonstrators led by Amir Biki, an Islamic leader and regime critic. The demonstration took place in the context of new policies to restrict the place of Islam in Indonesian politics. According to some estimates, 400 people were killed by the military.

4   In the same report, Komnas HAM also recommended the 1965 violence to be resolved through non-judicial means.

was rejected by the Attorney General who argued that it was 'difficult to investigate cases which have happened that many years ago' (*Voice of America* 2012).

While the argument put forward by the Attorney General reflects a preference for non-judicial mechanisms, which has received renewed attention under the current presidency of Joko Widodo (see below), their establishment at the national level has been largely unsuccessful.[5] In 2004, parliament passed Law 27/2004 on the Truth and Reconciliation Commission (TRC) to settle cases of past human rights violations outside of the courts. Drafted to address cases that occurred before the enactment of the 2000 Human Rights Courts Law, it was anticipated that the TRC would also address the 1965 violence. However, a number of provisions in the Law were problematic, including that compensation for victims would only be offered in conjunction with an amnesty. Several human rights organisations then brought the Law to the Constitutional Court, which agreed that this provision contradicted the Constitution and the principles of international law. However, rather than annulling the particular article, the Constitutional Court cancelled the entire law, leaving Indonesia without a formal non-judicial mechanism to settle past human rights violations.

The ineffectiveness of transitional justice mechanisms in Indonesia has been attributed to both a lack of political will to address past human rights violations (Sulistiyanto 2007, 90; Wahyuningroem 2013, 126) and to a direct result of the continued presence of New Order players in today's political elite (Kimura 2015, 88). Elite continuity has been identified as a major constraining factor in transitional justice efforts (Posner and Vermeule 2004, 770–772). In Indonesia, the domination of 'old faces' in Indonesian politics has been attributed to the characteristics of authoritarianism. Hadiz and Robison (2013) have ascribed this to the destructive nature of the previous regime that 'disorganised civil society and destroyed liberal forces' (Hadiz and Robison 2013, 36). The lack of political and ideological alternatives has thus allowed New Order elites to continue to yield power and wealth, while new players continue to engage with the political practices of the past. Aspinall has argued that during the New Order, political and social forces were tolerated as long as they obeyed the rule of the regime and did not challenge it directly. This led to

---

5   It should be noted that, at a local level, there have been some successful reconciliation processes. See, for instance, Wahyuningroem 2013 and Kuddus 2017.

'semi-opposition', a combination of opposition and compromise, which has continued to influence the nature of the democratic transition and that explains why most key political forces after 1998 were either direct participants or marginal semi-oppositional players in the Suharto regime (Aspinall 2010, 21).

Both concepts draw relationships between present-day elite continuity and the nature of past authoritarianism. This has arguably limited the development of more liberal society and politics (Hadiz and Robinson 2013, 36) and led to low-quality democracy (Aspinall 2010, 32). In relation to human rights protections, this low-quality democracy is represented by significant institutional and legal reform on one hand, yet a lack of implementation on the other (Hadiprayitno 2010, 374; Setiawan 2016a, 5).

Diluting transitional justice: The Jokowi presidency

The 2014 election of Joko Widodo ('Jokowi') as president brought new hopes that past human rights violations would be addressed. This was influenced by the general, but inaccurate, perception[6] that Jokowi had limited links to the military, political and business elites, which, as discussed above, are considered a key obstacle in human rights reform. Moreover, Jokowi was the only presidential candidate who explicitly promised to deliver justice for past human rights violations in his campaign program (Hearman 2014). *Nawa Cita*, the nine-point priority agenda put forward by Jokowi and his running mate Jusuf Kalla, stated that 'the just finalisation of past human rights violations' was of utmost importance, as they represented a 'social and political burden' on the country. This document also identified numerous past human rights violations that were to be addressed by the government, including the 1965 violence.[7] Once installed as president, Jokowi repeated the importance of solving

---

6   While Jokowi has far less direct ties to the New Order regime than his rival in the presidential contest, Prabowo Subianto, many of his allies are members of Indonesia's political and business elites, including some with a poor human rights record (see Warburton 2016, 304–305, 314).

7   In addition to the 1965 violence, the campaign program identified the following cases: Talangsari; Tanjung Priok; the enforced disappearances of activists in 1997–1998; the May 1998 violence; and the Trisakti and Semanggi shootings.

past human rights cases in his 2015 State of the Nation address, stating that 'future generations may not be burdened by the past' (Sekretariat Kabinet Republik Indonesia 2015).

Many human rights activists supported Jokowi's campaign because of the promises made[8] and expected his administration to bring past human rights violations to court. Instead, several non-judicial mechanisms were introduced, starting with the establishment of a Reconciliation Committee in May 2015 to address past human rights violations, including the 1965 mass violence (Setiawan 2016b). However, this initiative was abandoned after the August 2015 appointment of retired general Luhut Panjaitan to the post of Coordinating Minister of Politics, Law and Security. While in April 2016 Panjaitan supported the organisation of a National Symposium on the 1965 violence,[9] opening dialogue between government officials, former members of the military and survivors, the recommendations of the symposium have not been released. Prospects for human rights reform became even more uncertain after the July 2016 appointment of retired general Wiranto as Coordinating Minister, replacing Panjaitan. Wiranto had been indicted by the United Nations in 2003 for atrocities committed in Timor-Leste. In early 2017, Wiranto announced the establishment of a National Harmony Council that would also be mandated to settle past human rights abuses (*The Jakarta Post* 2017).

The turn towards non-judicial mechanisms with little public participation and that shield those responsible for violations from being held to account can be explained by the ties that many members of the political elite have to organisations directly involved in human rights abuses. For example, Vice President Jusuf Kalla strongly denied rumours of a possible presidential apology ahead of the 50th anniversary of the 1965 violence. In the 1960s, Kalla had led the Indonesian Students Action Front in Makassar (South Sulawesi), which supported Suharto's rise to power. The strength of organisational ties was also evident among actors who were less directly involved than Kalla. Defence Minister Ryamizard Ryacudu, for instance, also rejected a possible apology. This position can be explained considering

---

8   At the same time, the support from many human rights activists for Jokowi can be understood as an effort to counter the rise of Prabowo Subianto, who was involved in human rights violations in East Timor and Papua, the enforced disappearances of democracy activists (1997–1998) and the 1998 violence.

9   It is likely that the symposium was organised in a response to heightened attention for the 1965 case domestically and abroad (McGregor and Purdey 2016).

his previous role (2000–2002) as head of the Army Strategic Command, which four decades earlier played a crucial role in the annihilation of the Communist Party.

Ongoing elite influence must also be seen in the context of Jokowi's limited political authority, a result of his marginal win in the presidential elections (Setiawan 2016b). This has forced Jokowi to use a number of strategies in order to increase his power, including the building of alliances with conservative elites (Warburton 2016, 315). This has enabled Jokowi to expand his administration's programs that are primarily focused on the economy. These favour infrastructure, deregulation and de-bureaucratisation, with the reducing of red tape to enhance infrastructure projects being a personal priority of Jokowi (Warburton 2016, 308). At the political level there is thus little room for considering questions of justice for past human rights violations. Moreover, societal support for transitional justice is limited, with a broad section of the population showing reluctance or even antipathy (Kimura 2015, 89; Warburton 2016, 315). Public discussions on the 1965 violence (including cultural events such book launches, photo exhibitions and film screenings) have been regularly shut down following pressure from the security forces or vigilante groups.[10] While it is difficult to identify a pattern in these occurrences as many events proceed without any problems, pressure on civil society actors illustrates that the challenges for transitional justice for the 1965 violence are not only in the political and legal spheres, but also in the broader societal context.

Beyond law and politics: Transitional justice as a societal process

It is evident that in so far as Indonesia is willing to answer claims for justice for past human rights violations in general, and the 1965 case in particular, it favours the establishment of non-judicial mechanisms. These state-led initiatives have largely focused on reconciliation, without much attention given to establishing what has happened. It has been observed that political factions generally oppose the notion of 'truth', even when

---

10   Examples are the forced cancellation of a series of panels on 1965 at the Ubud Writers and Readers Festival (2015), the *Belok Kiri* (Turn Left) Festival (2016) and the 2017 attack on the Legal Aid Foundation, following its organisation of an academic discussion on the 1965 violence.

they are more supportive of reform (Kimura 2015, 77–78). An example of that unease is that during the Jokowi presidency political discourses on historical justice have shifted from 'reconciliation' to 'harmony', with limited references to human rights frameworks or public participation. The primary concern of the Jokowi administration is to address these cases as quickly as possible: when the Reconciliation Committee was established, the government announced the committee would finalise its work within months. Both the administration's preference for the creation of short-term institutions and its emphasis on 'closure' reflect an approach towards transitional justice characterised by short-term mechanisms, overlooking the social legacies of mass violence.

To an extent, the tendency towards a state-centric and top-down approach in transitional justice processes in Indonesia reflects many of these efforts globally, which, according to McEvoy (2007), have been dominated by legalism. One aspect of legalism is the institutionalisation of transitional justice, often leading to the establishment of 'state-like' structures including specialised courts and commissions. While the development of institutional capacity is important in the transition to more democratic forms of governance, this is no guarantee for success. As argued by McEvoy, one of the shortcomings of the institutionalisation of transitional justice is the tendency that these render justice as the business of the state. In this process, the complexities of past violence are oversimplified and fail to take into account local sources of knowledge. Similarly, these structures often do not engage sufficiently with the community and civil society, which means that they do not appropriately respond to the needs of its intended beneficiaries (McEvoy 2007, 421–424). In the Indonesian context, the top-down and state-centred approach is even more problematic because of the strong political and societal resistance towards transitional justice: it has more to do with protecting vested political interests, rather than delivering to those who have been affected by past violence.

One of the challenges of transitional justice mechanisms, whether of a judicial (i.e. special tribunals) or non-judicial (i.e. truth commissions) nature, is to acknowledge that the consequences of violence continue long after the event and even after the delivery of formal justice. In her seminal work on truth commissions, Priscilla Hayner remarked that, while these institutions are often welcomed as a way to break through social silences and an opportunity for healing, they 'do not offer long-term therapy' (Hayner 2001, 135). There is thus no direct correlation between transitional justice mechanisms and healing. As such, it is crucial to differentiate between justice processes pursued at a national and political level, and individual reconciliation (Hayner 2001, 157). This is more difficult to achieve, if it is at all possible: those who 'have suffered the long hand of power may never be able to stitch their lives together' (Gómez-Barris 2009, 26). Taking these realities into account, it is evident that transitional justice mechanisms will be more effective when they are part of a longer-term healing process. This constitutes a call to rethink transitional justice, taking it beyond traditional parameters of law and politics. Instead, transitional justice should be conceptualised as a process that concerns both the settling of accounts after violent conflict *and* the coming to terms with damages that have been inflicted on a society (Brants 2016, 16).

Coming to terms with the past requires the creation of a physical space where the past can exist in the present. From this perspective, transitional justice is thus intrinsically linked to storytelling. Indeed, 'the story' has increasingly gained prominence in human rights work (Kurusawa 2007). As testimonial acts, stories have various roles to play in the pursuit of justice. Not only do they generate factual knowledge about what has happened, to whom and who is responsible, but stories are also 'voices against silence, interpretation against incomprehension, empathy against indifference and remembrance against forgetting' (Kurasawa 2007, 25). As such, stories are invaluable in 'restitching the social fabric' (Gómez-Barris 2009, 94) in order for both individuals and society to come to terms with the past.

Cases of historical violence have shown us that the intense and often deeply painful experiences of the past are not only relevant for those who experienced it directly. Focusing on the remembrance of the Holocaust, Marianne Hirsch (2008) has argued that postmemory plays a crucial role in the intergenerational transmission of trauma.[11] Postmemory is the relationship of individuals to experiences that preceded their births (Hirsch 2008, 103). It is thus not memory in a literal sense, but refers to a profound connection with the past that conveys the lasting presence of painful experiences. While postmemory is a generational structure of memory transmission taking place within the family, thus between first and subsequent generations, it also has a horizontal, or affiliative,

---

11   There are, of course, many differences between the Holocaust and the 1965 violence. In contrast to the Holocaust, there is not yet an authorised narrative on the 1965 violence that acknowledges the crimes, and to some extent survivors and their families continue to carry a stigma as a consequence of New Order propaganda.

component. In an affiliative sense, postmemories serve to connect with a person's contemporaries who may not have a familial link (Hirsch 2008, 114–115). In reactivating a distant past and bringing it to the present, raising awareness of the event, postmemory is crucial to civil society transitional justice efforts. This is all the more relevant as time passes, and the distance between the present and the event increases, and there is arguably more knowledge to be generated.

Postmemory is not only relevant as a trigger for human rights activism, but also because it provides insights into the long-term and intergenerational effects of violence. This has been conceptualised by Macarena Gómez-Barris (2009) as the 'afterlife' of violence. In contrast to 'aftermath', defined as the political and economic legacies of past human rights violations, afterlife constitutes the struggles and realities of people living through political violence. Afterlife thus represents the continuing and persistent symbolic and material effects of the original event of violence on people's daily lives, their social and psychic identities, and their ongoing wrestling with the past in the present (Gómez-Barris 2009, 6).

In providing insights into what it means to live with the legacies of past violence, the concept of postmemory also allows us to critically consider transitional justice efforts, particularly when those have given little space for truth-telling.

Digital storytelling on the 1965 violence

While justice efforts for the 1965 violence continue to be disputed or rejected at the national political level, there is a growing awareness of and interest in these events, fed by various civil society activities and scholarly studies both in and outside of Indonesia (Kuddus 2017, 80–81). This includes the emergence of digital storytelling websites: *1965setiaphari* ('1965 each day')[12] and *Ingat 65* ('Remember 65').[13] While there are differences between the two websites – *Ingat 65*, for instance, aims to develop 'a young people's movement'[14] whereas *1965setiaphari* is intended

---

12   The English-language component of the website is called *Living1965*. From 2018, *1965setiaphari* has primarily used social media, including Instagram (@1965setiaphari) and Twitter (@1965setiaphari).
13   Other websites include *Learning 65*, initiated by the Culture-Centred Approaches to Research and Evaluation Centre at the National University of Singapore and the Yogyakarta-based *Kotak Hitam Forum* (Black Box Forum), which was established in 2008 and mainly produces short documentaries.
14   Ingat 65 Concept Note, on file with author.

as an 'ongoing and living memorial' – there are also striking similarities. Both projects were initiated by individuals who have not experienced the events directly, or the non-witness generation. Similarly, many of the stories that appear on these websites have been contributed by young Indonesians reflecting on the 1965 violence, an event that they never directly experienced.

The use of digital platforms by civil society can be understood in the context of the global rise of digital technologies in general and in Indonesia in particular. With the fourth-highest number of Facebook users and Jakarta once named the most active city on Twitter, digital technologies in Indonesia are 'fast becoming the core of life, work, culture and identity' (Jurriëns and Tapsell 2017, 1). It is therefore unsurprising that civil society actors have turned towards these technologies. The popularity of social media is also important for the storytelling platforms as they largely rely on these avenues for the stories to be disseminated. In addition, the use of digital technology has numerous potential advantages, including that the projects are not situated in local contexts and are therefore not subject to some of the limitations of localised activism, such as the wider public's limited access to these efforts (Wahyuningroem 2013, 135). At the same time, it is important to recognise that most of Indonesia remains underdeveloped for digital technologies (Jurriëns and Tapsell 2017, 2) and thus not all Indonesians will be able to access the websites as intended by those who created them.

The emergence of the storytelling platforms on the 1965 violence should also be situated in a context where human rights issues remain highly contested. Discussing digital activism in the context of Papua, Postill and Saputro (2017) argue that digital technologies offer activists both a method to evade opposition from certain political and societal actors and a way to connect with like-minded people (Postill and Saputro 2017, 139). The digital storytelling platforms on the 1965 violence certainly avoid some of the challenges that many civil society actors have recently faced in the public sphere when attempting to debate the 1965 violence (Setiawan 2016c). Similarly, through the stories that are published on the websites, they raise awareness, particularly to an audience that generally lacks such knowledge about the 1965 violence and its afterlife. In so doing, the storytelling platforms create a new and alternative space, where voices and views excluded from mainstream discourses can exist, where they are not subject to censorship and physical intimidation, and where people can potentially connect across local and national boundaries.

Three generations removed: Grandchildren's stories

In this section, I will discuss the stories of two grandchildren of the witness generation, Puri Lestari and Rangga Purbaya. Puri is the granddaughter of one of generals killed, while Rangga is the grandson of a member of a leftist organisation who was disappeared. Their stories illustrate their strong connection to an event that occurred before they were born, or postmemory, and the impact it has had on their families, thus providing insights into the afterlife of 1965.

Puri Lestari's story *Ini kan buku komunis*? (Isn't this a communist book?) appeared on *Ingat65*. The story gives an insight into the family of Mayor General Sutoyo, who was killed on the night of 30 September 1965. For Puri, 1965 is significant not only because of her grandfather's fate, but also because of her father, Agus Widjojo. A reformist general, Widjojo was an open supporter of reconciliation (Kuddus 2017, 71) and in 2016 was one of the key drivers of the National Symposium. Yet, during Puri's childhood 1965 was barely spoken about. Despite the silence in the family, Puri was curious – particularly as a photo framed in her grandmother's home also featured in a history textbook. But she did not ask any questions, especially after her mother warned her not to upset her father, described by Puri as 'one of thousands, if not millions, who experienced fear, pain, anger, disappointment, sadness and trauma'. However, as a university student in Australia Puri read what her father called 'communist books' (the work of the late author and former political prisoner Pramoedya Ananta Toer) and learned about Indonesia's human rights record. Studying abroad proved to be a turning point for Puri, with the 2008 Apology to Australia's Stolen Generation[15] offering an example how states can face their dark pasts and ask forgiveness. Accompanying her piece with a photo of her father and her child, Puri concludes that it represents 'his [Widjojo's] motivation to make peace, move on, and attempt to address the 1965 tragedy for Indonesia's new generation' (Lestari 2016).

An absent grandfather is also at the heart of Rangga Purbaya's story *Di Mana Kakek?* (Where Is Grandpa?). Featured on *1965setiaphari*, Rangga's story concerns his grandfather Boentardjo Amaroen Kartowinoto,

---

15   The Stolen Generation are Indigenous children who, between 1910 and 1970, were forcibly removed from their families as a result of various Australian Government policies.

who was disappeared and presumably killed in 1965. In his essay, Rangga recalls his childhood visits to Yogyakarta and to his grandmother's grave, a common practice for Javanese families. However, he never visited his grandfather's grave, who, according to his father, was buried in Semarang. When Rangga was around eight years old, he looked at a family photo album with his father, finding a rather large picture of his grandfather. His father then told Rangga: 'If you see this person, talk to him immediately. Tell him you are his grandson, the son of Bima!' Surprised, Rangga asked his father 'but hasn't grandpa passed away?' The question was not answered and Rangga did not pursue it, but he realised later why his father was silent: '[he] was always hoping to find grandpa alive' (Purbaya 2016).

Both stories provide a glimpse into the intimate spaces of the family where the past continues to dwell. A striking resemblance between the two stories is that photographs of absent grandfathers triggered questions for both Puri and Rangga, illustrating that photographic images play a key role as a medium of postmemory (cf. Hirsch 2008, 115). The stories also illustrate the familial dimension of postmemory, as illustrated by the writers' conversations with their parents. At the same time, it is also through photographs that both essays bring the past into the present day. Puri Lestari uses a photo of her father and her child to position herself, as well as her father, in the political debate on the 1965 case. While Rangga's story does not have such an explicit message, his grandfather's disappearance has played a key role in his work as photographer, in which images of family members, personal objects (i.e. his grandfather's razor) and places (including sites of mass murder) prominently feature. As such, their stories and photographs also represent the affiliative aspect of postmemory, where past events transcend the space of the family and are shared in a larger context with contemporaries.

Through photos of their grandfathers, both Puri's and Rangga's stories evoke a sense of loss and the unknown. Puri's story, in particular, mirrors the experience of many young Indonesians who learned not to question official history and who only encountered alternative narratives following the fall of the New Order, or when studying abroad. Similarly, silence is also present in the story of Rangga, who during the New Order was unsure what had happened to his grandfather. However, as soon as Suharto stepped down, his father informed him about his grandfather's political affiliation.[16] Their stories also raise the question of who was affected and

---

16   Personal communication.

in what ways, as illustrated by Rangga's father's hope to find his father, and by Puri's comment that her father – the son of one of the 'Heroes of the Revolution' – was one of many who suffered, while not part of the leftist movement. Both stories thus give insights into the complex legacies of mass violence that continue to touch lives, including of those who were born many years later and never knew their grandparents.

Conclusion

While Indonesian governments since the end of authoritarianism have made tentative steps to address the violence of 1965, these efforts have largely consisted of the enactment of laws and establishment of short-term institutions. This legalistic but non-judicial approach has largely failed to address the societal legacies of the 1965 violence, which as this chapter has argued is a crucial aspect for both individuals and society to come to terms with the past.

The challenges of human rights reform in Indonesia, and particularly in the area of transitional justice, can largely be explained by the trajectory of democratisation that has been characterised by compromise and that has shielded those involved in human rights violations from being held accountable. In the area of human rights this has meant that while legal frameworks were established, their implementation leaves much to be desired. This can be attributed to the persistence of New Order elites that remain indifferent or even hostile towards transitional justice as a consequence of their political affiliations. The 1965 violence has been particularly complex in this context because the memory of the event was hijacked by the regime for its own political objectives. The argument that violence was justified in the interests of the nation, and by extension that thus there are no human rights issues to address, continues to command authority.

In this context, civil society actors have persistently challenged state narratives. They have made important contributions towards communicating the experiences of those who lived through the events of 1965 in an effort to raise awareness and enhance societal support for the justice process. In considering the recent emergence of digital storytelling platforms on the 1965 violence, this chapter has argued that they have both emerged as a response to the increased presence of digital technologies in Indonesians' lives, and the limited public space to discuss these events.

As such, through using digital technologies alternative public spaces have been created, where knowledge on the 1965 violence and its ramifications is generated and can be debated freely. What distinguishes the digital platforms discussed in this chapter from other civil society efforts is that they have given a specific space to the non-witness generation, descendants of those who were directly affected by the violence, to share their experiences and thoughts.

The stories discussed in this chapter illustrate the strong connection individuals have with an event that preceded their births. These postmemories thus resurrect a distant past, bringing it to the present. Their stories evoke a sense of lives that were lost, families torn apart, silences and unanswered questions. In so doing, the stories not only seek to engage audiences with events that happened more than 50 years ago, but also enhance understanding of the deep scars that violence has inflicted on a society. As works of postmemory, the digital storytelling platforms are calling for a reconsideration of transitional justice beyond the paradigms of law and politics. Rather, a young generation is arguing that justice must be rooted in historical and social awareness, where the past can openly exist in the present.

Bibliography

Aspinall, Edward. 2010. 'The Irony of Success'. *Journal of Democracy* 21 (2): 20–34. doi.org/10.1353/jod.0.0157.

Brants, Chrisje. 2016. 'Introduction'. In *Transitional Justice: Images and Memories*, edited by Chrisje Brants, Antoine Hol and Dina Siegel, 1–12. London and New York: Routledge.

Cammack, Mark. 2016. 'Crimes against Humanity in East Timor. The Indonesian Ad Hoc Human Rights Court Hearings'. In *Trials for International Crimes in Asia*, edited by Kirsten Sellars, 191–225. Cambridge: Cambridge University Press. doi.org/10.1017/CBO9781316221754.010.

Gómez-Barris, Macarena. 2009. *Where Memory Dwells*. Oakland: University of California Press.

Hadiprayitno, Irene. 2010. 'Defensive Enforcement: Human Rights in Indonesia'. *Human Rights Review* 11: 373–399. doi.org/10.1007/s12142-009-0143-1.

Hadiz, Vedi and Richard Robison. 2013. 'The Political Economy of Oligarchy and the Reorganisation of Power in Indonesia'. *Indonesia* 96: 35–57. doi.org/10.1353/ind.2013.0023.

Hayner, Priscilla. 2001. *Unspeakable Truths: Confronting State Terror and Atrocity*. Routledge: New York and London. doi.org/10.4324/9780203903452.

Hearman, Vannessa. 2014. 'Spectre of Anti-Communist Smears Resurrected against Jokowi'. *The Conversation*, 4 July 2014.

Hirsch, Marianne. 2008. 'The Generation of Postmemory'. *Poetics Today* 29 (1): 103–128. doi.org/10.1215/03335372-2007-019.

The Jakarta Post. 2017. 'Wiranto Backtracks on Harmony Council's Purpose'. 10 March 2017.

Jilovsky, Esther. 2015. *Remembering the Holocaust: Generations, Witnessing and Place*. New York: Bloomsbury Academic. doi.org/10.5040/9781474210942.

Jurriëns, Edwin and Ross Tapsell. 2017. 'Challenges and Opportunities of the Digital 'Revolution' in Indonesia'. In *Digital Indonesia: Connectivity and Divergence*, edited by Edwin Jurriëns and Ross Tapsell, 1–18. Singapore: ISEAS – Yusof Ishak Institute. doi.org/10.1355/9789814786003-007.

Kimura, Ehito. 2015. 'The Struggle for Justice and Reconciliation in Post-Suharto Indonesia'. *Southeast Asian Studies* 4 (1): 73–93.

Kuddus, Rohana. 2017. 'The Ghosts of 1965. Politics and Memory in Indonesia'. *New Left Review* 104: 45–92.

Kurasawa, Fuyuki. 2007. *The Work of Global Justice: Human Rights as Practices*. Cambridge: Cambridge University Press. doi.org/10.1017/CBO9780511619465.

Lestari, Puri. 2016. '"*Ini kan buku komunis?*" *Kisah cucu pahlawan revolusi* ["Isn't This a Communist Book?" The Story of a Grandchild of a Hero of the Revolution]'. Medium, 20 April. Available at medium.com/ingat-65/ini-kan-buku-komunis-d39a72da473f#.vb1iyis0n (accessed 4 October 2017).

McEvoy, Kieran. 2007. 'Towards a Thicker Understanding of Transitional Justice'. *Journal of Law and Society* 34 (4): 411–440. doi.org/10.1111/j.1467-6478.2007.00399.x.

McGregor, Katharine E. 2013. 'Mass Violence in the Indonesian Transition from Sukarno to Suharto'. *Global Dialogue* 15 (1): 133–144.

McGregor, Katharine E. and Jemma Purdey. 2016. 'Indonesia Takes a Small but Critical Step toward Reconciliation'. *Indonesia at Melbourne* (blog), 26 April. Available at indonesiaatmelbourne.unimelb.edu.au/indonesia-takes-a-small-but-critical-step-toward-reconciliation/ (accessed 13 November 2019).

Posner, Eric A. and Adrian Vermeule. 2004. 'Transitional Justice as Ordinary Justice'. *Harvard Law Review* 117 (3): 761–825. doi.org/10.2307/4093461.

Postill, John and Kurniawan Saputro. 2017. 'Digital Activism in Contemporary Indonesia: Victims, Volunteers and Voices'. In *Digital Indonesia: Connectivity and Divergence*, edited by Edwin Jurriëns and Ross Tapsell, 127–145. Singapore: ISEAS – Yusof Ishak Institute. doi.org/10.1355/9789814786003-014.

Purbaya, Rangga. 2016. '*Di Mana Kakek?* [Where is Grandpa?]'. *#1965setiaphari*, 1 May. Available at 1965setiaphari.org/1965setiaphari/di-mana-kakek (accessed 4 October 2017).

Sekretariat Kabinet Republik Indonesia. 2015. 'Pidato Kenegaraan Presiden Republik Indonesia Dalam Rangka HUT Ke-70 Proklamasi Kemerdekaan Republik Indonesia Di Depan Sidang Bersama DPR RI dan DPD RI, Jakarta 14 Agustus 2015 [State Speech of the President of the Republic of Indonesia on the Occasion of the 70th Anniversary of the Proclamation of the Independence of the Republic of Indonesia at the Joint Session of the DPR RI and the DPD RI, Jakarta 14 August 2015]', Transcript. Available at setkab.go.id/pidato-kenegaraan-presiden-republik-indonesia-dalam-rangka-hut-ke-70-proklamasi-kemerdekaan-republik-indonesia-di-depan-sidang-bersama-dpr-ri-dan-dpd-ri-jakarta-14-agustus-2015/ (accessed 18 May 2017).

Setiawan, Ken. 2016a. 'From Hope to Disillusion. The Paradox of Komnas HAM, the Indonesian National Human Rights Commission'. *Bijdragen tot de Taal-, Land- en Volkenkunde* 172: 1–32. doi.org/10.1163/22134379-17201002.

Setiawan, Ken. 2016b. 'The Politics of Compromise'. *Inside Indonesia* 123 (January–March). www.insideindonesia.org/the-politics-of-compromise-2.

Setiawan, Ken. 2016c. 'The Fear of Communism Still Haunts Indonesia'. *Indonesia at Melbourne* (blog), 3 March. Available at indonesiaatmelbourne.unimelb.edu.au/belok-kiri-fest-fear-of-communism-still-haunts-indonesia/ (accessed 13 November 2019).

Suh, Jiwon. 2016. 'The Suharto Case'. *Asian Journal of Social Science* 44: 214–245. doi.org/10.1163/15685314-04401009.

Sulistiyanto, Priyambudi. 2007. 'Politics of Justice and Reconciliation in Post-Suharto Indonesia'. *Journal of Contemporary Asia* 37 (1): 73–94. doi.org/10.1080/00472330601104623.

Voice of America. 2012. 'Korban Peristiwa 1965–66 Kecewa dengan Kejakasaan Agung [Victims of the 1965–66 Event Disappointed with Attorney General]', 12 November.

Wahyuningroem, Sri Lestari. 2013. 'Seducing for Truth and Justice: Civil Society Initiatives for the 1965 Mass Violence in Indonesia'. *Journal of Current Southeast Asian Affairs* 32 (3): 115–142. doi.org/10.1177/186810341303200306.

Warburton, Eve. 2016. 'Jokowi and the New Developmentalism'. *Bulletin of Indonesian Economic Studies* 52 (3): 297–320. doi.org/10.1080/00074918. 2016.1249262.

Part 2 – Cambodia and Myanmar

4

The evolution of Cambodian civil society's involvement with victim participation at the Khmer Rouge trials

Christoph Sperfeldt and Jeudy Oeung

In the scholarly literature on the role of civil society in transitional justice processes there seems to be broad agreement that civil society actors can make important contributions to these processes (Backer 2003; Duthie 2009). However, the scope and nature of civil society's involvement is rarely examined by way of more in-depth case studies. This chapter looks at the case of Cambodian non-governmental organisations' (NGOs) involvement with victim participation at the Extraordinary Chambers in the Court of Cambodia (ECCC) with a view to examining civil society's contributions in more detail.

The ECCC is a hybrid criminal court, combining national and international elements, established in 2003 through an agreement between the United Nations and the Cambodian Government. Based on Cambodia's national law, the ECCC introduced provisions that allow victims of crime to participate in its proceedings as civil parties and thus beyond a role as a witness. Civil parties at the ECCC are considered parties to the proceedings with a range of participatory rights, including the right to request investigations (McGonigle Leyh 2011). It is this aspect of the ECCC's mandate that attracted local NGOs' attention. The influx of development aid in the aftermath of the withdrawal of the United Nations Transitional Authority in Cambodia (UNTAC), at the beginning of the 1990s, led to the creation of a comparatively strong and diverse local NGO community in Cambodia (Hughes 2009; Dosch 2012). With the establishment of the ECCC, some of these local NGOs began to develop activities in support of the Khmer Rouge trials.

This chapter takes an evolutionary perspective in that it explores how local civil society engagement with the ECCC's victim participation scheme has changed over time. Internationalised criminal trials often span a long time period. An evolutionary perspective allows capturing over time the dynamic development of different forms of NGO engagement with a formal transitional justice mechanism, such as the ECCC. In doing so, the chapter builds upon and expands arguments, which have been published previously by the authors (Oeung 2016; Sperfeldt 2012a; Sperfeldt 2013a). The focus is here on Cambodian NGOs and their involvement with victim participation at the ECCC, and not on the contributions of the many international NGOs or other Cambodian NGOs' work in related transitional justice areas.

The chapter begins by providing an overview of the four different phases of NGO engagement to date, and examines the various roles that these actors have progressively assumed in supporting and complementing the Court's victim participation scheme. The case of the ECCC is an example of extensive NGO involvement, including in areas of the judicial process that would normally fall within the responsibility of a court. At a point where the ECCC's trial proceedings in its second and largest case are coming to an end, this chapter concludes with a discussion of the opportunities and limitations that come with such wide-ranging NGO involvement.[1]

---

1   At the time of writing the ECCC is pursuing four cases – often referred to as Case 001, 002, 003 and 004 – but only the first two cases have moved to the trial stage.

The evolution of Cambodian civil society's involvement with the ECCC's victim participation scheme

Phase I: Advocacy and early outreach (2003–2007)

Following the Cambodian Government's request to the United Nations in 1997 for assistance 'in bringing to justice those persons responsible for genocide and crimes against humanity during the rule of the Khmer Rouge from 1975 to 1979',[2] it took years to negotiate this agreement and establish a tribunal. Throughout the negotiation process, Cambodian and international civil society organisations advocated for a survivor-friendly tribunal. Once the ECCC started its operations in 2005/2006, discussions began within civil society regarding the future procedural rules of the Court (Acquaviva 2008). Cambodian NGOs showed a keen interest in this process. Members of the Cambodian Human Rights Action Committee (CHRAC),[3] an umbrella organisation of Cambodian human rights NGOs, suggested that the ECCC's Internal Rules include a mechanism that might address the survivors' suffering, arguing that such provisions would restore survivors' dignity and provide recognition of what happened during the Khmer Rouge period (CHRAC 2005).

Many Cambodian NGOs spoke out in favour of a model where victims could participate as *parties civiles*, or civil parties – such a model, inspired by the French criminal code, also exists under Cambodian national law.[4] In May 2006, NGOs met with the Deputy Prime Minister Sok An and ECCC officials, and provided them with a list of recommendations favouring the incorporation of provisions for a civil party system in the ECCC Internal Rules (see Collectif pour les Victimes des Khmer Rouges 2006). These NGOs' actions were guided by the belief that 'victim participation will help bridge the gap between the Court and the people and will give victims a voice in this important process' (CHRAC 2006, 7).

---

2   Letter dated 21 June 1997 from the First and Second Prime Ministers of Cambodia addressed to the Secretary-General, republished in UN doc. A/51/930-S/1997/488 of 24 June 1997, Annex.
3   Established in 1994, CHRAC is coalition of 21 local NGOs working in the fields of human rights, democracy and legal aid in Cambodia.
4   Authors' interview with Hisham Mousar, former project manager of the Khmer Rouge Tribunal Project at the Cambodian NGO ADHOC, Phnom Penh, 1 May 2013.

On 12 June 2007, the Judges Plenary adopted Internal Rules that made the ECCC the first internationalised criminal court with a victim participation scheme based on the civil party model.[5]

Moreover, these NGOs emphasised the importance of an active role for civil society in any future victim participation process. CHRAC noted that 'Cambodian NGOs are eager to assist the Court' (CHRAC 2006, 9). Similar views were expressed by a number of ECCC officials. David Boyle, who was closely involved in the drafting of the Internal Rules, wrote in 2006, 'active participation by Khmer Rouge victims, *aided by NGOs*, will constitute one of the essential conditions for impartial and independent trials before the [ECCC]' (emphasis added by the authors) (Boyle 2006, 313). These remarks already foreshadowed the active role NGOs would play in the ECCC's future victim participation scheme.

This account shows that civil society organisations played an instrumental role in advocating for the inclusion of victim participation into the Khmer Rouge trials. Considerations of local ownership and the potential legacy for Cambodia's domestic judiciary led many, but not all, NGOs to speak out in favour of the civil party system. Moreover, the majority of these NGOs were motivated by the firm belief that victim participation could make a positive contribution to social reconstruction, healing and reconciliation among survivors and the Cambodian society at large.[6]

These expectations would remain hollow, however, if Cambodians were unaware of the Khmer Rouge trials. The Open Society Justice Initiative (OSJI) was one of the earliest proponents for comprehensive outreach to local populations. Considering the limited budget of the ECCC and the strength of local civil society, OSJI recommended:

> [to] use existing NGOs already operating throughout the country to help with outreach. Existing non-governmental organizations have already established communication mechanisms with the people they serve. Establishing credibility and a positive working relationship with local NGOs will engender more trust with victims and witnesses (OSJI 2004).

---

5   ECCC Internal Rule 23 states that 'the purpose of Civil Party action before the ECCC is to (a) participate in criminal proceedings against those responsible for crimes within the jurisdiction of the ECCC by supporting the prosecution; and (b) allow victims to seek collective and moral reparations, as provided in this Rule'.
6   Also at author's interview with Youk Chhang, Director of DC-Cam, 17 May 2013.

OSJI called therefore on Cambodia's main donors to 'complement ECCC efforts with appropriate initiatives from civil society' (OSJI 2006). By that time, Cambodian NGOs had already started to engage in outreach activities. A 2006 report found that nearly a dozen NGOs had ECCC-related activities (Penh et al. 2006, 7). Cambodian NGOs, including the Documentation Center of Cambodia (DC-Cam), the Cambodian Association for Human Rights and Development (ADHOC) and CHRAC, had started with radio broadcasts about the Khmer Rouge trials as early as 2002 and further intensified their activities from 2005 onwards. CHRAC added a monthly newsletter in Khmer language with information about the ECCC, while the Center for Social Development (CSD) began to organise public dialogue forums in Cambodia's provinces. These outreach efforts demonstrate the enthusiasm among Cambodian NGOs about the Khmer Rouge trials, as well as the capacity to design new activities and raise funds in support of ECCC-related work. These and subsequent nationwide outreach activities also contributed to increasing awareness among the Cambodian population of the Khmer Rouge trials (Pham et al. 2011a, 21). Through their established relations of trust, NGOs had access to communities that would often be out of reach to official institutions, such as a temporary court. These outreach activities in turn laid the foundation for subsequent victim participation activities.[7]

Phase II: Extensive NGO support – limited ECCC capacity (2007–2009)

The ECCC struggled to keep pace with the developments during this formative phase. A victim participation process was initially not planned and not budgeted. The Victims Unit (later renamed as the Victims Support Section, VSS) began its operation with limited capacities in January 2008. However, it took almost another two years, and only after receiving earmarked funding from the German Foreign Office, for the unit to be able to operate at a more considerable threshold (ECCC 2008). A new Practice Direction, issued by the ECCC in October 2007, provided a so-called 'Victim Information Form', which survivors interested in participating in the trials had to complete. The complexity of the form combined with the lack of outreach indicated that most survivors, especially those residing in rural areas, would encounter considerable difficulties with filling in and submitting the form.

---

7   Interviews with Youk Chhang, 17 May 2013, and Leakhena Nou, 30 June 2013.

Support to the application and participation process

Against this background, NGOs feared that only a few survivors would be able to participate. Following the announcement of the first indictments at the ECCC in 2007, these NGOs expanded their initial outreach activities to include information about victim participation at the ECCC. Eventually, around a dozen Cambodian NGOs became involved in different aspects of victim participation activities (Sperfeldt 2013a, 348–350). Some of these local NGOs gradually assumed the role of 'intermediaries' between the ECCC and participating survivors. Such intermediary functions related initially to facilitating the application process and communication between the Court and victims.

The first three Cambodian intermediary NGOs that began assisting survivors with the application process from late 2007 onwards, were DC-Cam, ADHOC and the Khmer Institute of Democracy (KID). After only a few months – by February 2008 – the ECCC's Victims Unit had already received more than 600 applications, providing an indication of the capacity of NGO provincial outreach networks (CHRAC 2008). DC-Cam even set itself the ambitious goal of assisting more than 10,000 survivors in submitting complaints to the ECCC (Kinetz and Yun 2008). These NGOs adapted their existing project structures for the purposes of ECCC-related outreach: DC-Cam undertaking provincial missions from their head office in Phnom Penh; ADHOC making use of its extensive provincial office network; and KID mobilising its provincial volunteer network.

There was no doubt that for many non–legally trained intermediary staff, the process was a steep learning curve. The challenges were particularly acute during the application process, where NGOs struggled with the difficult victim information form. The completeness of forms submitted by NGOs varied greatly, although the quality improved over time. This situation was exacerbated by a lack of guidance from the ECCC, requiring many intermediary NGOs to go back and forth between applicants and the Court to seek supplementary information or further proof of identity.[8] Yet, through their intermediary role, Cambodian NGOs established important channels of communication between the Court and the participating survivors. In doing so, they helped to bridge the gap between the majority of survivors who reside in rural areas and

---

8   Interview with Long Panhavuth, 27 May 2013.

the ECCC. Youk Chhang, Director of DC-Cam, argues that 'it created a space for the victims to walk through, come to the court ... it creates communication lines with the court. This, to me, can be considered a success'.[9]

In early 2008, the ECCC recognised the first civil parties who now sought legal representation. Following inquiries by civil party applicants and NGOs, the ECCC administration declared that it did not intend to establish a legal aid scheme for civil parties (Kinetz and Prak 2008). In a country where most survivors lacked the means and an appropriate education to follow the proceedings by themselves, this would be a major obstacle to active participation (Thomas and Chy 2009). Local intermediary organisations, fearing that civil parties were not able to exercise their right to participate, reached out to local legal aid NGOs, such as the Cambodian Defenders Project (CDP) and Legal Aid of Cambodia (LAC) (Sperfeldt, Oeung and Hong 2010). These Cambodian lawyers, often in conjunction with international pro bono lawyers, began representing the first civil parties before the ECCC.

These NGOs and individual lawyers used their involvement to direct attention to issues that were initially neglected by the ECCC, including sexual and gender-based violence as well as crimes against minority populations (Nguyen and Sperfeldt 2014). For instance, NGOs were crucial in working with civil party lawyers in getting the ECCC to investigate the crime of forced marriage and include it as part of the indictment (Studzinsky 2012). One of the most innovative non-judicial NGO activities was the so-called 'women's hearing' initiated by the NGO CDP (Ye 2014). Thus, local NGOs and their collaboration with lawyers and survivor groups were essential in complementing the ECCC's investigative activities and painting a more complete historical account of the crimes committed under the Khmer Rouge regime.

Against the background of a growing backlog of unprocessed forms at the Victims Unit, considerable delay in notifying applicants of the status of their applications and the lack of a court-funded legal aid scheme, a number of Cambodian NGOs decided that they needed to bring their engagement to another level. The main concern cited by NGO workers was that many Khmer Rouge survivors would lose out on the opportunity to be part of the ECCC process. Yet coordination among NGOs was difficult

---

9   Cited from interview with Youk Chhang, 17 May 2013.

(Oeung 2012, 40). NGOs are by their nature independent organisations, each with their specific goals and approaches. The only systematic effort of coordination among NGOs took place within the CHRAC network and its extended membership. CHRAC's member organisations established a coordinated support scheme for victim participation.[10] The support scheme consisted of three components: assisting interested survivors with completing and submitting the ECCC Victim Information Form;[11] sending these forms to the CHRAC Secretariat, as focal point for quality control and coordination; and offering legal representation to unrepresented civil parties, through two legal aid member organisations and in collaboration with international pro bono lawyers (see Figure 4.1).[12]

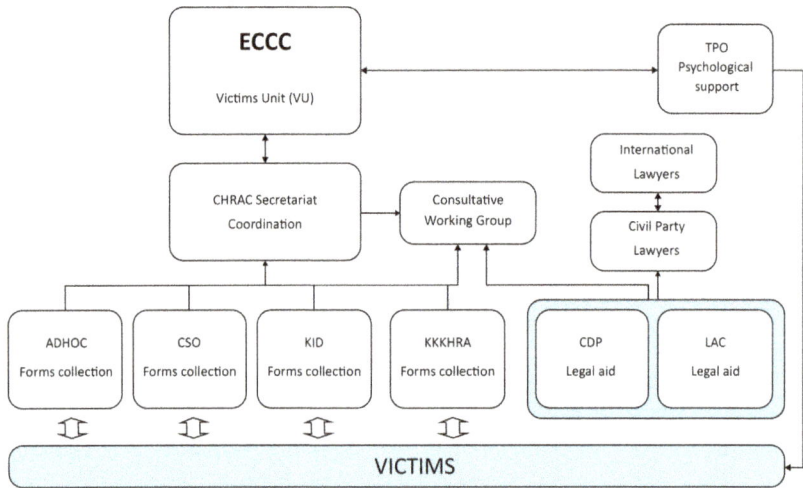

Figure 4.1: Chart of the CHRAC Support Scheme.
Source: Oeung and Sperfeldt (2010).

10   These coordination efforts were influenced positively by the fact that a number of local NGOs engaged in ECCC-related work and received funding through a comprehensive donor support program, implemented by the German Development Service (DED, later merged into GIZ).

11   These NGOs included the Cambodian Human Rights and Development Association (ADHOC), the Khmer Institute of Democracy (KID), the Center for Social Development (CSD, whose responsibilities were later carried on by the Center for Justice and Reconciliation, CJR) and the Khmer Kampuchea Krom Human Rights Association (KKKHRA).

12   The legal aid organisations were the Cambodian Defenders Project (CDP) and Legal Aid of Cambodia (LAC). Two lawyers from each organisation were involved in representing civil parties before the ECCC, often in partnership with various international pro bono lawyers. In addition, CDP lawyers later specialised in representing victims of gender-based violence. The only other NGO providing a continuous presence of two Cambodian lawyers was Avocats Sans Frontiers (ASF) France.

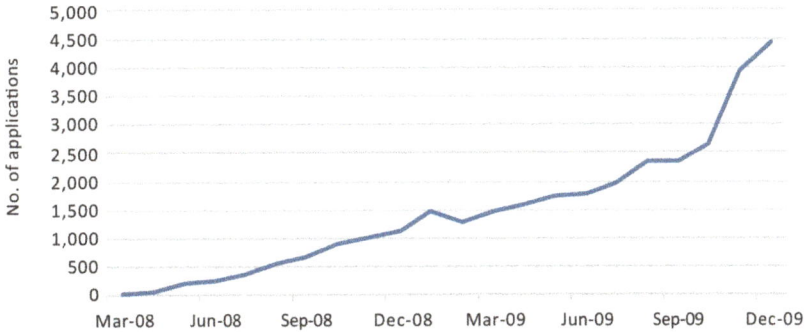

Figure 4.2: Accumulated submissions by CHRAC of ECCC Victim Information Forms.

Source: Oeung and Sperfeldt (2010).

From its inception in March 2008 until the deadline for Case 002 civil party applications in December 2009, more than 4,440 applications were submitted to the VSS through the CHRAC support scheme (see Figure 4.2, Oeung and Sperfeldt 2010). The majority of those applicants were female (63 per cent), and more than 60 per cent applied for civil party status, with the rest submitting general complaints. Based on statistics provided by the VSS, an estimated 60 per cent of all application forms were submitted to the VSS through the CHRAC support scheme and its member organisations.

Data from the VSS confirm the prominent role played by NGOs in facilitating the victim participation process at the ECCC. Of the more than 8,200 victim information forms received by the VSS in Case 002 in total, more than 80 per cent were submitted through NGO intermediaries (ECCC OCIJ 2010, para. 11). Apart from the Cambodia-based intermediaries, outreach among the Cambodian diaspora has also contributed to this achievement.[13]

In response to a perceived lack of ECCC capacities, many intermediary NGOs gradually expanded their involvement with the victim participation process, taking on ever greater responsibilities. Initial straightforward outreach projects developed into more comprehensive victim support programs including activities such as notifying survivors of the status of their applications, facilitating legal representation for civil parties and supporting civil parties with travel and other logistics

---

13   Interview with Leakhena Nou, Phnom Penh, 30 June 2013.

(Sperfeldt 2013a, 350–351). These NGOs simply had not anticipated that, after the initial application stage, they would be left to deal with numerous follow-up activities, which they had expected to fall within the responsibility of the Court.

NGOs at their zenith – comprehensive support in Case 001

The ECCC's first trial in Case 001 against Kaing Guek Eav, alias Duch, proved to be the zenith of NGO support to victim participation. More than 90 civil parties in Case 001 benefited from various forms of NGO assistance ranging from help with their application and visits to the ECCC, to facilitating legal representation and arranging meetings with their lawyers. All civil parties eventually found a legal representative, with little assistance from the Court and mostly through NGO facilitation. These lawyers often worked on a pro bono basis and had no further resources available to meet with their clients. It was left to NGOs to organise regular meetings between lawyers and their clients and to provide support for civil parties and other victims who wished to attend the trial hearings. This presence in the courtroom throughout the trial hearings increased understanding among civil parties of the issues at trial and provided a forum for consultations.

In addition, psychological care through Cambodian mental health workers of the local NGO Transcultural Psychosocial Organization (TPO) assisted in minimising negative side effects from the participation process (Strasser et al. 2011a). As the ECCC did not retain any in-house counselling capacity, it signed a Memorandum of Understanding with TPO, making the NGO responsible for providing mental health services to survivors participating in the Court's proceedings. Working in close cooperation with the VSS and the Witness and Expert Support Unit, TPO counsellors delivered psychological support to approximately 90 civil parties and 31 witnesses during the trial of Case 001 (Strasser et al. 2011b).

Cambodian NGOs' engagement with victim participation in Case 001 showed how far-reaching NGO support can be, as well as the extent to which an internationalised criminal court has ultimately relied on such assistance. The fact that some NGOs assumed roles as intermediaries compensated, to some extent, for the lack of preparedness and services from the ECCC in this phase. In a study conducted among civil parties who testified at the trial in Case 001, 'all of the civil parties said that their primary connection to the court was not through the Victims Unit but through their lawyers and local NGOs' (Stover, Balthazard and Koenig 2011, 14).

There is evidence of a correlation between extensive NGO support to victim participation and the attitudes of civil parties to the justice process as a whole. A survey conducted by Pham and colleagues among Cambodian civil parties in Case 001, found that 63 per cent of the respondents felt 'extremely' supported by NGOs during the application process, and 68 per cent received information from NGOs at least once a month (Pham et al. 2011b, 273–277). The authors of this study conclude that 'despite some disappointments in the Duch trial outcomes, civil parties felt positive about their overall participation, suggesting the importance of that process' (Pham et al. 2011b, 284–285). These results highlight the importance of support services to enable a satisfactory participation process.

Phase III: Decrease in NGO capacity – more ECCC activities (2010–2013)

Prior to the beginning of the ECCC's second trial in Case 002 the balance between NGO and ECCC activities began to shift. A steady decline of NGO support was accompanied by an expansion of capacity at the ECCC. A number of reasons may explain these changes, including (i) a rebalancing in the flow of external donor funding, with further earmarked funding allowing the VSS to expand its activities, while donor funding to NGOs saw a considerable decrease;[14] (ii) a recognition among ECCC officials that the Court had to deliver some minimal victim support measures in view of the large number of civil parties participating in Case 002, most visibly manifested in the fact that the ECCC now provided a limited legal aid capacity for unrepresented civil parties; and (iii) organisational changes among NGOs, with some organisations ceasing their operations,[15] accompanied by frustration among intermediaries about the limited progress in enhancing the collaboration between the Court and NGOs.

---

14   The German Government extended its earmarked funding to the VSS twice, while larger EU-funded projects to ADHOC and KID came to an end, without replacement at a similar level.
15   CSD, and later CJR, and KKKHRA ceased their ECCC-related operations sometime in 2009 and 2010.

Paradoxically, this decline in NGO activities occurred in a context of growing needs with almost 4,000 civil parties now requiring support for their participation in Case 002. The major donors to the ECCC showed little far-sightedness when they cut their complementary funding to civil society in the midst of ongoing trials and with little coordination among themselves – eventually donor fatigue prevailed.[16] In response to these constraints, some NGOs decided to scale back and consolidate their activities. During the trial of Case 002, NGO support was, by and large, limited to two larger intermediaries, ADHOC and DC-Cam, complemented by specialised NGO programs for vulnerable victim groups, such as victims of gender-based violence and those from minorities.[17]

Against these odds, and considering the much larger number of participating victims in Case 002, some NGOs became inventive. ADHOC amended its victim support scheme and devised, in 2010, a countrywide network for the approximately 1,800 civil parties that had applied through the NGO. From among these civil parties, the NGO identified so-called civil party representatives (CPRs), who were directly involved in the communication process. These CPRs benefited from capacity-building and served as focal points in their respective geographic area, where they facilitated communication with ADHOC, the ECCC and lawyers. This network not only empowered survivors by directly involving them in participation activities, it also represented the most comprehensive communication effort with civil parties during the trial phase of Case 002/01, from 2011 to 2014, covering nearly half of all civil parties before the ECCC (Balthazard 2013).

Although Cambodian NGOs supported ECCC victim participation with a high level of good will, care should be taken, however, to avoid underestimating the divergences within the relationship between NGOs and survivors – particularly when NGO representatives claim to speak on behalf of victims. Even though NGOs and survivor groups often share a number of common objectives, they are rarely unified in their opinions

---

16   The only continuous donor program around the ECCC with a focus on civil society was implemented, since 2007, by the German Development Service's Civil Peace Service Program and later continued under the auspices of the GIZ.

17   CDP was able to expand its support for victims of gender-based violence, while LAC maintained a small support project for Khmer Krom and ethnic Vietnamese minority civil parties. DC-Cam continued to implement a special project for the Cham population.

and attitudes. Nascent victim associations, such as Ksem Ksan, struggled to find a foothold in Cambodia's competitive civil society sector and were often left to fend for themselves.

Despite the decrease in funding, Cambodian NGOs involved in the ECCC's victim participation scheme continued their advocacy around victims' rights. NGOs organised numerous advocacy events and radio call-in shows. During the phase from 2010 to 2013, many Cambodian NGOs stepped up their advocacy especially regarding the ECCC's collective reparations mandate with the aim of achieving more tangible outcomes for the participating survivors.

Phase IV: NGO engagement with collective reparations (2014–2018)

The most recent phase saw a further decline in NGO outreach capacities – ADHOC's vital civil party representative scheme ended its operations in 2015, citing a lack of sufficient donor support. Suddenly, half of the civil parties before the ECCC were cut off from their most important platform for information and engagement with the trials. The combined decrease in support to outreach and to non-ECCC Cambodian lawyers, who nominally still represented the majority of civil parties, left many civil parties without the ability to contact their lawyers (Oeung 2016). Sporadic ECCC provincial outreach fora never fully compensated for the waning NGO support. As a result, many civil parties know little about the proceedings in Case 002 (Sperfeldt, Hyde and Balthazard 2016).

While activities that had dominated a decade of NGO involvement with the Khmer Rouge trials were gradually coming to an end, NGO interest in the ECCC's evolving collective reparations scheme was on the rise. Alongside the International Criminal Court (ICC), the ECCC is one of the few internationalised criminal courts with a reparations mandate (Sperfeldt 2012b). The ECCC's Internal Rule 23 limits the scope of reparations in that civil parties are only allowed to seek 'collective and moral reparations', thus excluding individual reparations. In 2010, ECCC judges amended the Internal Rules with a view to providing for more flexibility in designing and implementing collective reparations measures in relation to Case 002 and beyond. The Internal Rules now empower the VSS to identify and design projects, which give effect to the reparations awards sought by civil parties.[18] The rules specifically mention that the VSS can collaborate with NGOs in developing and implementing such projects.

Local NGOs and survivors alike have put much hope in the reparations process, and it is foreseeable that the ECCC will not be able to satisfy all expectations. After a slow start, a number of Cambodian NGOs began working with the VSS to see a few symbolic measures materialise. At the preparatory stages for Case 002, these NGOs provided space for discussions, facilitated input from external stakeholders, and submitted multiple proposals to the Court with the aim of exploring options for the implementation of collective reparations (Sperfeldt and Winodan 2009). Moreover, intermediary NGOs' support was vital for facilitating consultations with civil parties about their preferences for collective reparations measures. The result of these consultations fed into the consolidated reparations request in Case 002, where civil parties requested measures in relation to remembrance and memorialisation, rehabilitation, documentation and education, and a few other projects (Kirchenbauer et al. 2013, 38–44).

From the 13 reparations projects proposed by the civil parties in Case 002/01, 10 projects involved NGOs as implementers and some projects were associated with initiatives from the Cambodian diaspora. External donors contributed more than US$770,000 to the 11 reparations projects ultimately recognised by the Trial Chamber in Case 002/01. Both the ECCC and the NGOs benefited from this arrangement: the Court was able to take credit for almost a dozen reparations projects it could never have implemented on its own, and NGOs were able to improve their standing and raise additional funding. The relative 'success' of this scheme meant that more NGOs became involved – further broadening NGO participation in Case 002/02 reparations projects beyond the group of NGOs that had engaged in ECCC-related work over the first decade of the tribunal's existence. Considering the lack of outreach capacities, however, the impact of these reparations initiatives on survivors is less certain.

NGOs' involvement with this type of restorative and rehabilitative work has expanded the possibilities of the ECCC's legacy, especially in the fields of memory culture, documentation and education. For instance, DC-Cam is building a new genocide education and research hub – the

---

18   ECCC Internal Rules 12*bis* (2) and (3), and Rule 23*quinquies*.

Sleuk Rith Institute – while smaller NGOs, such as Youth for Peace and Kdei Karuna, work with youth and community-based approaches in promoting storytelling, art projects and exhibitions to learn about and remember Khmer Rouge atrocities. Many of these projects have a pilot character and provide valuable lessons for future up-scaling in a post-ECCC memory and education environment (Oeung 2016, 120).

Harnessing civil society involvement in official transitional justice mechanisms

By complementing a purely retributive justice process with some restorative justice elements, transitional justice mechanisms like the ECCC have created both new opportunities and challenges for the institutions involved and the participating survivors (McGonigle Leyh 2009). In particular, the participation of a large number of survivors creates demand for a whole range of associated services that may exceed a court's resources or expertise. In some contexts, local civil society may be well positioned to support victim participation and serve some of the many demands of complex participation schemes.

The ECCC provides a case for studying extensive NGO support to victim participation in an official transitional mechanism (Hermann 2010). The observations in this chapter suggest that courts should be encouraged to utilise the comparative advantage of local civil society organisations, including their knowledge of the local context, proximity to target populations and their generally less cost-intensive activities. In relation to the ECCC, Pham and colleagues recommended that 'NGOs who have been the backbone of victim participation should be further supported and recognized in their role as intermediaries between the court and the victims' (Pham et al. 2011b, 285).

Thus, while reaching out to civil society appears advantageous, the observations in this chapter also suggest that such an engagement with actors outside the courts requires a more structured collaborative process. No strategic approach to collaboration developed between the ECCC and intermediary NGOs.[19] Sporadic meetings between the VSS and intermediary NGOs were only replaced at the beginning of 2010 by more

---

19   Interviews with Long Panhavuth, 27 May 2013, and Youk Chhang, 17 May 2013.

regular outreach coordination meetings with the ECCC Public Affairs Section. The Court simply failed to recognise that it would benefit from playing a lead role in coordinating NGO activities of relevance to the implementation of its mandate on victim participation. As a result, the civil party process lacked a joint outreach and victim strategy from the ECCC and civil society (ICTJ 2010, 11–18).

Stover and colleagues therefore suggest that 'it may even behove courts to formalize their relationship with such NGOs and facilitate the creation of an official or unofficial network of local organizations to meet the needs of victim participants' (Stover, Balthazard and Koenig 2011, 43). Courts need to develop a forward-looking approach towards collaboration with civil society and states, lead the planning process and, where necessary, assist with capacity-building. Such an approach to collaboration would ultimately contribute to making victim participation and outreach processes more efficient. In view of increasing workloads with large-scale victim participation and stagnant budgets, it may even be one of the few avenues available to implement a court's mandate in these areas (Sperfeldt 2013b, 1111–1137).

Yet, the evolutionary perspective applied in this chapter has also shown that this will not be possible, if transnational justice donors – domestic or international – do not begin with rebalancing their assistance. This is best illustrated by the fact that only 9 per cent of international assistance to transitional justice in Cambodia between 2002 and 2012 was going to civil society, while the ECCC absorbed US$250 million in the same time period – around 91 per cent of that assistance (Arthur and Yakinthou 2015, 6). Thus, even if local NGOs engage in advance planning and offer more coordinated support activities, they ultimately cannot guarantee the continuation and reliability of these services. Such decisions remain in the hands of mostly external donors who have to deal with fiscal uncertainties and often do not display the endurance required by lengthy internationalised criminal justice processes. NGOs' dependency on external funds ultimately proved to be their Achilles heel. It also introduced dynamics that were not always driven by the needs of the victim participation process, but instead by the availability of funds and changing donor priorities.

While many donors question the sustainability of longer-term civil society engagement, they have not shown that sole reliance on state-centric approaches delivers better or locally more relevant outcomes. Diversifying transitional justice initiatives among multiple actors in society may assist with spreading risks and opportunities, as well as mobilising greater segments of the population to engage with transitional justice mechanisms and thereby increasing local ownership of their outcomes. Such an approach may produce more positive and sustainable legacies than temporary mechanisms, including internationalised courts, can achieve on their own.

Bibliography

Acquaviva, Guido. 2008. 'New Paths in International Criminal Justice? The Internal Rules of the Cambodian Extraordinary Chambers'. *Journal of International Criminal Justice* 6: 129–151. doi.org/10.1093/jicj/mqm085.

Arthur, Paige and Christella Yakinthou. 2015. 'Funding Transitional Justice: A Guide for Supporting Civil Society Engagement'. Public Action Research.

Backer, David. 2003. 'Civil Society and Transitional Justice: Possibilities, Patterns and Prospects'. *Journal of Human Rights* 2 (3): 297–313. doi.org/10.1080/14754830032000132999.

Balthazard, Mychelle. 2013. 'Khmer Rouge Tribunal Project Evaluation Report, 2010–2012'. Consultant report, August 2013.

Boyle, David. 2006. 'The Rights of Victims: Participation, Representation, Protection, Reparation'. *Journal of International Criminal Justice* 4: 307–313. doi.org/10.1093/jicj/mql006.

CHRAC (Cambodian Human Rights Action Committee). 2005. 'Internal Report about the Delegation Visit to the ECCC'. Copy on file with the authors.

CHRAC. 2006. 'Comments on the ECCC Draft Internal Rules'. Submitted to the 2nd ECCC Plenary, Phnom Penh, 17 November 2006.

CHRAC. 2008. 'CHRAC Workshop on Complaints Procedures'. Workshop held on 22 February 2008 in Phnom Penh. Report prepared by Christoph Sperfeldt and Lach Sreytouch.

Collectif pour les Victims des Khmer Rouges. 2006. 'Propositions Relatives aux Droits des Victimes des Khmer Rouges devant les Chambres Extraordinaires Cambodgienes'. Paris, April 2006.

Dosch, Joern. 2012. 'The Role of Civil Society in Cambodia's Peace-building Process: Have Foreign Donors Made a Difference?'. *Asian Survey* 52 (6): 1067–1088. doi.org/10.1525/as.2012.52.6.1067.

Duthie, Roger. 2009. *Building Trust and Capacity: Civil Society and Transitional Justice from a Development Perspective*. New York: International Center for Transitional Justice.

ECCC (Extraordinary Chambers in the Court of Cambodia). 2008. 'Germany Pledges 1.5 Million Euro to Victim Support Unit'. Media Alert, 26 November 2008.

ECCC OCIJ (Office of the Co-Investigating Judges). 2010. 'Closing Order'. Case 002, D427, 15 September 2010.

Hermann, Johanna. 2010. 'Reaching for Justice: The Participation of Victims at the Extraordinary Chambers in the Courts of Cambodia'. *Centre on Human Rights in Conflict Policy Paper* No. 5. University of East London, September 2010.

Hughes, Caroline. 2009. *Dependent Communities: Aid and Politics in Cambodia and East Timor*. Ithaca: Cornell University Press.

ICTJ (International Center for Transitional Justice). 2010. 'Outreach Strategies in International and Hybrid Courts'. Report of the ICTJ-ECCC Workshop, Phnom Penh, 3–5 March 2010.

Kinetz, Erika and Yun Samean. 2008. 'DC-Cam Team Searching for KR Complainants'. *Cambodia Daily*, 17 March 2008, 35.

Kinetz, Erika and Prak Chan Thul. 2008. 'ECCC Struggling To Cover Victims' Legal Costs'. *Cambodia Daily*, 15 February 2008, 1–2.

Kirchenbauer, Nadine, Mychelle Balthazard, Latt Ky, Patrick Vinck and Phuong Pham. 2013. *Victim Participation before the Extraordinary Chambers in the Courts of Cambodia: Baseline Study of the Cambodian Human Rights and Development Association's Civil Party Scheme for Case 002*. Phnom Penh and Cambridge, MA: Cambodian Human Rights and Development Association and Harvard Humanitarian Initiative, Harvard University.

McGonigle Leyh, Brianne. 2009. 'Two for the Price of One: Attempts by the Extraordinary Chambers in the Courts of Cambodia to Combine Retributive and Restorative Justice Principle'. *Leiden Journal of International Law* 22: 127–149. doi.org/10.1017/S0922156508005669.

McGonigle Leyh, Brianne. 2011. *Procedural Justice? Victim Participation in International Criminal Proceedings*. Cambridge/Antwerp: Intersentia.

Nguyen, Lyma and Christoph Sperfeldt. 2014. 'Victim Participation and Minorities in Internationalised Criminal Trials: Ethnic Vietnamese Civil Parties at the Extraordinary Chambers in the Courts of Cambodia'. *Macquarie Law Journal* 14: 97–126.

Oeung, Jeudy. 2012. 'Roles of Civil Society in Civil Party Participation: Development toward Victim Participation'. In *Conference Report on Hybrid Perspectives on Legacies of the ECCC*, edited by Simon Meisenberg, Ignaz Stegmiller and Jeudy Oeung, 39–40. Phnom Penh: ECCC and CHRAC.

Oeung, Jeudy. 2016. 'Expectations, Challenges, and Opportunities of the ECCC'. In *The Extraordinary Chambers in the Courts of Cambodia: Assessing their Contributions to International Criminal Law*, edited by Simon Meisenberg and Ignaz Stegmiller, 103–121. The Hague: T.M.C. Asser Press. doi.org/10.1007/978-94-6265-105-0_5.

Oeung, Jeudy and Christoph Sperfeldt. 2010. *Victim Participation at the Extraordinary Chambers in the Courts of Cambodia: Third CHRAC Monitoring Report*. Phnom Penh: Cambodian Human Rights Action Committee.

OSJI (Open Society Justice Initiative) and Working Group on the Extraordinary Chambers. 2004. 'International Standards for the Treatment of Victims and Witnesses in Proceedings before the Extraordinary Chambers in the Courts of Cambodia for the Prosecution of Crimes Committed during the Period of Democratic Kampuchea'. Phnom Penh, May 2004.

OSJI. 2006. 'Memorandum to the Group of Interested States: Priority Issues for the Extraordinary Chambers in the Courts of Cambodia (ECCC)'. Open Society Justice Initiative, October 2006.

Penh, Buntheng, Kimmao Chhouk, Chansokol Men, Sovuthikar Invong and Chea Piseth Ly. 2006. *National Reconciliation after the Khmer Rouge*. Phnom Penh: Center for Advanced Studies.

Pham, Phuong, Patrick Vinck, Mychelle Balthazard and Sokom Hean. 2011a. *After the First Trial: A Population-Based Survey on Knowledge and Perception of Justice and the Extraordinary Chambers in the Courts of Cambodia*. Berkeley: Human Rights Center. doi.org/10.2139/ssrn.1860963.

Pham, Phuong, Patrick Vinck, Mychelle Balthazard, Judith Strasser and Chariya Om. 2011b. 'Victim Participation and the Trial of Duch at the Extraordinary Chambers in the Courts of Cambodia'. *Journal of Human Rights Practice* 3 (3): 264–287. doi.org/10.1093/jhuman/hur022.

Sperfeldt, Christoph and Vinesh Winodan, eds. 2009. *Conference Report on Reparations for Victims of the Khmer Rouge Regime*. Phnom Penh: CHRAC and ECCC Victims Unit.

Sperfeldt, Christoph, Oeung Jeudy and Daniel Hong. 2010. 'Legal Aid Services in Cambodia: Report of a Survey among Legal Aid Providers'. Cambodian Human Rights Action Committee, November 2010.

Sperfeldt, Christoph. 2012a. 'Cambodian Civil Society and the Khmer Rouge Tribunal'. *International Journal of Transitional Justice* 6 (1): 149–160. doi.org/10.1093/ijtj/ijr037.

Sperfeldt, Christoph. 2012b. 'Collective Reparations at the Extraordinary Chambers in the Courts of Cambodia'. *International Criminal Law Review* 12: 457–489. doi.org/10.1163/157181212X648888.

Sperfeldt, Christoph. 2013a. 'The Role of Cambodian Civil Society in the Victim Participation Scheme of the Extraordinary Chambers in the Courts of Cambodia'. In *Victims of International Crimes: An Interdisciplinary Discourse*, edited by Thorsten Bonacker and Christoph Safferling, 345–372. The Hague: T.M.C. Asser Press. doi.org/10.1007/978-90-6704-912-2_21.

Sperfeldt, Christoph. 2013b. 'From the Margins of Internationalized Criminal Justice. Lessons Learned at the Extraordinary Chambers in the Courts of Cambodia'. *Journal of International Criminal Justice* 11 (5): 1111–1137. doi.org/10.1093/jicj/mqt069.

Sperfeldt, Christoph, Melanie Hyde and Mychelle Balthazard. 2016. *Voices for Reconciliation: Assessing Media Outreach and Survivor Engagement for Case 002 at the Khmer Rouge Trials*. Honolulu: East-West Center and WSD HANDA Center for Human Rights and International Justice.

Stover, Eric, Mychelle Balthazard and Alexa Koenig. 2011. 'Confronting Duch: Civil Party Participation at the Extraordinary Chambers in the Courts of Cambodia'. *International Review of the Red Cross* 93 (882): 1–44. doi.org/10.1017/S1816383111000439.

Strasser, Judith, Julian Poluda, Mychelle Balthazard, Chariya Om, Sotheary Yim, Sophea Im, Kok-Thay Eng and Christoph Sperfeldt. 2011a. 'Engaging Communities – Easing the Pain: Outreach and Psychosocial Interventions in the Context of the Khmer Rouge Tribunal'. In *We Need the Truth: Enforced Disappearances in Asia*, edited by Katharina Lauritsch and Franc Kernjak, 146–159. Guatemala: ECAP.

Strasser, Judith, Julian Poluda, Chhim Sotheara and Phuong Pham. 2011b. 'Justice and Healing at the Khmer Rouge Tribunal: The Psychological Impact of Civil Party Participation'. In *Cambodia's Hidden Scars: Trauma Psychology in the Wake of the Khmer Rouge*, edited by Beth Van Schaak, Daryn Reicherter and Youk Chhang, 149–171. Phnom Penh: Documentation Center of Cambodia.

Studzinsky, Silke. 2012. 'Neglected Crimes: The Challenge of Raising Sexual and Gender-Based Crime before the Extraordinary Chambers in the Courts of Cambodia'. In *Gender in Transitional Justice*, edited by Susanne Buckley-Zistel and R. Stanley, 100–113. Basingstoke: Palgrave Macmillan. doi.org/10.1057/9780230348615_4.

Thomas, Sarah and Terith Chy. 2009. 'Including Survivors in the Tribunal Process'. In *On Trial: The Khmer Rouge Accountability Process*, edited by John D. Ciorciari and Anne Heindel, 214–293. Phnom Penh: Documentation Center of Cambodia.

Ye, Beini. 2014. 'Transitional Justice Through the Cambodian Women's Hearings'. *Cambodia Law and Policy Journal* 2: 23–38.

5

Showing now: The Bophana Audiovisual Resource Centre and the Extraordinary Chambers in the Courts of Cambodia[1]

Rachel Hughes

The Bophana Centre is an audiovisual archive, a training centre and a venue for free film screenings in the centre of Phnom Penh, capital of Cambodia. The centre was founded in 2006 by two Cambodian film-makers, Rithy Panh and Pannakar Ieu.[2] In the same year, the United Nations–supported Khmer Rouge Tribunal – formally the Extraordinary Chambers in the Courts of Cambodia (ECCC) – was also established in Phnom Penh. Although vastly different initiatives, the organisation and tribunal share a concern to work towards some form of justice for victims of Khmer Rouge crimes and to foster dialogue about how to constitute a better present and future in light of this and other historical conflicts in the country.

---

1   The fieldwork that forms the basis of this chapter was conducted in Cambodia in November 2016–January 2017 and June 2017 and was funded by an Australian Research Council Discovery Early Career Research Award [DE160100501].
2   Originally trained in France, Ieu had assisted King Sihanouk's film-making in the heyday of Cambodian film-making from the mid-1960s to the early 1970s (Ly and Muan 2001, 150). At the time he co-founded Bophana, Ieu was responsible for the cinematic division of the Ministry of Culture and Fine Arts (Jarvis 2015, 528).

This chapter is based on fieldwork conducted in and around the ECCC between late 2011 and early 2017. It introduces the work of the Bophana Centre as a unique Cambodian organisation and critically explores its relationship to the ECCC in the wider context of what is generally termed Cambodian civil society. It argues that the practices fostered at Bophana are ontologically and epistemologically at variance with transitional justice theory and practice. The creative labour of Bophana's film- and app-makers is cultural, material and relational. These kinds of practices have seen Bophana play a key role in the outreach and reparation activities of the ECCC, and in turn has changed the nature of these activities.

Ten years after its inception, Bophana is a relatively large and well-organised NGO, with both international and Cambodian-based donors and upwards of 25 paid staff. Its exhibitions, public events and weekly film screenings are well-attended. The Centre's Hanuman audiovisual archive (of film and audio material produced in or about Cambodia) is an excellent resource for students and researchers, being well-organised, centrally located in Phnom Penh and free to access. Conferences hosted by the centre also aim wide – to 'better understand Cambodian history, its culture, architecture, traditions [and] current challenges [as well as] image analysis and film-making' (Bophana 2016).

Counter to the exclusively project-based, developmentalist approaches of many NGOs in Cambodia, Bophana offers a long-term, modest, creative arts–based program of action, with some supplementary project work. The usual subjects of international development interventions and transitional justice in Cambodia – what Alexander Hinton identifies in his critical analysis of Cambodian transitional justice as 'victims [who] remain wounded and unhealed, awaiting rescue' (see Hinton 2013, 191) – are not found at Bophana. Rather, the centre emphasises shared creative labour, questioning of and dialogue about the past, and film appreciation. In and through this organisation, film-making and film-screening practices assemble diverse subjects, objects and affects. In this chapter, I first offer some observations about Bophana's prominent co-founder, Rithy Panh, before turning to the unique relationship between Bophana and the ECCC in the context of more than a decade of so-called transitional justice and civil society activity in Cambodia.

Rithy Panh

Rithy Panh was 12 years old when the Khmer Rouge came to power on 17 April 1975. He was forced from Phnom Penh to work as a farmer in Battambang in the country's north. He suffered greatly from starvation and illness due to overwork during the following years and lost many family members, including both his parents and his siblings. After the Khmer Rouge were ousted in 1979, Panh travelled to the Thailand–Cambodia border and was eventually resettled in Grenoble, France (Jarvis 2015, 527). After trying his hand at woodcarving, he studied film-making. He made 18 films between 1989 and 2016. Many of these films take a specific geographical place of personal (and also wider Cambodian) experience as their documentary subject matter. His 1989 film, *Site 2*, returns to life in the Cambodia–Thailand border camps, while his 2002 film, *S-21: The Khmer Rouge Killing Machine*, details the horror of a high school-turned-security centre in Phnom Penh. An earlier film of Panh's – *Bophana: A Cambodian Tragedy* (1996) – traced the fate of two young lovers, one of whom, a young woman named Bophana, was eventually interrogated, tortured and killed at the S-21 complex. Bophana has now lent her name to the Centre, and her painted portrait hangs in the main stairwell that takes visitors and staff from the street to the first-floor digital archive.

Of Panh's larger body of work, comparative literature scholar Panivong Norindr argues that it is:

> through the sounds of everyday life and 'filmed speech' [that] Rithy Panh succeeds in bringing to the fore, and through the voice of putatively unsophisticated subjects, some of the most tragic and under-acknowledged truths of our time (Norindr 2010, 189).

It is also true that the element of filmed silence or 'non-speech' has contributed to Panh's popularly acknowledged title of 'Cambodia's greatest living film-maker'. Helen Jarvis adds that Panh's films and books contribute 'penetrating silences' (Jarvis 2015). Some of the most affecting of these are silences between speech, when a subject of his film cannot or does not speak. However, media scholar Dierdre Boyle's characterisation of Panh's work as 'shattering [official] silence', may be misplaced praise. It is not true that 'official silence' followed the Khmer Rouge regime, because the successor state in Cambodia – the People's Republic of Kampuchea – initiated multiple forms of public memory about the genocide. As well, speech and silence, like memory, is culturally specific. As Carol Kidron argues in relation to silence in Canadian–Cambodian intergenerational interaction, 'the lived experience of the silent or silenced past may not always be politically motivated, performed as acts of resistance, or as capitulation to hegemonic indoctrination' (Kidron 2012, 726–727; see also Kent 2016). Panh himself has explained one moment in his film *S-21* where his subject had no words with which to explain his past events:

> I told [one former Khmer Rouge guard] 'you can complete your words by showing me what happened' ... I just try to take the memory out of the body, what your body keeps, what your body feels (Panh and Bataille 2012, 41).

Such scenes in *S-21* nonetheless complete more than words. Filmed gestures, of former perpetrators especially, complete – in the sense of *join up* – viewing and embodied memory. This 'being shown' is more intimate, and more shocking, than 'being told'. Although film critics and scholars have lauded such scenes, terming them 're-enactments', Panh has stated that the term 're-enactment' 'is not the right word' for his work (Panh in Oppenheimer 2016, 244).

Panh is probably best known outside of Cambodia for his 2013 film *The Missing Picture*, which won 10 international film awards, including at the Cannes and Toronto Film Festivals. *The Missing Picture* takes as its starting point and abiding challenge the absence or impossibility of 'a picture' of Khmer Rouge rule in Cambodia, particularly an evidentiary photograph. In an English-language trailer a narrator states: 'I seek my childhood like a lost picture, or rather it seeks me'. In a French version, it is stated:

> For many years ... I have been looking for the missing picture: a photograph taken between 1975 and 1979 by the Khmer Rouge when they ruled over Cambodia ... On its own, of course, an image cannot prove mass murder ... I searched for it vainly in the archives, in old papers, in the country villages of Cambodia. Today I know: this image must be missing ... So I created it ... (Panh 2013).

The film supplements historical footage with images and sequences of painted miniature clay figures – the work of sculptor Mang Sarith – set in dioramas. These figures populate and animate a remembered rather than recorded past. The scenes show rather than tell of life under Khmer Rouge rule; though poignant and incriminating, they avoid simplistic indictments.

Bophana and the ECCC

Bophana has been one of many NGOs to assist Cambodia's internationalised tribunal, the ECCC (see Sperfeldt 2013). Following a Memorandum of Understanding between itself and the tribunal, Bophana has provided audiovisual support for the legal outreach activities of the Public Affairs Section (PAS) of the tribunal. Since 2009, the PAS has been running a specific legal outreach program known as the Khmer Rouge Study Tour (hereafter Study Tour). The first part of a Study Tour involves PAS officers travelling from Phnom Penh to a provincial city, town or village to hold a Memory Night of film screenings and presentations about the ECCC. Bophana technicians travel with PAS staff to the location of the Memory Night, usually a central, open-air, public space. There they erect a large white screen, locate a power source and set up the film projector and recruit speakers necessary for the PAS presentations and film screenings (see Figure 5.1).

Later that night or the next morning, the community is invited to board free buses to Phnom Penh (see Figure 5.2), taking in the Tuol Sleng Genocide Museum (the former S-21 site), the Choeung Ek 'killing field' memorial and the ECCC itself (see Elander 2012). The PAS outreach staff, accompanied by Bophana staff, have taken the Study Tour to scores of provincial communities, and tens of thousands of Cambodians have subsequently passed through the ECCC Public Gallery to observe or hear about the work of the tribunal. In this way, Bophana is facilitating larger ECCC outreach efforts to inform and engage Cambodians in a legal process that is unfolding, for a great many people, in distant chambers.

Bophana has also played a key role in ECCC outreach by way of its development of the audiovisual materials that are screened at the Study Tour Memory Nights. Bophana has produced a short Khmer-language film for children, *The Hermit and the Tiger*, which uses animal characters (played by child actors) to tell the story of a quest for justice. This film is shown early in the night's proceedings, so that children might see it before they fall asleep on mats and laps. Both of the award-winning documentaries that are routinely shown as the main feature at Memory Nights – *About My Father* (2010) and *Red Wedding* (2012) – were directed or co-directed by Bophana-trained film-makers and produced by Bophana. Both films follow women victims of the Khmer Rouge – Phung-Guth Sunthary in *About My Father*, and Pen Sochan in *Red Wedding*. Painful events, including gender-based and sexual violence in the form of forced marriage, are remembered or uncovered in the films as these women participate in cases before the ECCC.

Figure 5.1: Bophana technicians and PAS staff setting up for an outdoor ECCC Memory Night in Kompong Chhnang, Cambodia.

Source: Photo by author.

Figure 5.2: Free ECCC outreach bus taking villagers from Kompong Chhnang to Phnom Penh.
Source: Photo by author.

About My Father and *Red Wedding* have been received by critics as being 'in the tradition of Rithy Panh' (Chan in Titi-Fontaine 2013). One of the co-directors of *Red Wedding* has said in interview that Panh taught her 'to be especially close to … characters and to go deep into the questioning of subjects' (Chan in Titi-Fontaine 2013). Lida Chan's statement speaks to a learned empathic intimacy as a means for eliciting words or gestures from her subjects. To capture 'many voices' or 'penetrating silences', one must be 'close' and 'go deep into the questioning'. To fully understand Bophana's work in and around the Memory Nights, however, recognition must be given to the organisation's critical familiarity with colonial and neo-colonial cinematic traditions in Cambodia.

Film screening

Public screening of films to Cambodian audiences, in both urban and village settings, dates back to at least the early twentieth century. Cambodia scholars Daravuth Ly and Ingrid Muan note that cinema first arrived in Cambodia during the French protectorate period, and historian Penny Edwards reports that by 1916 a small cinema catered to

Phnom Penh's 1,600 Europeans (Edwards 2007, 59). A General Mission of Cinema of the colonial Government of Indochina reportedly passed through the country in 1917–18, screening to Cambodian audiences in open-air venues (see Ly and Muan 2001, 143). Two striking images in Ly and Muan's book depict the General Mission 'in the field'. One of these images shows a group of men raising a large outdoor screen – white fabric stretched taut inside a frame of bamboo poles (see Figure 5.3). A similar object is used by Bophana technicians at present-day Memory Nights. Although the technology of film production and projection has changed enormously, the kinds of objects onto which images are projected – large, portable, open-air screens – are largely unchanged.

Figure 5.3: The General Mission of Cinema of the colonial Government of Indochina setting up for an outdoor screening.

Source: Image courtesy of Daravuth Ly and Ingrid Muan.

Little is known of the actual films shown during this General Mission, but the use of film as a method of pacification and propaganda-dissemination was gaining traction in the French empire at the time (see Slavin 2001, 59). Four to five decades on, after Cambodia gained independence from France in 1954, the United States Information Service (USIS) 'cinecars' travelled through the country projecting films on American life, health, education and contemporary domestic and foreign affairs to village audiences (Ly and Muan 2001, 145).

These accounts confirm that Cambodian audiences – like many other populations in colonial and Cold War South-East Asia – have long been audiovisually enrolled in imperial and geopolitical projections of power. As the Cambodian population is still predominantly rural, and because of the colonial segregation of viewing subjects – whereby Europeans watched films inside theatres while indigenous populations were offered 'wandering cinema' in rural areas (Campbell and Power 2010, 178) – the latter form of cinema survives in the country to the present day. Those best placed to produce 'wandering cinema' in the present, however, are not ruling or meddling powers but Cambodians themselves.

Film-making in Cambodia

Film-making in Cambodia has always been an internationalised affair. The USIS ran a film-making training program in Phnom Penh in the 1950s and 1960s, taking in students from various ministries, the Police, and the Army (Ly and Muan 2001, 145–146). Cambodia's King Sihanouk, himself an avid film-maker, presided over the first International Film Festival of Phnom Penh in 1968, a year before Cambodia's first National Film Festival in November 1969 (Ly and Muan 2001, 153–154). By the 1960s and into the early 1970s both film-making and film-viewing (in cinemas) were well-established practices in Phnom Penh. As the war between the advancing Khmer Rouge and ruling US-backed Lon Nol forces came closer to the city, cinemas (like other businesses) closed up, fearing for the safety of their patrons (Ly and Muan 2001, 154).

Film-making during Khmer Rouge rule (April 1975 to January 1979) was an insular practice – largely limited to the regime's own experimentation with film production. The films were subsequently shown in some areas of the country. These propaganda films – showing large-scale infrastructure worksites of hundreds of workers, including children, moving earth without the help of machinery, and often without shoes – were recently shown at the ECCC as evidence of Khmer Rouge crimes against humanity. These films can be found in Bophana's Hanuman archive, and Rithy Panh, along with many other film-makers – including Public Affairs officers at the ECCC – have included these grainy black and white film sequences as opening shots in their contemporary films.

In the period immediately following Khmer Rouge rule, efforts to revive Cambodian film-making met with limited support. Two Cambodian film-makers who survived the Khmer Rouge period and returned to Phnom Penh – Yvon Hem and Ly Bun Yim – spoke in 2001 of their frustration with the lack of official interest in re-establishing a Cambodian film industry in the post-conflict period (see Ly and Muan 2001). Over the last decade, Bophana has led efforts to accumulate a significant audiovisual archive and organise the means for its public access and the capacity for professional audiovisual training and services to once again be offered in Phnom Penh.[3] Importantly too, Bophana has fostered the creative talent of a group of young Cambodian film-makers, not least by providing them with technologies of film-making (see Hamilton 2013).

Bophana and Cambodian civil society

Cambodia has, since the United Nations Transitional Authority period of 1991–1993, played host to a significant number of international and Cambodian NGOs. Peace studies scholar Caroline Hughes (2009) and others (Ear 2013; Slocomb 2010; Springer 2015) point to the growing inequality and aid dependency brought about by 30 years of liberalising Cambodia's economy, a shared priority of the Cambodian state and international interests in the country since the 1980s (see Slocomb 2010, 225). As economic historian Margaret Slocomb notes, Cambodian economic policy of the 1990s was dictated more from outside than from within Cambodia as a direct consequence of a 1994 Structural Adjustment Programme (SAP) with international creditors (Slocomb 2010, 235). With significant increases in inequality following this, experienced geographically as a further entrenched rural–urban divide, the SAP was subsequently replaced (by the same international fund and bank actors) with a Poverty Reduction Strategy Paper in 1999 (Slocomb 2010, 236). Through the 2000s, aid remained central to political priorities and economic policy. Aid dependency also elevated donor-preferred practices and competitive project-based funding that engaged NGO partners in fixed cycles of project design, monitoring and evaluation (Hughes 2009). Geographer Tim Frewer argues that NGOs in Cambodia have recently found a new and expanded role thanks to

3   Like Bophana, Khmer Mekong Films, also founded in 2006, offers full film production services in Phnom Penh, but does not engage in archival work or regular public film screenings.

donor emphasis on civil society and good governance, and that NGOs in Cambodia are generally considered by donors, think tanks and local scholars to be playing a positive role – so much so that recent government attempts to regulate the NGO sector have been understood as an 'attack' on civil society (Frewer 2013, 99).

Like many other Cambodian NGOs, the Bophana Centre receives international funding, but is also significantly embedded in Cambodia in terms of staffing, training and cooperation with various state and non-state actors. Bophana advertises that it offers archive and production services to 'individuals, civil society organisations, enterprises and State institutions' (Bophana 2016). In this statement, the organisation positions itself as a service provider to Cambodian civil society. Bophana has also engaged with the ECCC as a service provider. As discussed above, Bophana has assisted with both the content and operation of the PAS Study Tour. The PAS has in turn assisted Rithy Panh by granting many hours of interview access to Duch, defendant in ECCC Case 001, out of which Panh made his film, *Duch: Master of the Forges of Hell* (see Panh and Bataille 2012).

Panh was also involved in a key discussion with the ECCC over the filming of the tribunal for livestreaming and recording purposes. Footage from six cameras in the ECCC courtroom is edited in situ into a single stream of images to be sent to live screens around the public gallery, as well as to the media room situated below the public gallery, and to the web via the ECCC livestream. Panh advised that footage from all cameras be preserved, such that it would be possible to record and later show simultaneous occurrences in different parts of the chambers (Helen Jarvis, pers. comm., Phnom Penh, Cambodia, 15 June 2017). For example, he felt strongly that a camera should be trained on the defendants at all times, to record their responses to the evidence and arguments being presented, and that this footage should be preserved in perpetuity (ibid.). Unfortunately, Panh's advice and offer of Bophana's help with this approach was not taken up by the non-Cambodian group responsible for ECCC filming, with the result that footage not used in the livestream feed is generally discarded.

Unlike many development and good governance–focused NGOs, Bophana does not explicitly appeal to liberal democratic conceptualisations of civil society that have been 'influential in guiding the "good governance" agendas among development agencies' (McIlwaine 2007; see also Frewer

2013).[4] Bophana eschews the general separateness-with-suspicion between international NGOs and the Cambodian state, whereby the Cambodian state is understood as the current government, and the current government as Cambodia's ruling party. By taking a wide historical and cultural view of the audiovisual arts, Bophana implicitly supports a politics of polyphony in the present as well as *a l'histoire sa polyphonie* (see Norindr 2010, 189). Just as subjects in Panh's films – and in those of his students – are given space to speak and gesture their truths, so does Bophana create a space for multiple, coexisting audiovisual activities that are always already political.

While Cambodian civil society is dominated by humanitarian and human rights–based work, Bophana appears to step back from these normative approaches, offering instead an emphasis on practice, study and enquiry, and on dialogue within and about creative processes. Because memory is part of the creative process, this is also dialogue about memory – personal memory, public memory, social memory and memory that exceeds these categorisations. It is in this sense that Bophana, unlike most civil society actors operating in and around the ECCC, does not participate straightforwardly in the discursive field of 'transitional justice'. The emphasis on creative practice at Bophana does not cleave to the priorities of the interventionist and technical enterprise denoted as 'transitional justice' in Cambodia (and elsewhere). Creative enquiry and experimentation is more open in its approach, and its effects more uncertain, potentially wide-ranging and longer-term, than is countenanced by the prescriptions and evaluations of transitional justice. Focusing on the work Bophana does on a daily basis, following the approach taken by Claire Mercer and Maia Green elsewhere, allows for an understanding of how 'civil society' or 'transitional justice' approaches 'dovetail with [Cambodian] agendas, and with local histories … that provide further templates for action' (Mercer and Green 2013, 107). I close my analysis with a discussion of yet another shared focus of Bophana and the ECCC that again shows the difference of Bophana's work, a difference that can be thought about by recourse to the tension between the terms 'technical' and 'technological'.

---

4   Bophana does appeal to notions of 'capacity building' in the form of education and training of Cambodians in film direction, production and film production services.

App-learning on Khmer Rouge history

Bophana is currently developing an internet-based application, a project known as 'App-learning on Khmer Rouge history' (hereafter KR-app). This is a multimedia offering that combines archival audiovisual material with Bophana-developed text, drawn images, film sequences and interactive elements. It aims to educate Cambodians, especially youth, about the rise, rule and fall of the Khmer Rouge regime via their internet-enabled devices, especially smartphones and tablets.[5] By compiling and writing this history, incorporating filmed and transcribed survivor testimony, and by newly (audio)visualising many historical details and events, the KR-app also aims to assist the healing of survivors, generate dialogue (especially between younger and older Cambodians) and encourage Cambodians to read the existing historical sources on this period (interview with Chea Sopheap, Phnom Penh, 9 December 2016). The project has been formally endorsed by the Ministry of Education, Youth and Sports so that it may be incorporated into schools nationwide (ECCC 2017, 10). The KR-app is a proposed reparation project of ECCC Case 002/02, under the 'guarantee of non-repetition' measure. As well as finding funding through the New Zealand–based Rei Foundation, Bophana was successful in its bid for European Union funding (via UNOPS, the United Nations Office for Project Services) that was earmarked for ECCC reparations.[6] The KR-app has been developed with assistance from the two sections of the ECCC responsible for victim participation and reparation requests, the Civil Party Lead Co-Lawyers Section and the Victims Support Section.

While the UNOPS call for proposals did not explicitly use the phrase 'transitional justice', the background section of the document refers to a general state of 'injustice and lack of understanding' in Cambodia about the Khmer Rouge past, a gross simplification of the politics of the past in Cambodia since 1979, but one often perpetuated in transitional justice discourses about Cambodia and its tribunal. Although calling for proposals

---

5   A 2015 research report showed that 39.5 per cent of Cambodians own at least one smartphone (up from 26.1 per cent in 2014), with smartphone ownership rates higher among urban residents (51.7 per cent) than rural residents (34.4 per cent), and very high amongst those studying for or holding a university degree (82 per cent) (Phong and Solá 2015, 7). In the same study, 28.6 per cent of Cambodians claimed to access the Internet using their own phone and use of the Internet was also found to decrease dramatically with age, from 51.6 per cent of those aged between 15 and 25 to 10 per cent of those aged 40 and 65 (Phong and Solá 2015, 16).

6   The Call for Proposals was titled 'Awareness & Education on Khmer Rouge History Programme – Supportive Educational Resources Development' and was made in December 2015 for projects to be completed over 2016–2017.

that might 'remedy' this situation 'nation-wide', supporting information delivery was the main aim of the grant. The call for proposals stated that the successful project will 'provide supportive educational resources to be disseminated to high schools and university students' (UNOPS n.d., 2). In reality, Bophana is developing a high-quality creative and interactive educational resource that will likely be used far more widely than in high schools and universities.

The development of the KR-app is in itself a creative process. Both its content and software development are labour intensive, with more than 20 staff affiliated to the project over 2016–2017. The KR-app will have eight 'chapters', dealing in loose chronological order with the rise, rule and fall of the Khmer Rouge. Bophana has convened a 'Scientific Committee' for the project that regularly advises the lead writer and project manager. Committee members are Cambodian academics and experts with research and publication backgrounds in Khmer Rouge history. Monthly meetings of the Scientific Committee allow for new content that has been developed by the writers to be debated, improved or corrected. Consensus or compromise on wording and explanation is attempted on a sentence-by-sentence basis, a laborious but ultimately highly productive arrangement that also has the potential to enhance research capacity and scholarly networks between committee members, as well as between Bophana and allied organisations dedicated to preserving and promoting critical engagement with Cambodia's past.

Bophana has also produced bespoke images and film content for the KR-app, employing artists and film-makers to draw, sculpt, photograph and film objects and images that will (audio)visually enhance the text-based content of the app (see Figure 5.4). The process of this creative visualisation work is described by the project manager in the following way:

> our artists listen to the memory of the survivor and, under the supervision of the writers ... recreate the story and then the film-makers film it ... some images you cannot find [in the archives], so we have to draw ... to recreate (interview with Chea Sopheap, Phnom Penh, 9 December 2016).

Figure 5.4: Website image advertising the KR-app.
Source: Image courtesy of Bophana Centre.

Although transitional justice discourses imagine information dissemination and awareness raising to be largely technical processes, the significant and creative technological and cultural aptitude of an organisation like Bophana demands far greater attention to processes of understanding, rendering and deliberating past events and claims to truth. This attentiveness is part of the professionalism of the organisation, but it is also generated within the creative process, as a part of being enrolled in the affective and highly material process of working with archival material and survivor memory for public memorialisation, broadly conceived. This is a therapeutic *practice* that extends outward through technologically mediated relations with diverse others and materialities, not inward towards a perceived fragile ego (see Boyd 2017). Such practice goes largely unrecognised within a development project approach that emphasises 'objectives', 'stakeholders', 'target activities' and 'evaluation'.

While the UNOPS call required successful applicants to 'be recognised by the ECCC as a Judicial Reparation project', this is a wholly separate ECCC process with additional conditions. Recognition as a reparation project can only be granted in a judgement handed down by the Trial Chamber or Supreme Court Chamber of the ECCC. Reparation projects relating to a specific trial of the ECCC can be proposed to these chambers by the Civil Party Lead Co-Lawyers if certain criteria have been met – namely that the proposed project will involve and benefit participating victims (known as 'civil parties'), is directly related to a crime being prosecuted in the case and has already found full funding. The UNOPS requirement for reparation *recognition* effectively added additional conditions for potential applicants, and asked that they guarantee something they could not.[7]

ECCC civil parties have been involved in the development of Bophana's KR-app. The app development team has also consulted ECCC documents – including case files, civil party testimonies, and judgements – and has also conducted new interviews with civil parties (interview with Keo Duong, Phnom Penh, 30 December 2016). The reported benefit to civil parties of the KR-app is largely one of participating in the development of its content, of contributing their story to a multimedia source that will educate fellow Cambodians and others over coming years. The UNOPS requirement that the project benefit Cambodian youth, however, demands that Bophana consult with young people as well as civil parties (who are predominantly older).

It is difficult to imagine how this careful work of producing high-quality and interactive audiovisual content, technological functionality across multiple devices,[8] and continuous public engagement and testing of 'beta' versions (with civil parties and youth) is adequately covered by the original EU and Rei Foundation (NZ) funding and two-year project duration. This project-based work, emerging out of international donors' desire to support the restorative justice aims of an internationalised tribunal, risks (perhaps unwittingly) entering into the exploitation of Cambodian NGO staff in a manner akin to multinational corporations sourcing software development in parts of the developing South (see Harindranath 2002, 57–58; Potter et al. 2012, 143).

Conclusion

As critical development scholars have long argued, NGOs are highly specific to particular places and times, despite their appeal to broader – and sometimes global or universal – ideals. With such emplaced specificity comes a complex role in the politics of development, but acknowledgement of this remains largely outside mainstream NGO literatures (Mercer

---

7   Organisations could commit to applying – and seeking to meet the criteria required by the Civil Party Lead Co-Lawyers (CPLCLs) for proposed reparation projects – but recognition is a matter for ECCC judges, it is beyond the control of either the organisations or the CPLCLs.

8   The aim is to have the app accessible on iOS, Android and Windows systems (for both phones and tablets) and in two languages, English and Khmer.

2002; Mercer and Green 2013). Rather than understanding NGOs as key agents of civil society, this paper has considered 'civil society' and 'transitional justice' to be key rationales for the continued existence and salience of NGOs already well entrenched in Cambodia's society and economy. The Bophana Centre provides an example of how organisations intervene in these largely discursive, albeit economically consequential, fields, such that there is both the realisation and refusal of different kinds of work (Mercer and Green 2013).

What is the nature of Bophana's intervention, specifically? I have echoed here the observations of others on the importance of 'filmed speech' and 'filmed gesture' in Panh and his students' work. Some of this work pre-dates both the Bophana Centre and the ECCC. The terms 'testimony' (speech or gesture that aims to 'voice' a direct experience) and 'witnessing' (as film-making and film-viewing) are often attributed to this work. After the ECCC, these terms have specific legal meanings and resonances in contemporary Cambodia and, as such, are often discussed in legal and transitional justice literatures in relation to an individual subject (see Elander 2012; Hughes 2016). Testimony and witnessing at Bophana, however, are distributed or shared practices.

At Bophana, old and new cinematic and communication technologies coexist in productive, creative tension. Here, speech and silence are relational processes, rather than opposed and individualised states. Relationships between people, families, communities, animals, spirits, visions and objects are given representation, as is violence and suffering. As a film-maker, Panh has taken his belief 'in form, in colors, in light, in framing and editing [and] in poetry' (Panh and Bataille 2013, 247) and has widened the horizon of contemporary Cambodian engagement with its various pasts and presents. At the Bophana Centre, 'Uncle Rithy' has situated his own work and teaching within this horizon and, in doing so, practices a different kind of organisation.

Bibliography

Bophana Centre. 2016. Website. bophana.org/ (accessed 20 September 2016).

Boyd, Candice. 2017. *Non-Representational Geographies of Therapeutic Art Making: Thinking Through Practice*. Basingstoke: Palgrave. doi.org/10.1007/978-3-319-46286-8.

Campbell, David and Marcus Power. 2010. 'The Scopic Regime of Africa'. In *Observant States: Geopolitics and Visual Culture*, edited by Fraser MacDonald, Rachel Hughes and Klaus Dodds, 167–195. London: I.B. Tauris.

Ear, Sophal. 2013. *Aid Dependence in Cambodia: How Foreign Assistance Undermines Democracy*. New York: Columbia University Press. doi.org/ 10.7312/columbia/9780231161121.001.0001.

ECCC (Extraordinary Chambers in the Courts of Cambodia). 2017. *Civil Party Lead Co-Lawyers' Final Claim for Reparation in Case 002/02*, Document E457/6/2/1, 30 May. Available at eccc.gov.kh/sites/default/ files/documents/courtdoc/2017-06-01%2010:57/E457_6_2_1_EN.pdf (accessed 15 June 2017).

Edwards, Penny. 2007. *Cambodge: The Cultivation of a Nation 1860–1945*. Honolulu: University of Hawai'i Press.

Elander, Maria. 2012. 'The Victim's Address: Expressivism and the Victim at the Extraordinary Chambers in the Courts of Cambodia'. *The International Journal of Transitional Justice* 7: 95–115. doi.org/10.1093/ijtj/ijs028.

Frewer, Tim. 2013. 'Doing NGO Work: The Politics of Being 'Civil Society' and Promoting 'Good Governance' in Cambodia'. *Australian Geographer* 44 (1): 97–114. doi.org/10.1080/00049182.2013.765350.

Hamilton, Annette. 2013. 'Witness and Recuperation: Cambodia's New Documentary Cinema'. *Concentric: Literary and Cultural Studies* 39 (1): 7–30.

Harindranath, Ramaswami. 2002. 'Software Industry, Religious Nationalism and Social Movements in India: Aspects of Globalisation?'. In *Citizenship and Participation in the Information Age*, edited by Manjunath Pendakur and Roma Harris, 56–64. Ontario: University of Toronto Press.

Hinton, Alexander. 2013. 'Transitional Justice Time: Uncle San, Aunty Yan and Outreach at the Khmer Rouge Tribunal'. In *Genocide and Mass Atrocities in Asia: Legacies and Prevention*, edited by Deborah Mayersen and Annie Pohlman, 185–208. Hoboken: Taylor and Francis.

Hughes, Caroline. 2009. *Dependent Communities: Aid and Politics in Cambodia and East Timor*. Ithaca: Cornell University Press.

Hughes, Rachel. 2016. 'Victims' Rights, Victim Collectives and Utopic Disruption at the Extraordinary Chambers in the Courts of Cambodia'. *Australian Journal of Human Rights* 22 (2): 143–166.

Kent, Lia. 2016. 'Sounds of Silence: Everyday Strategies of Repair in Timor-Leste'. *Australian Feminist Law Journal* 42 (1): 31–50. doi.org/10.1080/132 00968.2016.1175403.

Kidron, Carol. 2012. 'Alterity and the Particular Limits of Universalism: Comparing Jewish-Israeli Holocaust and Canadian-Cambodian Genocide Legacies'. *Current Anthropology* 53 (6): 723–754. doi.org/10.1086/668449.

Jarvis, Helen. 2015. 'Panh, Rithy'. In *Modern Genocide: The Definitive Resources and Documentation Collection*, edited by Paul Bartrop and Steven Jacobs, 527–528. Santa Barbara: ABC-CLIO.

Ly, Daravuth and Ingrid Muan. 2001. *Cultures of Independence: An Introduction to Cambodian Arts and Culture in the 1950s and 1960s*. Phnom Penh: Reyum Publishing.

McIlwaine, Cathy. 2007. 'From Local to Global to Transnational Civil Society: Re-framing Development Perspectives on the Non-State Sector'. *Geography Compass* 1 (6): 1252–1281. doi.org/10.1111/j.1749-8198.2007.00061.x.

Mercer, Claire. 2002. 'NGOs, Civil Society and Democratization: A Critical Review of the Literature'. *Progress in Development Studies* 2 (1): 5–22. doi.org/ 10.1191/1464993402ps027ra.

Mercer, Claire and Maia Green. 2013. 'Making Civil Society Work: Contracting, Cosmopolitanism and Community Development in Tanzania'. *Geoforum* 45: 106–115. doi.org/10.1016/j.geoforum.2012.10.008.

Norindr, Panivong. 2010. 'The Sounds of Everyday Life in Rithy Panh's Documentaries'. *French Forum* 35 (2–3): 181–190. doi.org/10.1353/frf. 2010.0004.

Oppenheimer, Joshua. 2016. 'Perpetrators Testimony and the Restoration of Humanity: *S21*, Rithy Panh'. In *Killer Images: Documentary Film, Memory and the Performance of Violence in Brink*, edited by Joram Ten and Joshua Oppenheimer, 243–255. London and New York: Wallflower Press.

Panh, Rithy, writer-dir. 2013. *The Missing Picture* (feature film). Phnom Penh: Bophana Productions.

Panh, Rithy with Christopher Bataille. 2012. *The Elimination: A Survivor of the Khmer Rouge Confronts His Past and the Commandant of the Killing Fields*, translated by John Cullen. London: Profile Books.

Phong, Kimchhoy and Javier Solá. 2015. *Mobile Phone and Internet Use in Cambodia*. Phnom Penh: Asia Foundation.

Potter, Rob, Dennis Conway, Ruth Evans and Sally Lloyd-Evans, eds. 2012. *Key Concepts in Development Geography.* London: SAGE. doi.org/10.4135/9781473914834.

Slavin, David Henry. 2001. *Colonial Cinema and Imperial France, 1919–1939: White Blind Spots, Male Fantasies and Settler Myths.* Baltimore and London: Johns Hopkins University Press.

Slocomb, Maragaret. 2010. *An Economic History of Cambodia in the Twentieth Century.* Singapore: NUS Press.

Sperfeldt, Christoph. 2013. 'The Role of Civil Society in the Victim Participation Scheme of the Extraordinary Chambers in the Courts of Cambodia'. In *Victims of International Crimes, An Interdisciplinary Discourse*, edited by Thorsten Bonacker and Christoph Safferling, 345–372. The Hague: Asser Press. doi.org/10.1007/978-90-6704-912-2_21.

Springer, Simon. 2015. *Violent Neoliberalism: Development, Discourse, and Dispossession in Cambodia.* New York: Palgrave McMillan.

Titi-Fontaine, Sandra. 2013. 'La mariée était en rouge [The Bride Was in Red]', *Human Rights Tribune*, 8 March. Available at www.nouvelobs.com/rue89/rue89-monde/20130308.RUE4771/au-cambodge-sous-pol-pot-la-mariee-etait-en-rouge.html (accessed 14 June 2017).

UNOPS (United Nations Office for Project Services). n.d. *Call for Proposals Awareness and Education on Khmer Rouge History Programme – Supportive Educational Resources Development.* Copy on file with author.

6

Myanmar's transition without justice

Catherine Renshaw

The rape and murder of Maran Lu Ra and Tangbau Hkawn Nan Tsin, which took place in January 2015 in a small village in Shan State, Myanmar, became a focal point for civil society activism around issues of justice and impunity during Myanmar's transition to democracy.[1] There are several reasons for this. Of note, first, is the character of the victims. Ra and Tsin were young female schoolteachers and members of one of Myanmar's minority ethnic groups, the Kachin. From the 1960s until 1994, the Kachin Independence Army (KIA) waged war against Myanmar's military, seeking greater autonomy for Kachin State (Sadan 2015). During the decades of insurgency, Kachin women and children experienced severe human rights violations at the hands of both Myanmar's military and ethnic armies. A ceasefire between the government and the KIA broke down in 2011, leading to the displacement of civilians and to increasing levels of human rights violations. Ra and Tsin came to represent, for many, the suffering of women and children during the government's long-running civil conflict with armed ethnic organisations.

---

1   Throughout the chapter, the term 'Burma' is used when the text refers to the country and 'Burmese' for the people, before 1990. 'Myanmar' is used for the country after this date, as the country was officially renamed in 1990. The same applies to 'Rangoon' and 'Yangon'. 'Myanmar' refers to citizens of the country as a whole. 'Bamar' is used to describe the ethnic group that has dominated governance of the country and is the most numerous in the country.

Second, the suspected perpetrators were members of the military's Light Infantry Battalion 503, which had been stationed in the village at the time of the crimes. The inadequate police investigation into the case highlighted the fact that Myanmar's democratisation, which began in 2010 with the election of a nominally civilian government, had not ended military impunity. Legal and administrative barriers to justice remained in place: the military was not subject to the jurisdiction of national courts; the police force lacked institutional independence; and the judiciary was not impartial. The perfunctory and flawed investigation into the rape and murder of Ra and Tsin and the failure on the part of authorities to charge anyone for the crimes reflected the systemic justice failures that persisted into Myanmar's transition.

Third, Ra and Tsin were members of the powerful Kachin Baptist Convention (KBC), a Christian religious organisation dominant in Kachin State and across Myanmar's largely Christian north. In the wake of the crimes against Ra and Tsin and the subsequent police investigation, the KBC formed its own Truth-Finding Committee and conducted its own investigation into the crimes. The KBC investigation established serious procedural failures by the police and uncovered evidence that strongly suggested the culpability of the military. The case of Ra and Tsin brings to the fore the role assumed by civil society in the pursuit of truth and justice during Myanmar's transition, in a context where the primary political actors – the military and the country's major democratic political party, the National League for Democracy (NLD) – have strong reasons not to pursue a transitional justice agenda. In the face of resistance from these actors, the KBC and other civil society organisations articulate a unique and powerful perspective on the forms and processes that justice could take during Myanmar's transition to democracy.

This chapter shows how measures to advance justice during Myanmar's transition are being led from the bottom up by community-based groups, local religious organisations and non-governmental organisations (NGOs), without support from key political actors in the transition.[2] The conception of justice put forward by organisations such as the KBC focuses on securing justice in individual cases such as those of Ra and Tsin, in order to deter further crimes, end military impunity and bear

2   In this chapter, I use the term 'civil society' and 'civil society organisations' to refer to different forms of civil activism between the family and the state, including faith-based organisations (Heidel 2006).

witness to the wrong done to victims. There are also, however, broader and more complex forms of justice that are also promoted by civil society organisations. The statements from local organisations, particularly religious organisations and women's groups, have linked the conflict in Kachin State and elsewhere to the economic exploitation of the people, and they have demanded a form of justice that includes constitutional reform, genuine federalism and protection of minority rights. As well as retributive justice in individual cases, many civil society organisations call for the return of traditional ownership of land, measures to safeguard the environment, the protection of language, culture and religion, and an end to discrimination against ethnic minorities: the demand is for a form of justice that is both specific (addressing individual cases such as those of Ra and Tsin) and broad (addressing structural social and economic inequalities). In the early years of Myanmar's transition, the government was deficient in addressing both forms of justice.

As several scholars have pointed out, narrow definitions of 'civil society organisations' and 'community-based organisations' are not useful in the Burmese context, because they impede a full understanding of social organising and social change in the country (Kramer 2011; Prasse-Freeman 2012; see also Lidauer 2012). From 1962, under the rule of General Ne Win, three main types of civil society organisation were permitted to exist: (1) organisations affiliated with the government, whose activities were restricted largely to the promotion of literature and culture; (2) the Buddhist monkhood (*sangha*); and (3) Christian churches. It was not until the early 1990s that United Nations agencies and international NGOs began sponsoring the activities of local NGOs, focusing mainly on healthcare and health education services, HIV/AIDS prevention, child protection and microfinance (South 2008). In the late 1990s, as economic difficulties and the crushing sanctions policies of the United States and the European Union undermined the livelihood of millions of Burmese (Renshaw 2017), independent local charitable organisations emerged. In 2008, in the wake of Cyclone Nargis, local community organisations carried out the work of rescue and repair in large parts of the country (Renshaw 2014). Turnell argues that even before transition began, civil society organisations were indispensable parts of the Burmese political economy, providing social goods and essential services that the military was incapable of delivering (Turnell 2008; Prasse-Freeman 2012). Following the 2010 election and the liberalisation of laws relating to freedom of association, the space for civil society organisations dramatically increased across the country, and since then they have played a powerful and shifting role in Myanmar's transition to democracy. In this chapter, I use the expression 'civil society organisations' (CSOs) to refer to voluntary, autonomous associations and networks of organised civil activism existing between the family and the state (Hann 2011; South 2008) including faith-based groups but not private economic actors or political parties. On this definition, on one count, Myanmar has more than 200,000 civil society organisations (Heidel 2006, 43).

South, in his study of civil society organisations in Myanmar, distinguishes between NGOs and community-based organisations (CBOs). CBOs are locally managed grassroots organisations where members are the main beneficiaries. NGOs, in contrast, are not necessarily from the community – though they work for community members – and they may be local, national or international. One of my purposes in this chapter is to demonstrate this difference and to highlight the way in which the nature and characteristics of different civil society organisations shape the way they respond to questions of transitional justice. I focus on one of Myanmar's ethnic minority states, Kachin, to explore the transitional justice work being undertaken by CSOs and NGOs in that state. In Kachin, both NGOs and CBOs have been active in progressing debate about transitional justice – but in notably different ways. From the perspective of a community-based organisation, I consider the transitional justice work of the Kachin Baptist Convention, which is the most influential church in a state in which more than 90 per cent of the Kachin population is Christian (two-thirds Baptist and one-third Roman Catholic) (Jacquet 2015). I also consider the work of a prominent NGO with international links, ND-Burma, and its efforts to record and collate evidence of historic and ongoing human rights abuses carried out by the military.

This chapter begins by analysing the dynamics of Myanmar's transition to democracy, and explains why in the early years of the transition the major political actors had no appetite for questions of transitional justice. It then discusses the 'peace before justice' argument in the context of Myanmar. It then charts the rise and significance of civil society organisations within Kachin State and explains why organisations such as the KBC carry such legitimacy within local communities. Finally, the chapter outlines the singular contribution of community-based organisations in advocating for justice during the early years of Myanmar's transition to democracy.

The nature of Myanmar's transition to democracy

Myanmar is in the early years of democratic transition. In 2010, after 22 years of direct rule, Myanmar's military government withdrew to make way for elections and the assumption of power by a nominally civilian government. The democratic opposition party, the NLD, boycotted the elections, which were won by the military-backed Union Solidarity and Development Party (USDP).[3] There was deep scepticism, in the immediate aftermath of the 2010 elections, about whether the military intended to allow genuine democratic reform. But between 2010 and 2015, under President Thein Sein, the new government undertook a program of liberalisation, releasing political prisoners, legalising trade unions, allowing public political gatherings, easing press censorship and permitting the teaching of ethnic minority languages in schools across Myanmar (Renshaw 2016). The government also made renewed efforts to end decades-long civil conflict with ethnic armies. In 2011, Aung San Suu Kyi, leader of the NLD, declared that she trusted President Thein Sein to pursue further democratisation and she urged the people to do likewise. In 2012, the NLD contested seats in federal by-elections and Aung San Suu Kyi herself was elected to parliament. In the general elections of 2015, the NLD swept to power. Suu Kyi, who was married to a British citizen and whose sons hold British passports, was barred from becoming president by a special provision in the Constitution that precludes anyone whose spouse or children 'hold allegiance to a foreign power'. In 2016 Suu Kyi appointed herself Special Counsellor of State, a role that she said was 'above the President' (Holmes 2016).

Myanmar's transition is 'liberation from above' or 'regime-initiated liberalisation' (Huntington 1991). It is the result of a decision on the part of the military to withdraw from direct rule and affect an orderly transfer of power to a civilian government. From the military's perspective, the success of the transition depended on four factors: (i) cooperation from the country's pro-democracy political party, the NLD, and its iconic leader Aung San Suu Kyi, in the timing and mode of transition; (ii) guarantees about preserving the autonomy of the military and a political role for

---

3   Electoral laws required the National League for Demcocracy (NLD) to expel Aung San Suu Kyi, because she had a criminal record. The NLD refused to do this, which meant that the party could not be registered or stand candidates.

the military in the life of the state; (iii) a guarantee that there would be no prosecution of military officers for crimes committed while the military was in power; (iv) achieving peace with the various armed ethnic groups that had been in conflict with government military forces since the country gained independence from the British at the end of the Second World War (Renshaw 2013).

Between 2010 and 2015, transition proceeded in accordance with the script laid out by the military. First, Suu Kyi convinced hardliners within her party that the NLD should be a junior partner in the military-led process of gradual democratic reform. The NLD abandoned its longstanding demand for the reinstatement of the results of the 1990 elections, which the NLD won but the military refused to recognise, and ended its campaign of civil disobedience and unlawful gatherings. The new government's strongest claim to credibility – both domestically and internationally – was Suu Kyi's endorsement of the government's plan for democratisation (Myers 2011).

Second, the military ensured that reform would take place within the framework of the 2008 Constitution of the Union of Myanmar, which preserves a central political role for the military. The Constitution provides that 25 per cent of members of state and federal parliaments must be serving army officers appointed by the commander-in-chief, and that the Constitution cannot be amended without the approval of more than 75 per cent of parliament. Under the Constitution, the commander-in-chief has a decisive say in the appointment of the president and two vice-presidents. Certain key cabinet positions (such as Home Affairs and Defence) are confined to active military personnel. The army is fiscally and administratively autonomous. Article 445 of the 2008 Constitution provides immunity for members of the former military government in relation to any act done in the execution of duty; article 20(b) of the Constitution states that the Defence Service has the right to independently administer and adjudicate all affairs of the armed forces; article 343 provides that in the adjudication of military justice, the decision of the Commander-in-Chief of the Defence Services is final and conclusive. In 2016, before the NLD assumed power after the November 2015 elections, Senior General Min Aung Hlaing reminded the people at the Armed Forces Day Parade that a political role for the military was essential to the stability and prosperity of the state (Reuters 2016b).

Third, Suu Kyi has constantly reassured the military that she does not wish to see the prosecution of military officers for acts committed during the years of military rule. Suu Kyi publicly reiterated that she preferred processes that lead to healing rather than to opening wounds, that she had no desire for retribution and that she does not want to see anyone in the military stand trial for the human rights violations of the past. When she discussed mechanisms for accountability, which was rarely and reluctantly, it was in the form of a truth and reconciliation commission, similar to the South African commission. But in Suu Kyi's view, there was no urgency for the creation of such an institution (Naing 2012). Conscious of the need to placate the military during the period of transition, Suu Kyi embraced Myanmar's military, the *Tatmadaw*, as 'her father's army' and declared that she was 'very fond' of the army (BBC 2013).

Finally, the government intensified efforts to sign ceasefire agreements with ethnic minority armies. An official ceasefire with the Shan State Army-South (SSA-South) was signed at the end of 2011 (Oo 2011). On 12 January 2012, the government signed a ceasefire with the 19-member Karen National Union, to end hostilities between the military and the Karen National Liberation Army. The government also continued negotiations with the Chin National Front. In 2015, the government signed a Nationwide Ceasefire Agreement with eight armed ethnic organisations. Negotiations were complicated by decades of mistrust and by continuing uncertainty about whether the military was actually under the control of the government. In Kachin State, for example, a 14-year-long ceasefire came to an end in 2011, when the Kachin Independence Army refused to accede to a request that it transform its military forces into a Border Guard force under the control of the *Tatmadaw*. President Thein Sein's orders that the army not launch attacks on ethnic armed groups in northern Kachin State were defied (*Burma Partnership* 2012).

For the Kachin, the NLD's victory in the elections of November 2015 changed little. Even as preparations got underway for another nationwide peace conference in August 2016, and at the same time that Aung San Suu Kyi was making a pledge to the nation that peace with ethnic groups was her first priority, the *Tatmadaw* was intensifying attacks on KIA positions. Hundreds of thousands of civilians were displaced. Government forces were accused of committing grave human rights violations. These include firing on unarmed civilians, including those sheltering in refugee camps; desecrating churches; the abduction and disappearance of villagers suspected of belonging to the KIA; razing homes, pillaging properties; using antipersonnel mines; conscripting forced labour; enlisting children to serve as army porters; torture; and rape (Human Rights Watch 2017).

From the perspective of the military, the NLD and leaders of armed ethnic organisations, the success of Myanmar's transition to democracy depended on the exclusion of the institutions and processes of transitional justice. The military's interest in defraying justice is comprehensible. Myanmar's transition was not the result of a change of guard among the top military leadership: prosecuting those ultimately responsible for war crimes and crimes against humanity would mean prosecuting the people who were driving transition. Aung San Suu Kyi and the NLD understood that focusing on retribution – or even calling for recognition of the crimes committed by the former military regime through the establishment of a truth commission – could destabilise the political situation and undermine prospects for further democratisation and peace. For leaders of ethnic armies, the primary demand was not for retribution or acknowledgement of the wrongs of the past – it was for a strong form of federalism that would preserve the autonomy and rights of ethnic states to manage their own governance and resources. The Nationwide Ceasefire Agreement did not include provisions for the establishment of criminal proceedings in relation to crimes committed by the military (or crimes committed by ethnic armies), nor did it refer to the establishment of truth commissions, nor did it refer to reparations. It did, however, refer to the pursuit of social and economic goals (protection of the environment, improvements to health and education, and addressing the chronic drug problem that exists in many ethnic states).

The 'political stability before justice' argument in the context of Myanmar

In 1991, Samuel Huntington set out the considerations that new democratic regimes must take into account in deciding how to address crimes committed by officials of the predecessor regime (Huntington 1991). In Huntington's view, the decision to prosecute and punish, or forgive and forget, did not turn on moral or legal arguments about societal obligations to truth, justice and the rule of law. Instead, the decision was determined by the nature of the democratisation process and the distribution of political power during and after transition. In Huntington's view, in circumstances where democratic transformations were initiated and guided by leaders of the existing authoritarian regime, assurances regarding non-prosecution – amnesties – were essential to prospects of democratic consolidation. Put simply, no authoritarian leader would enable transition if they anticipated being prosecuted as a result. Amnesty was the price of peaceful transformation. The question of whether prosecuting perpetrators of crimes in former regimes undermines prospects for democratic consolidation became one of the key debates in the scholarship on transitional justice (O'Donnell and Schmitter 1986; Huntington 1991; D'Amato 1994; Akhavan 2009; Snyder and Vinjamuri 2004; Kim and Sikkink 2010).

Recent scholarship has moved the debate about peaceful democratic transition *versus* pursuit of justice in different directions. First, *via* historical analysis of the different circumstances in which trials, amnesties or truth commissions contribute to stabilising new democracies, scholars have drawn attention to institutional combinations that appear to be effective in promoting democratic consolidation (for example, trials and truth commissions; amnesties and truth commissions) (Salehi and Williams 2016). Second, scholars have been attentive to temporal and sequencing issues in the establishment of transitional justice institutions and policies. Dancy and Wiebelhaus-Brahm, for example, in their study of transitions in Latin America, conclude that amnesties followed by trials, or trials followed by amnesties, are both sufficient conditions for democratic consolidation (Dancy and Wieblhaus-Brahm 2015). Third, the concept of transitional justice itself has been interrogated. Scholars have unpacked assumptions about the form that transitional justice should take and paid attention to local experiences, priorities and practices (Shaw and Waldorf 2010; Jeffrey and Kim 2014).

In Myanmar, the 'political stability versus justice' debate did not feature in public discourse during the early years of Myanmar's transition to democracy. This is because the military, which under the 2008 Constitution is not subject to civilian control, remained central to the transition, central to the governance of the state and central to the peace process with ethnic armies. It was clear to all primary political actors that retribution – and even truth-seeking, if implemented too early – would undermine prospects for transition. This understanding shaped Myanmar's transition in two key ways.

First, for the military, a broad amnesty was a precondition for withdrawal from power. The constitutional immunity from prosecution for Myanmar's former military rulers, and their agents and personnel, and the Defence Service's right to independently administer and adjudicate all affairs of the armed force, was a non-negotiable condition of the bargain between the key actors in the transition. Immunity from prosecution for the military was one of the terms on which transition took place. Suu Kyi and her party understood that to challenge this would be to risk a resumption of power by the military and unravel the democratic advances that had been made (which included a relatively fair and free election in 2010, and a parliament dominated by a democratic political party after the 2015 election).

Myanmar's political history was instructive for Suu Kyi and Myanmar's pro-democracy leaders. In general elections held in 1990, the NLD, led by Aung San Suu Kyi, won a sweeping victory, securing more than 50 per cent of the popular vote. The military, however, refused to transfer power to the NLD. The reason for this – in popular legend at least – was an offhand comment from U Kyi Maung, chairman of the NLD, who in a post-election press conference referred to 'Nuremberg-style tribunals' while explaining to a foreign journalist that the NLD did *not* intend to seek accountability for what the army had done to the people during its period of rule. 'Here in Myanmar', said Kyi Maung, 'we do not need any Nuremberg-style tribunals' (Jones 2014). Many people in Myanmar believe that one of the primary reasons why the Burmese military refused to relinquish power after the 1990 elections was because the generals feared they would be tried for crimes committed during the period of dictatorship (Kaung 2011; Jones 2014). The NLD was determined to ensure that history would not repeat itself and that in the 2012–2015 elections, the generals would not be frightened once again into retreating from reform. For Suu Kyi and the NLD, the high-level prosecution of members of the military was not a political possibility.

There are civil society organisations in Kachin State, and among the Kachin diaspora in Thailand, the United States and elsewhere, who still call for the establishment of the traditional mechanisms of transitional justice: in the first place, a UN-backed independent Commission of Inquiry on the human rights abuses being committed against the Kachin and other peoples, to put an end to impunity. But in the early years of transition even the United Nations seemed prepared to defer accountability and give democracy a chance to take root. In 2010, for example, the Special Rapporteur on the situation of human rights in Myanmar reported that the people of Myanmar had endured gross and systematic human rights violations that possibly amounted to crimes against humanity or war crimes under the terms of the Rome Statute of the International Criminal Court. The Rapporteur suggested the possible establishment of a Commission of Inquiry (United Nations General Assembly, Human Rights Council 2010, 2014). The United States and several other countries supported this suggestion. But after 2012, when Suu Kyi entered parliament, calls from within the UN for the establishment of a Commission of Inquiry abated. In 2013, the Special Rapporteur recommended merely the consideration of the establishment of a truth commission, to 'inform continuing democratic reform and national reconciliation' (United Nations General Assembly 2013).

Second, Myanmar's transition to democracy was complicated by the ongoing civil conflict with ethnic armed organisations. Civil war stood as a grave threat to democratic consolidation because while there was a prospect that conflict could lead to the secession of some ethnic states, the military would preserve its political independence and power to ensure the country remained unified. Myanmar's Deputy Minister for Foreign Affairs, His Excellency U Khin Maung Win wrote in 2004:

> Myanmar is a Union composed of more than one hundred different national races, each with its own culture and traditions. Politically, there cannot be lasting peace and stability in the country without national unity. Unfortunately, the divide and rule policy practiced by the British colonialists resulted in suspicion and discord among the national races. This subsequently led to armed insurgency that spread to various parts of the country for decades. The question of achieving national unity and bringing to an end the armed insurgency are vital issues for any government, past, present and future (Win 2004).

Again, the history is instructive. The 1962 military coup in Burma took place amid uprisings in ethnic states, because the military feared that unless they assumed control of the country the Union would disintegrate. Farrelly notes that 'anxiety about the potential for territorial fragmentation is the principle motivation for those who consider the military's role essential to national survival' (Farrelly 2014, 313). In 2010, the military's historical priority of preserving national unity was overlaid with the substantial economic interests of the military and their cronies, and of the Burmese and Chinese businesses who sought to preserve their investments (Renshaw 2017).

The moral argument for deferring justice, made by the primary actors in the transition, was that the preservation and consolidation of democracy, within a united Myanmar, and all the goods that flow from democracy, requires peace and stability. Development, to improve the health, education and living standards of the people, also requires peace. Therefore, ran the argument, those who were genuinely interested in protecting human rights must support peace and political stability at all costs and if justice (by which they meant policies that sought accountability for past acts of the military) stood in the way of peace then justice should be deferred or sacrificed.

Transition without justice: Leaving truth until tomorrow and leaving today to the rule of law

What was offered to the people of Myanmar after the 2015 elections, instead of historical justice, were two things: (1) attention to the rule of law as a means for ensuring that abuses do not continue; and (2) a promise from Suu Kyi that, at some point in the future, there would come a time for seeking and telling the truth about Myanmar's past.

Over the past quarter of a century the precise nature and substance of 'the rule of law' has been the subject of vigorous debate (Krygier 2010). For Suu Kyi, throughout the long years of dictatorship, 'the rule of law' stood in opposition to the arbitrary exercise of state power by the military. The rule of law meant the enforcement of just laws, enacted with the authority of a democratically elected legislature, interpreted by an independent judiciary and enforced by an impartial police service.[4] Under any commonly accepted understanding of the rule of law, these features are a centerpiece (Fuller 1964). In Myanmar, since 2012, the rule of law has been championed by both the military and Suu Kyi as a panacea for the ongoing abuses of power that accompanied military action in ethnic conflict zones. In 2016, for example, when the United Nations reported that military action in Rakhine State could amount to

---

4   See Nick Cheesman, *Opposing the Rule of Law: How Myanmar's Courts Make Law and Order* (Cambridge: Cambridge University Press, 2016) for an illuminating study of the conflation of the rule of law with law and order in Myanmar. Cheesman's argument is that law and order is neither consonant with the rule of law, nor a negative of the rule-of-law ideal; it is, in fact, what he calls 'asymmetrically opposed' to the rule of law.

ethnic cleansing, Suu Kyi said: 'The Myanmar government is responding to the issue of Rakhine state based on the principles of the rule of law' (Funakoshi 2016).

For civil society organisations, an early test case of the potential for 'the rule of law' to bring justice was the government's response to public protests against the Letpadaung copper mine. In 2010, a company owned by the military, the Union of Myanmar Economic Holdings Ltd, confiscated 1,356 hectares of farmland in order to develop a copper mine in partnership with a Chinese industrial and arms manufacturer. On 29 November 2012, security forces violently dispersed a peaceful protest organised by Buddhist monks and local farmers whose land had been confiscated. Tear gas, smoke bombs and fire were used against the protesters as they slept in the early morning. The international media reported that the police used white phosphorous against protesters (Lwin 2013). The raid was justified by Myanmar's authorities on the grounds that permission had not been sought for the public protest. Suu Kyi visited the protest site immediately following the incident and told protesters that she would seek to negotiate a solution between mine operators and local communities.

In the wake of the incident, President Thein Sein formed a Parliamentary Commission to establish the facts and inquire whether mining should continue at Letpadaung. Aung San Suu Kyi was asked to chair the commission. In March 2013, the commission handed down its report. The report acknowledged that the mine had environmental consequences and that farmers were forcibly evicted from their land to make way for the project (Weng and Aye 2013a). But the report did not recommend the closure of the copper mine. Nor did it expose the perpetrators of the violence carried out on 29 November. Instead, the report advised the protesters to desist and the company to do three things: (1) provide jobs for people in local communities; (2) maintain a healthy environment; and (3) provide educational and healthcare benefits for local people. Aung San Suu Kyi told farmers that Myanmar could not afford to shut down the mine and risk turning away foreign investors, and that their protest was illegal: 'you all have to ask permission from the government if you protest as our country has the rule of law now. Those who do not respect the rule of law, they could get punished' (Weng and Aye 2013b).

Since her ascension to power, Suu Kyi has invoked the rule of law without necessarily being attentive to the legitimacy of laws themselves. The NLD, like the military, has used section 66(d) of the Telecommunications Law, introduced in 2015, to stifle criticism on social media (*Free Expression Myanmar* 2017). Section 66(d) provides for up to three years in prison for 'extorting, coercing, restraining wrongfully, defaming, disturbing, causing undue influence or threatening any person using a telecommunications network'. Provisions of the State Secrecy Act and the Unlawful Associations Act have also been used numerous times against citizens and members of community-based organisations. In July 2015, interfaith activists U Zaw Zaw Latt and Daw Pwint Phyu Latt were sentenced to four years imprisonment each – two under the Unlawful Associations Act and two under the 1947 Immigration Emergency Provisions Act – for participating in an interfaith peace trip to territory controlled by the Kachin Independence Army (Lwin 2016).

In the case of the 2015 murder and rape of the two young Kachin schoolteachers, described at the beginning of this chapter, the military published a statement shortly after the incident, denying military involvement and stating that the *Tatmadaw* would take action based on the rule of law against anyone who alleged soldiers were involved in the crimes (Weng 2015). The President's Office supported the *Tatmadaw*'s position, claiming that an accusation against an individual solider was an accusation against the *Tatmadaw* as an institution, and warning that the *Tatmadaw* had a right to defend itself by prosecuting those who make unfounded accusations (Weng 2015). The threat was not an idle one. In 2014, a team of journalists reported that chemical weapons were being produced in a secretive army installation in Pakokku Township. The three reporters, the journal's editor and its chief executive officer were charged under the State Secrets Act and sentenced to 10 years imprisonment with hard labour (Mann 2014). In another case, 25-year-old Chaw Sandi Tun posted a comment on Facebook likening the colour of Aung San Suu Kyi's dress to the colour of the military's uniform. She was charged with defamation under article 34(d) of the Electronic Transactions Law, which carries a penalty of up to five years in prison (Zin 2015). During the early years of Myanmar's transition, the 'rule of law' was invoked not to serve the people but to constrain their freedom.

The limited conception of the rule of law, as invoked by both the military and by Aung San Suu Kyi, suggests a political morality that may be out of kilter with the needs of a society that has been subjected to authoritarian rule and massive violations of human rights. In the aftermath of transitions from dictatorship and oppressive rule, the capacity of citizens (and their leaders) to distinguish between right and wrong, just and unjust, can be severely diminished (Minow 1998; Dyzenhaus 2000). One of the primary purposes of transitional justice is to assist societies to reconstruct the moral foundations necessary for a future stable democracy. Unless this is achieved, liberal values proclaimed by the new democratic regime risk sliding into what Dimitrijević describes as 'ritual facades without any legitimising and practical authority' (Dimitrijević 2006, 374).

One example serves to illustrate the profoundly negative consequences of the decision made by Myanmar's leaders to adopt silence as a response to systemic human rights abuses that took place under military rule. In October 2016, the government announced that the military was commencing what it called a 'clearance operation' in northern Rakhine State, home to Myanmar's population of Rohingya Muslims, in response to an attack by armed insurgents on three border guard posts (Reuters 2016a). The area was sealed off, movement within the area was restricted and humanitarian agencies were denied access. The operation lasted from 9 October 2016 until 9 February 2017 (Republic of the Union of Myanmar, President's Office 2017). During that period, according to the High Commissioner for Human Rights, government forces carried out a series of atrocities against local Muslim populations (OHCHR 2017). These included the burning and looting of Rohingya villages; the murder of Rohingya men, women and children; summary execution of imams, religious scholars and community leaders; rape and torture. The military used helicopters to fire bullets and drop grenades on villagers as they were working on their farms, shopping in markets or fishing. Tens of thousands of villagers fled across the border to Bangladesh. 'Now is the worst it has ever been', said one Rohingya villager. 'We have heard from our grandparents that there were bad things happening in the past too, but never like this' (OHCHR 2017, 43).

What baffled observers of Myanmar's transition was the almost universal failure of Myanmar's leaders, including Aung San Suu Kyi, and large sections of Myanmar's public, to recognise the nature of the military's actions and the fact that the persecution of the Rohingya was of the same order as the persecution that they and their families had endured at the hands of the *Tatmadaw* during the decades of military rule. The response of much of the public to the Rohingya crisis, which was captured in print, social media and in large rallies held in support of the *Tatmadaw*'s actions, speaks to an urgent need to transform the political culture of Myanmar. There is an argument that providing processes that permit people to acknowledge and understand the atrocities that mark a country's past, and uncover the systematic nature of violations and the motivational patterns that led to violations, helps both political leaders and citizens rebuild the moral foundations of their society (Minow 2002). Put simply, it must be publicly stated that there was no justification for the murder, rape, torture and disappearance of tens of thousands of people during the decades of military rule. Truth commissions, in other parts of the world, have contributed to this task; though the evidence of their impact is still debated (Crocker 1999; Brahm 2007). In Myanmar's case, the atrocities perpetrated over so many years across the entire country might tend to suggest a need for multiple commissions, or multiple strands to a commission's mandate. For example, there have been demands for the investigation of crimes committed in ethnic states in order to terrorise local populations and suppress insurgencies; acknowledgement of crimes of torture, extrajudicial killing, disappearance and false imprisonment to contain political opponents of the regime; and acknowledgement, apologies and reparation for gender-based crimes against women. Myanmar's leaders, however, argued that there were other national priorities that outweighed the need to recognise and repair past violence. There are no immediate prospects for the establishment of an official truth commission in Myanmar.

The contribution of civil society organisations to transitional justice in Myanmar

In the immediate aftermath of the murders of Ra and Tsin, the KBC organised a procession to accompany the two-day journey of the coffins from Shan State to the Kachin State capital Myitkyina. As the coffins processed through the countryside, large crowds stood by the side of the road to watch and pray. When the coffins reached Myitkyina, enormous crowds gathered for multifaith prayer services in honour of the two teachers. Since then, each year, on the anniversary of their deaths, the KBC has held prayer services across the Kachin region and in Kachin communities around the world, to remember the women and affirm the need for justice in relation to their deaths (Nyein 2018). The significance of these actions can only be understood if one appreciates the scale of abuse that took place in Myanmar during military rule: the routine brutality of the military in its treatment of villagers; the uncounted numbers of men, women and children who were killed and whose bodies were buried without markers; the fear of arbitrary torture, rape and imprisonment with which ordinary people lived their everyday lives (KWAT 2011). The military presence within the village where the two girls were staying and the grossly inadequate police investigation mirrored thousands of other cases that had taken place during the years of military rule. Ra and Tsin came to stand for all of them. By memorialising the deaths of two individuals such as Ra and Tsin, the KBC was making a statement that the truth of wrongs must be told and that each individual life is of value. The deep grief and outrage that marked the community's response to the death of the two schoolteachers was a deeply authentic and powerful response. People from across Kachin State, Shan State and throughout Myanmar, recognising the innocence of the victims, their youth, their vocation as teachers and the brutality of their murders, identified with the tragedy and, under the leadership of the KBC, shaped their response as a political one.

In Kachin, from the mid-1990s, the leadership of religious and community-based organisations became more pronounced in the wake of disillusionment with the political leadership of armed ethnic organisations. A peace deal signed between the military and the Kachin Independence Organisation (KIO) in 1994 brought with it the potential for local Kachin political leaders to make large amounts of money. Local Kachin strongmen exploited the natural resources of the state in collaboration with the *Tatmadaw* and Chinese companies. The business methods of the KIO were often indistinguishable from those of the *Tatmadaw*, and included cronyism, land-grabbing, exploitation and tactics of terror against local populations. There was little consultation between KIO leaders and the people about economic decisions that affected their lives (Woods 2011). Community leadership during this period came from the local churches, schools and community-based organisations. During the period of the ceasefire, the KBC was a major provider of healthcare and education services to the Kachin people. The KBC, with other religious leadership groups such as the Kachin Catholic Bishops Conference, has through the KBC Committee for Peace and Reconciliation led demands for the political rights of the Kachin. The demands are principally for political autonomy for Kachin through a federal political structure. The KBC has also pressed for accountability in relation to specific human rights violations such as the murders of Ra and Tsin. In the wake of the murders, the KBC announced that it had created a 15-member committee, composed of leaders of the KBC, other religious leaders, civil society representatives and lawyers, to independently investigate the crime. The military cooperated, to an extent, with the KBC investigators, although it did not permit the KBC Committee to ask questions directly to Burmese military officers (Gam 2017). The KBC investigation into the deaths of Ra and Tsin is ongoing.

The KBC is not the only CSO focused on the issue of transitional justice. The work of ND-Burma is particularly notable. ND-Burma was founded in 2004 with the objective of training local organisations in the collection and management of human rights documentation. ND-Burma coordinates members' input into a common database and engages in advocacy campaigns, seeking accountability in individual cases and broader justice (government recognition, redress and guarantees of non-recurrence for victims of human rights violations). Its vision is explicitly political – 'a peaceful, democratic and federal Burma that has acknowledged past human rights violations and has implemented measures to uphold the dignity of victims and guard against recurrence' (ND-Burma 2018). It membership includes both local organisations (Assistance Association for Political Prisoners – Burma; Kachin Development Networking Group; Human Rights Foundation of Monland; Kachin Women's Association Thailand; Palaung Women's Organization; Ta'ang Students and Youth Organization; Tavoyan Women's Union) and affiliate members based outside Myanmar with strong international connections (such as EarthRights International and the International Center for Transitional Justice).

In relation to the murder of Ra and Tsin, ND-Burma (through its member organisation the Kachin Women's Association Thailand), like the KBC, made inquiries and investigations into the incident and aimed to produce its own report of what had taken place. There are significant differences, however, in the approach and purpose of the work of CBOs such as the KBC and ND-Burma, even when both are focused on the same issue.

ND-Burma self-consciously refers to itself as an 'Unofficial Truth Project' (ND-Burma 2015). Several of ND-Burma's various reports, including the milestone 'To Recognize and Repair: Unofficial Truth Projects and the Need for Justice in Burma' (ND-Burma 2015) were funded by Open Society Foundations. To provide a framework for collaboration among members, ND-Burma has developed a 'controlled vocabulary' of the categories of human rights violations on which the network focuses. Its aim is to collate the data that will one day be used by an official truth commission. The group recognises that while many parts of the country are still in conflict and the military still retains a significant degree of power, a state-led initiative is unlikely to be established and, even if it were, there would be serious and justifiable questions about its neutrality. In these circumstances, ND-Burma's approach is to engage local communities as active participants in the first stage of what they hope will eventually be a government-supported process (Holliday 2014).

ND-Burma operates with funding from international NGOs, with input from international donors, using a controlled vocabulary of wrongs, with a long-term vision of presenting evidence before an officially sanctioned Commission. Bickford (2007) notes that there is something potentially troubling about the similarities among Unofficial Truth Projects across the world, as it suggests 'an overly scientific approach to truth-telling, as if there is one way to do it, and all these efforts are converging on the formula'. Yet the point of grassroots measures is that there should be no formula – efforts should be context-driven and capture the specificity of local circumstances. With efforts to formalise data collection and record-keeping comes not just the problem of categorisation and formula – which arguably distances the victim from the truth of their story – but also an implicit promise that the story, so told, will eventually be officially recognised and form part of an official narrative. There is the potential for disillusionment if this promise to victims is not fulfilled.

The Kachin Baptist Convention and ND-Burma, together with other civil society organisations, advocate for redress of both current and historical wrongs committed by both the *Tatmadaw* and by ethnic armies. Unless there is an end to impunity, they argue, crimes such as those committed against Ra and Tsin will continue to be committed. From one perspective, this demand has been registered and responded to by both the military and the government of Aung San Suu Kyi. Both acknowledge the need for military accountability and both champion the rule of law as a tool for addressing human rights violations. The Kachin Baptist Convention requested, and was officially given, an active role in the investigation into the murder of Ra and Tsin. Yet in relation to calls for justice for historical wrongs, there is little appetite on the part of the military or Suu Kyi to institute any of the formal mechanisms of transitional justice. Nonetheless, by memorialising the death of victims such as Ra and Tsin, the KBC makes a profoundly significant contribution to transitional justice in Myanmar.

Both ND-Burma and the KBC form a discordant note in Suu Kyi's narrative that the military, ethnic leaders and the National League for Democracy must walk forward 'hand in hand' towards a new future, without looking back at the past. Both ND-Burma and the KBC draw a clear line between the failure to prosecute members of the military for crimes carried out in the past, and the continuing commission of crimes. There appears to be, from the outpouring of grief that marked the death of Tsin and Ra, and in the testimonies collected by ND-Burma, an urge to confront the past that is not in accord with Suu Kyi's emphasis on 'moving on' and 'healing not retribution'.

Conclusion

To date, there has been little justice, in any form, in Myanmar's transition to democracy. The explanation for this is threefold. First, Myanmar's transition to democracy is the result of indigenous top-down change, and not the result of revolution, or an unopposable groundswell of popular opposition or the efforts of the political opposition. The military remains a major player in the transition to democracy, and retains a significant degree of political power. The interests of the National League for Democracy are primarily to affect a peaceful and stable transition, and this goal is not seen as consistent with the establishment of strong accountability mechanisms. For this reason, unofficial truth projects and memorialisations are taking place in parts of Myanmar, but national-level justice projects are not on the agenda of any of the main political actors.

Second, justice as conceived by many people in Myanmar is broadly imagined, encompassing political reform (a federal structure with highly autonomous ethnic states) and economic reform (land redistribution and control of natural resources by the states). This is precisely the kind of justice that the country's new leaders, the National League for Democracy, will struggle to deliver in a context where the military must be appeased and the economic interests of powerful investors in Myanmar and China protected.

Third, armed conflict resumed in Kachin State at precisely the same time as the transition to democracy got underway. Questions of timing are crucial in matters of transitional justice. There are perceptions in states such as Kachin State and outside it that pressing too hard for historical justice might undermine prospects for peace.

The difficulty is that Myanmar's modern history is marked by political betrayal and the broken promises of the military: the failure to create a genuinely federal state in 1947 after independence; the failure to hand power to the NLD after the elections of 1990; and myriad other betrayals from land-grabbing to unfair trials. Many ethnic groups, such as the Kachin in the far north of Myanmar, have attempted in the past to follow the path of democracy and peace before justice. The dividends have been difficult to discern. Why, ask many, should they now trust the promise, made by both the *Tatmadaw* and Aung San Suu Kyi, that justice will follow peace and democracy? They argue that unless there is justice, peace will be impossible. There is a sense that transition is yet another elite pact, and that their suffering has no recognition. Furthermore, as military action in conflict zones increases, as evidence of current human rights abuses by the military grow, and as the foreign media and independent observers are prevented from witnessing what is occurring in conflict zones, the price of the pact between Suu Kyi and the *Tatmadaw* seems by some to be too high.

In relation to human rights abuses committed by the military during the decades of dictatorship, neither the military nor Aung San Suu Kyi have indicated that they will countenance retribution. Truth is a possibility, but it is a long way off. The focus of the military and Suu Kyi is on pursuing a path towards an imperfect but achievable form of constitutional democracy. They demand that victims of human rights violations forgo their right to revisit the past and seek a truthful accounting of, and justice for, the crimes of the past. What Suu Kyi and the military offer instead is piecemeal justice administered by the new government according to a narrow interpretation of the rule of law; and hopefully peace, so that a larger justice might be negotiated at some later point. What is clear is that, in this context, civil society organisations are critical actors in recording and articulating alternative expressions of what justice requires; and beginning the long process of recalibrating the political morality of post-transition society.

Bibliography

Akhavan, Payam. 2009. 'Are International Criminal Tribunals a Disincentive to Peace?: Reconciling Judicial Romanticism with Political Realism'. *Human Rights Quarterly* 31 (3): 624–654. doi.org/10.1353/hrq.0.0096.

BBC (British Broadcasting Corporation). 2013. 'Aung San Suu Kyi Tells of Fondness for Burma Army'. BBC News. Video, 27 January. www.bbc.com/news/av/world-asia-pacific-21224307/aung-san-suu-kyi-tells-of-fondness-for-burma-army.

Bickford, Louis. 2007. 'Unofficial Truth Projects'. *Human Rights Quarterly* 29: 994–1035. doi.org/10.1353/hrq.2007.0036.

Brahm, Eric. 2007. 'Uncovering the Truth: Examining Truth Commission Success and Impact'. *International Studies Perspectives* 8: 16–35. doi.org/10.1111/j.1528-3585.2007.00267.x.

Burma Partnership. 2012. '2012: A Year for Cautious Optimism'. *Burma Partnership* (blog), 9 January. www.burmapartnership.org/2012/01/2012-a-year-for-cautious-optimism/.

Crocker, David. 1999. 'Reckoning with Past Wrongs: A Normative Framework'. *Ethics and International Affairs* 13: 43–63. doi.org/10.1111/j.1747-7093.1999.tb00326.x.

D'Amato, Anthony. 1994. 'Peace vs. Accountability in Bosnia'. *American Journal of International Law* 88 (3): 500–506. doi.org/10.2307/2203717.

Dancy, Geoff and Eric Wiebelhaus-Brahm. 2015. 'Timing, Sequencing, and Transitional Justice Impact: A Qualitative Comparative Analysis of Latin America'. *Human Rights Review* 16 (4): 321–342. doi.org/10.1007/s12142-015-0374-2.

Dimitrijević, Nenad. 2006. 'Justice beyond Blame: Moral Justification of (the Idea of) a Truth Commission'. *The Journal of Conflict Resolution* 50 (3): 368–382. doi.org/10.1177/0022002706286952.

Dyzenhaus, David. 2000. 'Justifying the Truth and Reconciliation Commission'. *Journal of Political Philosophy* 8: 473–492.

Farrelly, Nicholas. 2014. 'Law, War, Politics: Reflections on Violence and the Kachin'. In *Law, Society and Transition in Myanmar*, edited by Melissa Crouch, and Tim Lindsey, 305–322. Oxford: Hart Publishing.

Free Expression Myanmar. 2017. Website. freeexpressionmyanmar.org/ (accessed 2017).

Fuller, Lon. 1964. *The Morality of Law*. New Haven and London: Yale University Press.

Funakoshi, Minami. 2016. 'Suu Kyi Says "Delicate" Myanmar Conflict Handled by Rule of Law'. *Reuters*, 3 November. www.reuters.com/article/us-myanmar-japan-idUSKBN12Y0B0.

Gam, Nmang. 2017. 'Two Years On, No Justice for Two Murdered Kachin Teachers'. *Kachinland News*, 20 January. www.kachinlandnews.com/?p=27451.

Hann, Chris. 2011. Zivilgesellschaft, In *Lexikon der Globalisierung*, edited by Fernand Kreff, Eva-Maria Knoll and Andre Gingrich, Bielefeld: Transcript Verlag.

Heidel, Brian. 2006. *The Growth of Civil Society in Myanmar*. Bangalore: Books for Change.

Holliday, Ian. 2014. 'Thinking about Transitional Justice in Myanmar'. *South East Asia Research* 22: 183–200. doi.org/10.5367/sear.2014.0204.

Holmes, Oliver. 2016. 'Aung San Suu Kyi Set to Get PM-Type Role in Myanmar Government'. *The Guardian*, 1 April.

Human Rights Watch. 2017. 'World Report: Burma: Events of 2016', www.hrw.org/world-report/2017/country-chapters/burma.

Huntington, Samuel P. 1991. *The Third Wave: Democratization in the Late Twentieth Century.* Norman: University of Oklahoma Press.

Jacquet, Carine. 2015. *The Kachin Conflict: Testing the Limits of the Political Transition in Myanmar*. Bangkok: Institut de Recherche sur l'Asie du Sud-Est Contemporaine (Research Institute on Contemporary Southeast Asia). doi.org/10.4000/books.irasec.241.

Jeffery, Renée and Hun Joon Kim. 2014. *Transitional Justice in the Asia-Pacific*. New York: Cambridge University Press.

Jones, Lee. 2014. 'The Political Economy of Myanmar's Transition'. *Journal of Contemporary Asia* 44 (1): 144–170. doi.org/10.1080/00472336.2013.764143.

Kaung, B. A. 2011. 'EC Chief Says NLD Threatened Junta with "Nuremburg-style" Trial'. *The Irrawaddy*, 29 July. www2.irrawaddy.com/article.php?art_id=21796.

Kim, Hunjoon and Kathryn Sikkink. 2010. 'Explaining the Deterrence Effect of Human Rights Prosecutions for Transitional Countries'. *International Studies Quarterly* 54 (4): 939–963. doi.org/10.1111/j.1468-2478.2010.00621.x.

Kramer, Tom. 2011. *Civil Society Gaining Ground. Opportunities for Change and Development in Burma*. Amsterdam: Transnational Institute (TNI)/Burma Centrum Netherlands (BCN).

Krygier, Martin. 2010. 'Four Puzzles About the Rule of Law: Why, What, Where? And who cares?'. *Nomos – American Society for Political and Legal Philosophy* 50 (64): 64–104. doi.org/10.18574/nyu/9780814728437.003.0004.

KWAT (Kachin Women's Association Thailand). 2011. *Burma's Covered Up War: Atrocities against the Kachin People*. Chiang Mai, Thailand: KWAT.

Lidauer, Michael. 2012. 'Democratic Dawn? Civil Society and Elections in Myanmar 2010–2012'. *Journal of Current Southeast Asian Affairs* 31 (2): 87–114. doi.org/10.1177/186810341203100204.

Lwin, Ei Ei Toe. 2013. 'Commission Stalls, Tension Rises'. *Myanmar Times*, 4 February. www.mmtimes.com/national-news/3965-commission-stalls-tension-rises.html.

Lwin, Si Thu. 2016. 'Interfaith Activists Convicted, Given Two Years in Prison'. *Myanmar Times*, 29 February. www.mmtimes.com/national-news/mandalay-upper-myanmar/19211-interfaith-activists-convicted-given-two-years-in-prison.html.

Mann, Zarni. 2014. 'Journalists Detained for Reporting Alleged Burmese Chemical Weapons Factory'. *The Irrawaddy*, 2 February. www.irrawaddy.com/news/burma/journalists-detained-reporting-alleged-burmese-chemical-weapons-factory.html.

Minow, Martha. 1998. *Between Vengeance and Forgiveness: Facing History after Genocide and Mass Violence*. Boston: Beacon.

Minow, Martha. 2002. *Breaking the Cycles of Hatred: Memory, Law, and Repair*. Princeton: Princeton University Press.

Myers, Steven Lee. 2011. 'In Myanmar, Government Reforms Win Over Some Sceptics'. *The New York Times*, 30 November. www.nytimes.com/2011/11/30/world/asia/in-myanmar-government-reforms-win-over-countrys-skeptics.html.

Naing, Saw Yan. 2012. 'Burma "Not Ready" for Truth Commission'. *The Irrawaddy*, 15 June. www.irrawaddy.org/human-rights/burma-not-ready-for-truth-commission.html.

ND-Burma. 2015. 'To Recognize and Repair'. nd-burma.org/to-recognize-and-repair/ (accessed 2018).

ND-Burma. 2018. 'About Us'. nd-burma.org/about-us/ (accessed 2018).

Nyein, Nyein. 2018. 'Three Years On, Still No Progress in Rape and Murder of 2 Kachin Teachers'. *The Irrawaddy*, 19 January. www.irrawaddy.com/news/burma/three-years-still-no-progress-rape-murder-2-kachin-teachers.html.

O'Donnell, Guillermo and Philippe C. Schmitter, eds. 1986. *Transitions from Authoritarian Rule*. Baltimore: Johns Hopkins University Press.

OHCHR (Office of the United Nations High Commissioner for Human Rights). 2017. *Report of OHCHR Mission to Bangladesh: Interviews with Rohingyas Fleeing from Myanmar since 9 October 2016*, 3 February.

Oo, Aung Naing. 2011. 'Give Peace in Burma a Chance'. *The Irrawaddy*, 13 December. www2.irrawaddy.com/article.php?art_id=22642&page=2.

Prasse-Freeman, Elliott. 2012. 'Power, Civil Society, and an Inchoate Politics of the Daily in Burma/Myanmar'. *The Journal of Asian Studies* 71 (2): 371–397. doi.org/10.1017/S0021911812000083.

Renshaw, Catherine. 2013. 'Democratic Transformation and Regional Institutions: The Case of Myanmar and ASEAN'. *Journal of Current Southeast Asian Affairs* 32 (1): 29–54. doi.org/10.1177/186810341303200102.

Renshaw, Catherine. 2014. 'Disasters, Despots and Gun-Boat Diplomacy'. In *The International Law of Disaster Relief*, edited by David D. Caron, Michael J. Kelly and Anastasia Telesetky, 164–189. Cambridge: Cambridge University Press. doi.org/10.1017/CBO9781107447844.015.

Renshaw, Catherine. 2016. 'Human Rights under the New Regime'. In *Constitutionalism and Legal Change in Myanmar*, edited by Andrew Harding, 215–234. Oxford: Hart Publishing/Bloomsbury.

Renshaw, Catherine. 2017. 'Myanmar and Sanctions'. In *The Business of Transition*, edited by Melissa Crouch, 228–254. Cambridge: Cambridge University Press.

Republic of the Union of Myanmar, President's Office. 2017. 'Tatmataw Ends Area Clearance Operations in Northern Rakhine'. www.president-office.gov.mm/en/?q=issues/rakhine-state-affairs/id-7288.

Reuters. 2016a. 'Clashes in Myanmar's Rakhine Raise Weekend Death Toll to about 30: State Media'. 14 November. www.reuters.com/article/us-myanmar-rohingya/clashes-in-myanmars-rakhine-raise-weekend-death-toll-to-about-30-state-media-idUSKBN1390H3.

Reuters. 2016b. 'Myanmar Army Reasserts its Key Political Role Ahead of Transition'. 27 March. www.reuters.com/article/us-myanmar-military/myanmar-army-reasserts-its-key-political-role-ahead-of-transition-idUSKCN0WT05N.

Sadan, Mandy. 2015. 'Myanmar: Ongoing Conflict in Kachin State'. In *Southeast Asian Affairs 2015*, edited by Daljit Singh, 246–259. Singapore: Institute of Southeast Asian Studies. doi.org/10.1355/9789814620598-017.

Salehi, Mariam and Timothy Williams. 2016. 'Beyond Peace vs. Justice: Assessing Transitional Justice's Impact on Enduring Peace'. *Transitional Justice Review* 1 (4): 96–123. doi.org/10.5206/tjr.2016.1.4.4.

Shaw, Rosalind and Lars Waldorf. 2010. 'Introduction: Localizing Transitional Justice'. In *Localizing Transitional Justice: Interventions and Priorities After Mass Violence*, edited by Rosalind Shaw and Lars Waldorf, 3–27. Redwood City, CA: Stanford University Press.

Snyder, Jack and Leslie Vinjamuri. 2004. 'Trials and Errors: Principle and Pragmatism in Strategies of International Justice'. *International Security* 28 (3): 5–44. doi.org/10.1162/016228803773100066.

South, Ashley. 2008. *Civil Society in Burma: The Development of Democracy amidst Conflict.* Washington DC: East-West Center. doi.org/10.1355/9789812309051.

Turnell, Sean. 2008. 'Burma's Economy 2008: Current Situation and Prospects for Reform'. Working Paper, Burma Economic Watch, Sydney, Australia.

United Nations General Assembly. 2013. *Report of the Special Rapporteur of the Commission of Human Rights on the Situation of Human Rights in Myanmar.* UN Doc. A/68/397 (23 September 2013).

United Nations General Assembly, Human Rights Council. 2010. *Progress Report of the Special Rapporteur on the Situation of Human Rights in Myanmar, Tomás Ojea Quintan.* UN Doc. A/HRC/13/48 (10 March 2010).

United Nations General Assembly, Human Rights Council. 2014. *Report of the Special Rapporteur on the Situation of Human Rights in Myanmar, Tomás Ojea Quintana.* UN Doc. A/HRC/25/64 (2 April 2014).

Weng, Lawi. 2015. 'Army Statement Warns against Linking Teachers' Murders to Troops'. *The Irawaddy*, 29 January. www.irrawaddy.com/news/burma/army-statement-warns-linking-teachers-murders-troops.html.

Weng, Lawi and Thet Swe Aye. 2013a. 'Activists, Locals Reject Letpadaung Inquiry'. *The Irrawaddy*, 12 March. www.irrawaddy.com/news/burma/activists-locals-reject-letpadaung-inquiry.html.

Weng, Lawi and Thet Swe Aye. 2013b. 'Stop Protests against Copper Mine, Suu Kyi Tells communities'. *The Irrawaddy*, 13 May. www.irrawaddy.com/news/burma/stop-protests-against-copper-mine-suu-kyi-tells-communities.html.

Win, H.E. U Khin Maung. 2004. 'Myanmar Roadmap to Democracy: The Way Forward' (2004) Paper presented at the Seminar on Understanding Myanmar Yangon, 27–28 January, Myanmar Institute of Strategic and International Studies.

Woods, Kevin. 2011. 'Ceasefire Capitalism: Military–Private Partnerships, Resource Concessions and Military–State Building in the Burma–China Borderlands'. *Journal of Peasant Studies* 38 (4): 747–770. doi.org/10.1080/03066150.2011.607699.

Zin, Salai Thant. 2015. 'Woman Faces 5 Years over Photo Likening Army Garb to Suu Kyi's Dress'. *The Irrawaddy*, 13 October. www.irrawaddy.com/news/burma/woman-faces-5-years-over-photo-likening-army-garb-to-suu-kyis-dress.html.

Part 3 – The Pacific Islands

7

The role played by reconciliation in social reconstruction in Bougainville

Joanne Wallis

In his final editorial in *The International Journal of Transitional Justice*, Harvey Weinstein lamented that, as a field, 'we have not been successful at promoting a research agenda that values the study of effectiveness' (Weinstein 2011, 1). Instead, much of the literature has assumed that transitional justice plays a positive role in the social reconstruction of conflict-affected societies. Much of the literature also assumes (either explicitly or implicitly) that this social reconstruction should be guided by liberalism, grounded in individual human rights protected by the rule of law. A nascent literature has evaluated the effect of truth commissions and criminal trials, particularly on efforts to establish respect for human rights. There has been little similar research to evaluate the effectiveness of local reconciliation practices, rather than prosecutions, and little research that challenges the assumption that social reconstruction should be guided by liberalism. My chapter evaluates the role played by local reconciliation practices in social reconstruction in Bougainville, including an analysis of what social reconstruction means in the Bougainville context. Local reconciliation practices are taken to mean local sociopolitical practices aimed at building and healing relationships so that formerly conflictual parties can live together peacefully.

Bougainville is an autonomous region of Papua New Guinea that endured a conflict between 1989 and 1997. Bougainville experienced only 'light' international intervention to end the war; near neighbours Australia and New Zealand provided small, unarmed truce and peace monitoring teams and the United Nations a minute observer mission (Regan 2010a). Bougainvillean political leaders opted to achieve peace by prioritising local reconciliation practices and by offering amnesties from prosecution, and pardons for those already prosecuted, for crimes (including human rights abuses) committed during the conflict as an incentive to former combatants to participate in reconciliation and weapons disposal. In the short term this approach appears to have worked; the conflict ended in 1997 and in 2001 a comprehensive political settlement, outlined in the Bougainville Peace Agreement, granted Bougainville extensive political autonomy and the right to vote on its political future (with the option of independence) between 2015 and 2020. A constitution-making process was undertaken between 2002 and 2004, and by 2005 Bougainvilleans had established the Autonomous Bougainville Government (ABG) (Wallis 2014). There has not been a major outbreak of violence since.

In this chapter, I consider some of the possible long-term consequences of the approach to reconciliation adopted in Bougainville for social reconstruction. As I focus on what social reconstruction means in Bougainville, I am particularly interested in the potential gap between, on the one hand, the liberal assumptions upon which much of the transitional justice literature is based and, on the other hand, the local context.

Internationally, civil society has been at the forefront of debates about how transitional justice should be conducted and the ends it should pursue. Encouraged by this international discourse, in Bougainville more formalised civil society organisations (CSOs) have tended to favour liberal approaches. For example, the Bougainville Human Rights Committee has argued that the lack of a formal transitional justice mechanism has created the impression that 'anyone can choose to perpetrate a crime with impunity' (Bougainville Human Rights Committee 2011). Consequently, these CSOs have called for a formal transitional justice mechanism, constituting either a truth and reconciliation commission or criminal trials, or combination of the two, to help address this growing culture of impunity and to establish the liberal principles of the rule of law and respect for human rights. In contrast, grassroots CSOs have tended to favour reconciliation grounded in local sociopolitical practices, not necessarily underpinned by liberal assumptions.

I begin by considering the literature relating to evaluating the impact of transitional justice, including local reconciliation practices. Building on that literature, I identify two criteria to evaluate the impact of reconciliation on the social reconstruction of a conflict-affected society: governance and justice. I then describe the conflict in Bougainville and the reconciliation that occurred. I then evaluate the role that reconciliation has played in social reconstruction in Bougainville against the two criteria and conclude that, while it has helped to create an environment in which relatively legitimate and effective institutions of governance have been created, it has undermined attempts to achieve justice by cultivating a culture of impunity. My analysis also highlights how attempts to evaluate the effect of reconciliation in Bougainville need to extend beyond an analysis of liberal principles and practices to incorporate the local sociopolitical principles and practices that continue to determine the nature of everyday life for many Bougainvilleans.

Evaluating the impact of transitional justice and reconciliation

Some form of transitional justice is now included in most peace processes, and has 'come to dominate debates on the intersection between democratization, human rights protections, and state reconstruction after conflict' (McEvoy 2007, 412). Transitional justice refers to the 'practices, mechanisms and concerns that arise following a period of conflict, civil strife, or repression, and that are aimed directly at confronting past violations of human rights and humanitarian law' (Roht-Arriaza 2006, 2). The most prominent mechanisms are truth commissions and criminal trials, but transitional justice can also include local reconciliation practices, reparations, memorialisation, and transitional legal and institutional reforms such as vetting and lustration (Thoms, Ron and Paris 2010). Truth commissions are temporary, usually state-sanctioned, bodies that investigate 'a pattern of abuses over a period of time, rather than a specific event' (Hayner 2001, 14) in order to 'supply narrative, rather than forensic, accounts of the past' (Thoms, Ron and Paris 2010, 334). Criminal trials aim to achieve 'truth, deterrence, punishment, reconciliation and promotion of the rule of law' (Thoms, Ron and Paris 2010, 333). They are premised on the belief that criminal punishment serves victims' needs by offering a sense of justice, catharsis and that 'their grievances have been addressed and can hopefully be put to rest' (Kritz 1996, 128).

I focus on reconciliation guided by local sociopolitical practices, which involves achieving 'negative peace' – that is, the cessation of violence and the (re)establishment of relationships that permit the coexistence of formerly hostile individuals or groups (Galtung 1990). It also aims to achieve 'positive peace', whereby it addresses 'conflictual and fractured relationships' in order to build and heal relationships (Hamber and Kelly 2004, 3; Lederach 1997). Reconciliation may take place at the interpersonal level, whereby relationships are restored between individual perpetrators and victims. It may also occur at the political level, to address wrongs committed by agents of the state, members of the opposition, separatist movements, militias or warring factions in the name of the organisation or cause with which they are affiliated, to establish societal and political processes that prevent a reversion to conflict (Philpott 2006). It is possible to achieve interpersonal reconciliation without political reconciliation, and vice versa, and the two may happen at the expense of each other. However, the two are interconnected, as rebuilding interpersonal relationships is often the key to facilitating broader political reconciliation between opposing individuals and groups. As unresolved resentments, underlying tensions and simmering hostilities have the potential to generate further conflict (Biggar 2003; Collier and Hoeffler 2004), it is claimed that reconciliation can be perceived as a panacea for past wrongs and as a form of social inoculation against a future return to violence (Long and Brecke 2003, 13). As noted, reconciliation is usually guided by local sociopolitical practices, which often prioritise 'restorative' over 'retributive' justice (Braithwaite 2003).

Thoms, Ron and Paris find that 'reliable empirical knowledge on the state-level impact of TJ [transitional justice] is still limited' (Thoms, Ron and Paris 2010, 331). Weinstein argues that the literature appears to have been reluctant to evaluate the impact of transitional justice because '"it is too soon" to look at what transitional justice actually accomplishes in the social reconstruction of a country' (Weinstein 2011, 1). This reluctance also reflects the implicit liberal assumption that criminal accountability is common sense and therefore does not need to be questioned.

There is also little agreement regarding what criteria should be used to evaluate the outcomes of transitional justice (Brahm 2007). While most scholars would agree that these outcomes should be peace and justice, there is no consensus regarding what these terms mean. Brahm has suggested two ways to evaluate the impacts of truth commissions: first, their effect on 'subsequent human rights practices'; and second, their effect on 'democratic development'. Thoms, Ron and Paris have suggested six criteria for evaluating the effects of trials and truth commissions: '(1) state respect for personal integrity rights … ; (2) levels of political violence; (3) adherence to the rule of law; (4) democratization; (5) popular perceptions of regime legitimacy; and (6) a political culture of human rights and diversity' (Thoms, Ron and Paris 2010, 331). Therefore, these scholars implicitly assume that the outcomes of transitional justice should be grounded in liberalism.

The liberal assumptions that have guided much of the transitional justice literature reflect the fact that much of the literature has its roots in liberal human rights discourse, with transitional justice mechanisms such as criminal trials and truth commissions seen as a way to combat impunity for human rights abuses. However, as illustrated below, universalist assumptions regarding the desirability or appropriateness of liberalism, particularly liberal human rights protections, do not necessarily hold in all conflict-affected contexts, nor do the highly technocratic, decontextualised and depoliticising approaches to transitional justice (such as truth commissions and trials) that they tend to generate.

With these caveats in mind, I identify two criteria as critical to evaluating the impact of reconciliation on the social reconstruction of a conflict-affected society: the establishment of effective and legitimate governance mechanisms, that is, mechanisms to manage the exercise of political power and provide opportunities for the people to influence the way that power is exercised; and the achievement of justice, that is, mechanisms aimed at eliminating arbitrary distinctions and establishing 'the structure of a practice of a proper balance between competing claims' (Rawls 1958, 165). Although these definitions are drawn from liberal theory, they are intended to be sufficiently broad to capture differing understandings, including those grounded in local sociopolitical practices, of what these governance mechanisms should look like and what a proper balance between competing claims involves.

While liberalism holds that governance should be democratic, to recognise the 'intrinsic equality' and 'personal autonomy' of individuals (Dahl 1989, 86), the critical peacebuilding literature has increasingly recognised that, to be effective and legitimate, governance mechanisms may need to combine both liberal and local sociopolitical principles in a process described as 'hybridity' (Richmond 2009). Similarly, liberalism holds that justice should be guided by the principle of the 'rule of law', which is based on the idea that the law must be universally and consistently applied – including to the government – by a formal regulatory system in which there is a clear hierarchy of law (Tamanaha 2004). The protection of human rights is linked to the rule of law, since human rights protections seek to ensure that the freedom and equality of individuals is protected against untrammelled majority rule and are usually enumerated in law and enforced via the courts. However, critical peacebuilding scholars are increasingly arguing that to be perceived as both effective and legitimate, justice may involve a range of both liberal and local mechanisms, and human rights protections may need to protect both group and individual rights (Boege, Brown and Clements 2009).

As noted, there is a nascent literature that has evaluated the effects of truth commissions and criminal trials, used individually or in conjunction with each other, on the social reconstruction of conflict-affected societies (Pham and Vinck 2007; Thoms, Ron and Paris 2010). Reflecting their basis in liberalism, one study that focused on criminal trials concluded that prosecutions for human rights violations led to subsequent improvements in human rights protections, and had a deterrent effect both in the society in question and beyond (Kim and Sikkink 2010). Another study concluded that claims that criminal trials 'threaten democracy, increase human rights violations, and exacerbate conflict' were not supported by empirical evidence from Latin America (Sikkink and Booth Walling 2007). Another found there is a 'justice balance', whereby truth commissions are unable to promote stability and accountability on their own, but can contribute to improvements in human rights protections when they complement and enhance amnesties and prosecutions (Olsen et al. 2010). Other studies have concluded that a failure to conduct criminal trials can generate a culture of impunity. A study of Guatemala found that a failure to prosecute violent crimes committed against women during the conflict, when the army was trained in the rape and torture of women, has contributed to subsequent impunity for these crimes and consequently to rising levels of murder of women in post-conflict Guatemala (Sanford and Lincoln 2011).

Studies of truth commissions on their own have reached more measured conclusions. One found that truth commissions can have a 'direct political impact' through the implementation of their recommendations, an 'indirect political impact' through their role in mobilising civil society, a 'positive judicial impact' by contributing to human rights accountability, and a 'negative judicial impact' by promoting impunity (Bakiner 2014, 26, 27).

A study of Liberia's Truth and Reconciliation Commission concluded that it has contributed to a perception of impunity because political elites, many of whom perpetrated human rights abuses during the conflict, have undermined its implementation, including its recommendations for criminal trials (Weah 2012).

There has been little substantive effort to evaluate the effect of local reconciliation practices on the social reconstruction of conflict-affected societies. As reconciliation is often presented as a locally driven alternative to the formal transitional justice models of truth commissions and criminal trials, the literature has tended to overlook the causal relationship between reconciliation and the social reconstruction of conflict-affected societies. One of the challenges of conducting a comparative evaluation of the effect of reconciliation across cases is that, while there are common understandings of what constitutes truth commissions and criminal trials, reconciliation is usually guided by local sociopolitical practices and therefore varies across societies. In addition, it is usually more straightforward to identify when truth commissions and criminal trials have concluded, and what their outcomes are, at least in terms of what 'truth' they uncover and prosecutions they achieve. In contrast, it is questionable whether reconciliation has an end date or a final outcome; it may be more accurate to see reconciliation as an open, ongoing process. Weinstein has asked whether 'closure [is] a valid concept and is the idea relevant across culture? Is resolution possible as an end-state?' (2011, 5). Opotow has similarly argued that 'labelling a conflict – particularly a violent, protracted, and deadly conflict – as reconciled can be dangerous' as it can 'raise hopes and expectations of victims, blunt bystander vigilance, and allow impunity to flourish' (Opotow 2001, 166). Moreover, if a more nuanced, context-specific approach to evaluating social reconstruction is adopted this is also likely to vary across cases, making comparison difficult.

One emerging consensus in the transitional justice literature informed by liberalism is that the increasing use of amnesties to facilitate reconciliation may have enhanced the risk of creating a culture of impunity. Indeed, one study that evaluated the consequences of reconciliation for social justice concluded that using amnesties to promote reconciliation can 'be particularly disheartening when it institutionalizes and legitimizes impunity' (Opotow 2001, 161). A culture of impunity – that is, 'exemption from accountability, penalty, punishment, or legal sanction for perpetrators of illegal acts' (Opotow 2001, 149; Afflito 2000; McSherry and Molina Mejia 1992; Penrose 1999) – is seen to undermine efforts to establish the rule of law and respect for human rights. While much of the literature is implicitly guided by the liberal assumption that transitional justice should pursue criminal accountability, and consequently that impunity refers to avoiding criminal sanction, a culture of impunity can also emerge when perpetrators are perceived to have avoided participating (or participating meaningfully) in reconciliation or sanctions dictated by local justice practices. Indeed, because local justice practices remain influential in Bougainville, many people who committed crimes or human rights abuses during the conflict have been subject to customary sanctions even though they have avoided criminal sanction.

Amnesties can go to the heart of the peace versus justice dilemma: on the one hand, amnesties are seen by some as a necessary sacrifice to achieve peace, by encouraging antagonistic groups to surrender their weapons and participate in reconciliation; on the other hand, others argue that meaningful peace cannot be achieved without justice (Mallinder 2007). In some cases, democratic governments have overcome amnesty laws to allow for criminal trials for past human rights violations (Lessa et al. 2014). When this does not occur, studies have concluded that impunity can be conferred on perpetrators 'under the guise of "reconciliation"', as occurred in Guatemala (Molina Mejia 1999, 61), or that 'impunity was called reconciliation' in Chile (Paz 1999, 25). While amnesties and other provisions that facilitate impunity might be seen as necessary to end conflict, reconciliation predicated on impunity may be short-sighted and trade 'short-term potential gains for a long-term continuation of impunity' (Roht-Arriaza 1996, 99). Despite this, advocates have argued that amnesties 'accompanied by traditional community-based justice mechanisms can co-exist with international prosecutions for those who are "most responsible"' for crimes. Amnesties can also be used 'in conjunction with restorative justice mechanisms to encourage perpetrators to participate without inculpating themselves', as occurred in South Africa (Mallinder 2007, 221). In these cases, amnesties could be granted on the condition that perpetrators comply with the penalties imposed by the restorative justice mechanism, such as public identification and apology, community service or financial compensation.

Since the late 1990s, the United Nations has maintained that amnesties that prevent prosecutions for war crimes, genocide, crimes against humanity and other gross violations of human rights are 'inconsistent' with states' obligations under the international human rights treaties, United Nations Policy and emerging principles of customary law

(OHCHR 2006). The United Nations' *Basic Principles and Guidelines on the Right to a Remedy* holds that victims have the right to 'equal and effective justice', 'adequate, effective and prompt reparation for harm suffered' and 'access to relevant information concerning violations and reparation mechanisms' (United Nations General Assembly 2005). Indeed, the International Criminal Court and ad hoc criminal tribunals established by the United Nations for Rwanda and the former Yugoslavia could disregard domestic amnesty laws and prosecute perpetrators of human rights abuses. States may also be legally obliged to prosecute under the Genocide Convention, Convention against Torture and Other Cruel, Inhuman or Degrading Treatment or Punishment and the Geneva Conventions (Orentlicher 1991).

Therefore, it has been argued that a 'justice cascade has emerged, along with global human rights and accountability norms, the institutionalization and enforcement of those norms and the demand for the implementation of those norms by domestic and international human rights advocates' (Lessa et al. 2014, 83). That is, at the international level transitional justice has been legalised and judicialised, and consequently accountability achieved via criminal trials is seen as the most legitimate means of achieving justice after conflict. Reflecting this justice cascade, there is increasing demand by international CSOs for criminal trials to overcome perceived impunity (Becker 2003; Loveman 1998). This demand has trickled down to CSOs in conflict-affected societies, in part because international CSOs have promoted these ideas, including via their funding. These interventions can have a distorting effect on CSOs in conflict-affected societies, as they can empower organisations willing (or able) to speak in the internationalised language of transitional justice and human rights, which usually consist of urban elites, while marginalising groups that are more focused on local sociopolitical practices, which usually operate at the grassroots level. As noted, conceptions of transitional justice guided by liberalism can also become highly technocratic and depoliticising, and with their relatively narrow focus on human rights obscure wider conversations about power, governance and justice. By arguing for criminal trials, which are usually conducted by the state against individual perpetrators in relation to individual victims, these conceptions can also reinforce both the state and the liberal emphasis on individualism.

In much of the transitional justice literature, 'civil society' is taken to include 'nongovernmental organizations (NGOs), individual activists and other social groups, including human rights, victim, student, neighbourhood and trade union organizations, that play an active role in generating conditions necessary to push governments to reckon with past atrocities' (Lessa et al. 2014, 76). This characterisation is also shaped by liberalism and focuses on the public sphere – that is, an arena of association that is concerned with state affairs, but which is not part of the formal state structure (Habermas 1996). The focus on the public sphere raises questions over its adequacy in contexts where there is an unclear line between the public and private spheres, and where CSOs are not formally part of the state structure, yet cannot be easily separated from the state, or from the private sphere. Moreover, while much of the transitional justice literature (and indeed the broader literature on civil society) assumes that CSOs are secular, this definition raises questions regarding its relevance in contexts where much of what would be classified as civil society is faith based. These questions grow louder in contexts, such as the Pacific Islands, where states themselves are only shallowly rooted in society and many people do not have a strong understanding of themselves as citizens of a state. This highlights how much of the transitional justice literature perpetuates liberal assumptions regarding the relevance and legitimacy of states as actors capable of facilitating or complying with formal transitional justice mechanisms.

Conflict and reconciliation in Bougainville

The Bougainville conflict was complex; while it is often described as a struggle between secessionist Bougainvilleans and the Papua New Guinea Government, it was also an internal conflict between – and within – pro- and anti-secessionist Bougainvillean elements, often based on localised concerns or criminal activity (Regan 2001; Boege 2009). Both Bougainvillean and international CSOs documented the many human rights abuses committed during the crisis.[1]

Civil society, broadly defined, in Bougainville is dominated by faith-based and women's organisations, although there is significant overlap between the two. The most prominent CSOs are centred on the three main churches (Catholic, Methodist and Seventh Day Adventist). Both during and since the conflict, Bougainvillean political leaders have sought counsel from

---

1   During the crisis, women's leader Marilyn Havini kept a record of human rights abuses that had been committed. Amnesty International also recorded abuses that occurred during the early stages of the crisis (Havini 1995, 1996; Amnesty International 1990).

the heads of the churches, and the current Bougainville president, John Momis, is a former Catholic priest who retains strong ties to the church. Church leaders play an important role in shaping public opinion via their sermons and, increasingly, via their ties to (or at least endorsements of) political candidates (interview with an ABG official, 22 January 2011). The fact that many schools and health facilities are run by churches, and some are jointly funded by the church and the autonomous government, also provides the churches with considerable political weight (interview with an international academic, 8 January 2010; Masono 2006). Indeed, one public servant noted that the churches are 'traditionally seen as the right hand of government in terms of development' and consequently the autonomous government pays them 'tithes' (interview with an ABG official, 22 January 2011). Their weight has been enhanced by the fact that they have begun to engage in commercial projects such as real estate, hotels, shipping, agriculture and plantations. The influence of the churches at the local level has also been enhanced by the fact that they have syncretised or 'interwoven' their beliefs and practices with Bougainvillean culture 'so that they combine custom and Christianity' (Boege and Garasu 2004, 573).

Women's CSOs are also active, including the secular Leitana Nehan Women's Development Agency, Bougainville Women for Peace and Freedom, and Bougainville Women's Federation and the faith-based Bougainville Inter-Church Women's Forum (Hakena, Nines and Jenkins 2006; Sirivi and Havini 2004). While some women's groups are nominally secular, the women involved are often church leaders and their platforms are influenced by faith-based norms. Many of these groups date back to the conflict, when they were formed to promote reconciliation (interview with a women's leader, 25 January 2011; interview with a women's leader, 2 February 2010). They then played an important role in promoting awareness of the peace process, and since autonomy have campaigned aggressively to promote women's rights and development.

According to local Bougainvillean sociopolitical practices, dispute resolution and societal cohesion follow a restorative justice approach guided by the principle of 'balanced reciprocity', which requires reconciliation – that is, truth-telling and forgiveness – and compensation to restore balance within the community (Regan 2005, 420). Consequently, local reconciliation practices have been prioritised, as they are seen as offering a way to 'reunite us to be one people again' and of ensuring that 'whatever happened during the war is not passed on to the next generation'

(Sister Lorraine Garrasu speaking in Thompson 2002). Utilising local customary practices to effect reconciliation means that it is 'irrevocable. Whatever we decide by these traditional means, will be guaranteed by society' (Jon Boboso speaking in Thompson 2002). Under the influence of faith-based CSOs, reconciliation ceremonies have combined local practices with Christian principles (Boege 2012). This combination has enhanced their legitimacy, and these reconciliation efforts 'have done more to consolidate popular commitment to peace than any other aspect of the process' (Regan 2001, 15).

Pragmatic decisions made during the peace process have limited the scope for Bougainvillean CSOs to advocate for a formal transitional justice mechanism. In order for the Bougainville parties to the conflict to agree to a common position on which to negotiate peace with the Papua New Guinea Government, the Australian and New Zealand governments facilitated a number of peace talks, which first resulted in an interim ceasefire. To make that ceasefire permanent, the Bougainville parties and Papua New Guinea Government agreed to offer amnesties and pardons to persons involved in offences related to the conflict. This offer was legally enshrined in the Bougainville Peace Agreement 2001, and subsequently in the Papua New Guinea Constitution. Granting amnesties and pardons was seen as necessary in order to encourage combatants to participate in the weapons disposal process created by the peace agreement, particularly as the agreement had left the political status of Bougainville open, with the region granted extensive autonomy and the possibility of independence determined by a later referendum.

To prepare Bougainville for the referendum, in 2008 the autonomous government developed a taskforce to support local reconciliation practices. Local-level reconciliation ceremonies had been ongoing throughout the conflict, had flourished during the peace process and have continued in the period since. Although they were not formally linked to the weapons disposal process, they helped to create an environment in which the process was deemed sufficiently advanced that the United Nations Observer Mission declared it completed in May 2005. However, many weapons remained in the community after autonomy. Consequently, in 2009 the autonomous government created a Ministry of Peace, Reconciliation and Weapons Disposal (later replaced by the Department of Bougainville Peace Agreement Implementation) and in 2012 it adopted a Peace, Security and Weapons Disposal Strategy. In 2013, Australia also began to fund the Bougainville Peace Building Strategy to encourage reconciliation and weapons disposal. In 2017, the autonomous government and Papua New Guinea Government created an independent Bougainville Referendum Commission to conduct the referendum.

Evaluating the effects of reconciliation in Bougainville

As described, I use two criteria to evaluate the effects of reconciliation on social reconstruction in Bougainville: governance and justice.

Governance

Reconciliation conducted before, during and since the peace process created space for a highly participatory constitution-making process during which Bougainvilleans negotiated the design of their governance institutions (Wallis 2014). They agreed that the Bougainville autonomous government would be a liberal institution, which includes a democratically elected legislature (the House of Representatives) and executive (the Bougainville President and Executive Council).

Bougainvilleans appear to have embraced liberal democracy at the regional level, indicated by high levels of electoral participation (Regan 2009; Commonwealth Secretariat and PIF 2005). The voting strategies utilised by Bougainvilleans also illustrate the growing influence of liberal democracy, as there is evidence that voters have developed political sophistication by gradually shifting their focus away from the issues of the conflict and towards the performance of the autonomous government, appearing to prioritise immediate concerns of local conflict, progress in the implementation of the Bougainville Peace Agreement and improvements in Bougainville's development (Regan 2010b). Evidence of growing acceptance of liberal democracy as a method of governance at the regional level is also provided by the fact that there has been no significant violence during, or after, autonomous government elections. Independent electoral observers have concluded that the elections were 'democratic, transparent, inclusive and credible' (Commonwealth Secretariat and PIFS 2010). One member of the autonomous government argued that this demonstrates the 'maturity' of Bougainvilleans in accepting the democratic process and moving away from conflict (Nisira 2010).

However, to look only at formal governance institutions presents an incomplete picture of social reconstruction in Bougainville. During the constitution-making process, Bougainvilleans agreed that at the village level local sociopolitical institutions should continue to perform much everyday governance. These local institutions consist of Village Assemblies at the level of the census village (of which there are approximately 600), which feed up into Councils of Elders (of which there are approximately 90). The councils have been the 'most effective governance institutions' below the autonomous government (Boege 2008, 28), as they connect the 'modern, formal' autonomous government with the traditional Village Assemblies (interview with a former member of the ABG, 2 November 2010) that continue to regulate the lives of the over 90 per cent of Bougainvilleans who live in rural areas (Finnroad 2008). The term 'Village Assembly' is used to describe these traditional systems of government, which are the (often loosely organised) methods by which traditional chiefs consult their people and perform their traditional administrative and dispute resolution role (Council of Elders Act, sections 9–10; interview with an ABG official, 22 January 2011). The Village Assemblies are also said to provide a 'pivotal link between the Council of Elders and the communities – and vice versa' (Sasa 2013, 53).

Wider acceptance of the role of liberal democracy in governance among ordinary Bougainvilleans is more limited. The Councils of Elders are only nominally democratic: to achieve balance between the liberal emphasis on democratic elections and local emphasis on customary authority, councils are 'mainly elective', but must also 'recognize the traditional role in governance of traditional chiefs and other traditional leaders' (ABG Constitution, section 49). In practice, these elections are more like 'selections', as there is no competition of candidates, with council members chosen in a consensual manner, reflecting local practices (Boege 2013, 19).

Therefore, to evaluate the role that reconciliation has played in social reconstruction in Bougainville it is necessary to examine both the role of liberal democratic and of local sociopolitical governance institutions. This highlights how a study of Bougainville guided solely by the transitional justice literature focused on the importance of liberal democracy would miss the important role that local sociopolitical practices play in governance. Applying a more nuanced analysis to Bougainville suggests that reconciliation has helped to establish both effective and legitimate liberal and local governance institutions, as it has created an environment in which Bougainvilleans have been able to negotiate and agree to the design of those institutions, and in which they have been able to peacefully work through them to govern Bougainville.

Justice

As with governance, there is a combination of both liberal and local sociopolitical justice mechanisms in Bougainville. At the regional level, the Bougainville Police Service seeks to enforce law and order, and the courts seek to uphold the rule of law. As a significant amount of court infrastructure was lost and many court files were destroyed during the conflict, during the early years of autonomy this challenged the ability of existing courts to function and the ability of the autonomous government to establish courts. As new court infrastructure has developed, the courts have been circuiting more regularly and they have made progress in clearing the backlog, particularly of serious criminal cases. The Office of the Public Solicitor also opened a new office in Bougainville in 2012 to provide legal advice to Bougainvilleans. Illustrating increasing awareness of the courts, there has been a rise in people seeking Interim Protection Orders in cases of violence against women and children.

However, looking only at the police service and courts presents a partial view of the way justice is achieved in Bougainville. During public consultations on the draft constitution, many Bougainvilleans stated that they 'want[ed] to see *kastom* [custom] built into, and recognised as part of, the justice system' (Bougainville Constitutional Commission 2004, 55). Consequently, the Bougainville police are mandated to strengthen customary authority, respect human rights and develop 'rehabilitatory and reconciliatory concepts of policing'. They are also required to 'work in harmony and partnership' with Councils of Elders, Village Assemblies and other traditional leaders 'to resolve disputes and maintain law and order in communities' (ABG Constitution, section 148(2)). Accordingly, the Bougainville Police Service incorporates the Bougainville Community Auxiliary Police Service, which is involved in 'community dispute resolution and peace building practices' as well as 'law and order and conflict prevention' (McGovern and Taga 2009; Dinnen and Peake 2013). The auxiliary police also utilise a 'community-based approach' to policing and work closely with the Council of Elders and traditional leaders to mediate local disputes, encourage reconciliation and prevent the escalation of conflict (interview with an international adviser to the ABG, 31 August 2010; Dinnen and Peake 2013).

The rule of law is also upheld by a combination of liberal and local justice mechanisms. The most established courts are the Village Courts created by Papua New Guinea law, which operate in most areas and have jurisdiction over any civil dispute arising in that area and over specified criminal matters (Village Courts Act 1973, sections 15, 23 and 25).[2] While Village Courts are formal institutions, since magistrates are untrained and lawyers do not appear in Village Courts, it is usual for magistrates to utilise a 'creative' mix of formal and customary law (Goddard 2000, 242; Boege 2008; interview with a former member of the ABG, 2 November 2010). Village Courts are said to perform a valuable role, as they are 'readily accessible', 'relatively unbiased' and offer a forum in which the local community 'can witness the righting of wrongs and the reasonable settlement of disputes' (Goddard 2000, 243). Village Courts are also able to provide outcomes that are 'highly contextualised and consequently of considerable local credibility and legitimacy' (Hegarty 2009, 3). However, Village Courts are said to be overworked and under-resourced,[3] as until the formal justice system becomes well established the Village Courts are being asked to deal with cases that extend well beyond their powers (Bougainville Human Rights Committee 2011).

While these multiple layers of liberal and local mechanisms seek to impose law and order and uphold the rule of law, there is evidence that the provision of amnesties and pardons for crimes that occurred during the conflict has cultivated a culture of impunity as it has 'given the impression to the general population that there is [sic] no consequences for abusing the rights of others' (Bougainville Human Rights Committee 2011), particularly as perpetrators are perceived to have avoided participating (or participating meaningfully) in local reconciliation practices. During public consultations on the new constitution, Bougainvilleans were 'generally supportive' of the amnesty and pardon provisions of the Bougainville Peace Agreement, but there was no consensus on how to otherwise deal with crimes that occurred during the conflict (Bougainville Constitutional Commission 2004, 251). Many Bougainvillean CSOs called for these amnesties to be conditional on a truth and reconciliation process involving 'public recognition of wrong done and forgiveness' (Sister Lorraine Garasu quoted in Howley 2002, 282), which reflects elements of local reconciliation practices. Ordinary Bougainvilleans expressed

2   Including motor vehicle offences, minor assaults, drinking, property damage and disturbing the peace.
3   In 2011, Village Court magistrates were paid K2 per week (less than US$1).

mixed views on this proposal; some called for a truth and reconciliation commission to tell 'the story of what happened', others favoured customary reconciliation initiatives that are seen as 'truly grounded in Bougainvillean culture' (Bougainville Constitutional Commission 2004, 252). Bougainvillean constitution-makers expressed less support, with some claiming that it would be 'contrary to custom' and could inhibit the weapons disposal process (Bougainville Constitutional Commission 2004, 114–115). Consequently, the Constitution reiterates the amnesty and pardon provisions of the Bougainville Peace Agreement (ABG Constitution 2004, section 187 and Schedules 6.1 and 6.2), recognises that human rights 'issues' occurred during the crisis and requires the autonomous government to formulate a policy for dealing with them, and for effecting reconciliation that utilises Bougainville 'customs and practices … so far as is possible' (ABG Constitution 2004, section 187).

Bougainvillean political elites have continued to favour reconciliation guided by local sociopolitical practices in relation to the conflict. However, there are questions over the conduct of many customary reconciliations. While many reconciliations have been 'inclusive affairs' that have 'brought entire communities together', they have often 'failed … to address the need for truth telling and justice for deeper healing', instead encouraging a 'forgive and forget' approach to past wrongs either because perpetrators were perceived to lack sincerity or because the compensation offered or sanctions imposed were inadequate (Bougainville Human Rights Committee 2011).

Reconciliations have also become increasingly commercialised, with monetary compensation, along with financial support for travel to the reconciliation ceremony and food to conduct the ceremony, often seen as more important than the act of reconciliation itself. Indeed, there is an emerging culture of former combatants seeking compensation from the autonomous government or international donors before they participate in reconciliation ceremonies, which has raised questions about their sincerity and undermined the perceived legitimacy of those ceremonies. There has also been 'no mechanism to ensure compliance' with reparation agreements and other reciprocal arrangements agreed during reconciliation ceremonies (Bougainville Human Rights Committee 2011). When this is combined with the fact that there has been no formal transitional justice mechanism to deal with crimes committed during the crisis, there is some evidence that a culture of impunity has developed with respect to crimes committed since autonomy. As a result, Bougainvilleans are said to be 'confused as to their rights to pursue justice in individual cases of severe abuse' (Bougainville Human Rights Committee 2011). In the face of this perceived impunity, some families of victims are engaging in increasingly violent forms of 'local justice', including 'horrific tortures and executions' as 'payback', which is also having a detrimental effect on the rule of law (Bougainville Human Rights Committee 2011).

Conclusion

Therefore, it appears that reconciliation coupled with amnesties and pardons has played a mixed role in the social reconstruction of Bougainville. Governance mechanisms have been established that combine liberal and local sociopolitical practices and appear to be viewed as relatively legitimate, albeit with varying levels of effectiveness. The pursuit of justice has been more mixed, as the pragmatic decision by Bougainvillean elites to favour reconciliation over a formal transitional justice mechanism has contributed to the emergence of a culture of impunity.

As described, some Bougainvillean CSOs have led a push to create a truth and reconciliation commission (interview with a Bougainvillean women's leader, 25 January 2011), noting that crimes and other human rights have been 'hardly talked about and hardly discussed' during the existing reconciliation process (Garasu in Howley 2002, 282). Yet the fact that the amnesty and pardon were enshrined in the Papua New Guinea and Bougainville constitutions means that they are 'obstinate amnesties' (Lessa et al. 2014, 85), which are difficult to wind back, although other cases have illustrated that sufficient momentum can lead to the repeal of such laws.[4]

However, questions have been raised about both these CSOs and their proposals. The increased influence of international CSOs, and their tendency to engage with and fund elite, Bougainvillean CSOs that speak in internationalised language of transitional justice and human rights, may be creating incentives for local CSOs to focus on such proposals. Only a small proportion of Bougainvilleans, mostly from educated, urban backgrounds, belong to such CSOs. Moreover, the individuals involved are often traditional or church leaders, or members of the autonomous government and local-level sociopolitical institutions. Therefore, it is

---

4   Such as in Argentina.

unclear whether these CSOs attract support because of this or because of the legitimacy of their proposals (Regan 2003). In addition, proposals to establish a formal transitional justice mechanism have largely failed to gain traction among ordinary Bougainvilleans, and consequently these CSOs have struggled to gain momentum for their proposals. Instead, a distinction may need to be drawn between the views of the primarily urban elites who are involved in CSOs, for whom international donors have created political space to advocate for such a commission, and those of people who are embedded within communities, who have more immediate developmental needs. Indeed, the Bougainville case highlights that, while international CSOs may advocate criminal trials as crucial to social reconstruction, many ordinary people in conflict-affected societies favour mechanisms that allow them to 'reconcile in order to survive' (interview with an international adviser to the ABG, 31 August 2010).

Bibliography

Afflito, F. M. 2000. 'Victimization, Survival, and the Impunity of Forced Exile: A Case Study from the Rwandan Genocide'. *Crime, Law and Social Change* 34: 77–97. doi.org/10.1023/A:1008367712285.

Amnesty International. 1990. *Papua New Guinea: Human Rights Violations on Bougainville, 1989–1990.* London: Amnesty International.

Backer, David. 2003. 'Civil Society and Transitional Justice: Possibilities, Patterns and Prospects'. *Journal of Human Rights* 2 (3): 297–313. doi.org/10.1080/1475483032000132999.

Bakiner, Onur. 2014. 'Truth Commission Impact: An Assessment of How Commissions Influence Politics and Society'. *The International Journal of Transitional Justice* 8 (1): 6–30. doi.org/10.1093/ijtj/ijt025.

Biggar, Nigel. 2003. 'Making Peace or Doing Justice: Must We Choose?'. In *Burying the Past: Making Peace and Doing Justice After Civil Conflict*, edited by Nigel Biggar, 3–24. Washington: Georgetown University Press.

Boege, Volker. 2008. *A Promising Liaison: Kastom and State in Bougainville.* The Australian Centre for Peace and Conflict Studies, Occasional Paper Number 12. Brisbane: University of Queensland.

Boege, Volker. 2009. 'Peacebuilding and State Formation in Post-Conflict Bougainville'. *Peace Review* 21: 29–37. doi.org/10.1080/10402650802690037.

Boege, Volker. 2012. 'Hybrid Forms of Peace and Order on a South Sea Island: Experiences from Bougainville (Papua New Guinea)'. In *Hybrid Forms of Peace: From Everyday Agency to Post-Liberalism*, edited by Oliver P. Richmond and Audra Mitchell, 65–76. Basingstoke: Palgrave Macmillan.

Boege, Volker. 2013. *Bougainville Report, Project: Addressing Legitimacy Issues in Fragile Post-Conflict Situations to Advance Conflict Transformation and Peacebuilding*. Brisbane: University of Queensland.

Boege, Volker, Anne Brown and Kevin Clements. 2009. 'Hybrid Political Orders, Not Fragile States'. *Peace Review* 21: 13–21. doi.org/10.1080/10402650802689997.

Boege, Volker and Lorraine Garasu. 2004. 'Papua New Guinea: A Success Story of Postconflict Peacebuilding in Bougainville'. In *Searching for Peace in Asia Pacific: An Overview of Conflict Prevention and Peacebuilding Activities*, edited by Annelies Heijmans, Nicola Simmonds and Hans van de Veen, 564–580. Boulder and London: Lynne Rienner.

Bougainville Constitutional Commission. 2004. *Report of the Bougainville Constitutional Commission: Report on the Third and Final Draft of the Bougainville Constitution*. Arawa and Buka: Bougainville Constitutional Commission.

Bougainville Human Rights Committee and Civil Society Bougainvilleans. 2011. *Universal Periodic Review: Bougainville Civil Society Stakeholder Shadow Report to OHCHR*. Buka: Bougainville Human Rights Committee and Civil Society Bougainvilleans.

Brahm, Eric. 2007. 'Uncovering the Truth: Examining Truth Commission Success and Impact'. *International Studies Perspectives* 8: 16–35. doi.org/10.1111/j.1528-3585.2007.00267.x.

Braithwaite, John. 2003. 'Principles of Restorative Justice'. In *Restorative Justice and Criminal Justice: Competing or Reconcilable Paradigms?*, edited by Andreas von Hirsch, Julian V. Roberts, Anthony E. Bottoms, Kent Roach and Mara Schiff, 1–20. Oxford: Hart Publishing.

Collier, Paul and Anke Hoeffler. 2004. 'Greed and Grievance in Civil War'. *Oxford Economic Papers* 56: 563–595. doi.org/10.1093/oep/gpf064.

Commonwealth Secretariat and PIF 2005. *General Election for the Autonomous Bougainville Government: Report of the Commonwealth–Pacific Islands Forum Expert Team*. Suva: Pacific Islands Forum/Commonwealth Secretariat.

Commonwealth Secretariat and PIFS. 2010. *General Election;* PIFS, *Report of the Pacific Islands Forum Secretariat's Election Observer Team to the 2010 Elections for the Office of President and Members of the House of Representatives of the Autonomous Region of Bougainville.* Suva: Pacific Islands Forum.

Dahl, Robert A. 1989. *Democracy and Its Critics.* New Haven: Yale University Press.

Dinnen, Sinclair and Gordon Peake. 2013. 'More Than Just Policing: Police Reform in Post-Conflict Bougainville'. *International Peacekeeping* 20 (5): 570–584. doi.org/10.1080/13533312.2013.853961.

Finnroad. 2008. *Papua New Guinea – Australia Transport Sector Support Program (TSSP) Supported by the Australian Government – AusAID: Socio-Economic Study – TSSP Provinces, Baseline Report.* Helsinki: Finnroad.

Galtung, Johan. 1990. 'Cultural Violence'. *Journal of Peace Research* 27 (3): 291–305. doi.org/10.1177/0022343390027003005.

Goddard, Michael. 2000. 'Three Urban Village Courts in Papua New Guinea: Comparative Observations on Dispute Settlement'. In *Reflections on Violence*, edited by Sinclair Dinnen and Alison Ley, 241–253. Canberra: Hawkins Press.

Habermas, J. 1996. *Between Facts and Norms: Contributions to a Discourse Theory of Law and Democracy*, translated by W. Rehg. Cambridge: MIT Press. doi.org/10.7551/mitpress/1564.001.0001.

Hakena, Helen, Peter Nines and Bert Jenkins, eds. 2006. *NGOs and Post-Conflict Recovery: The Leitana Nehan Women's Development Agency, Bougainville.* Canberra: ANU E Press. doi.org/10.26530/OAPEN_459395.

Hamber, Brandon and Gráiine Kelly. 2004. *A Working Definition of Reconciliation.* Belfast: Democratic Dialogue.

Havini, M. T. 1995. *A Compilation of Human Rights Abuses against the People of Bougainville 1989–1995, Vol. 1.* Sydney: Bougainville Freedom Movement.

Havini, M. T. 1996. *A Compilation of Human Rights Abuses against the People of Bougainville 1989–1996, Vol. 2.* Sydney: Bougainville Freedom Movement.

Hayner, Priscilla B. 2001. *Unspeakable Truths: Facing the Challenges of Truth Commissions.* New York: Routledge.

Hegarty, D. 2009. 'Governance at the Local Level in Melanesia – Absent the State'. *Commonwealth Journal of Local Governance* 3: 1–19. doi.org/10.5130/cjlg.v0i0.1099.

Howley, Pat. 2002. *Breaking Spears and Mending Hearts: Peacemakers and Restorative Justice in Bougainville.* London: Zed Books.

Kim, Hun Joon and Kathryn Sikkink. 2010. 'Explaining the Deterrence Effect of Human Rights Protections for Transitional Countries'. *International Studies Quarterly* 54: 939–963. doi.org/10.1111/j.1468-2478.2010.00621.x.

Kritz, Neil J. 1996. 'Coming to Terms with Atrocities: A Review of Accountability Mechanisms for Mass Violations of Human Rights'. *Law and Contemporary Problems* 59 (4): 127–152. doi.org/10.2307/1192195.

Lederach, Paul John. 1997. *Building Peace: Sustainable Reconciliation in Divided Societies.* Washington DC: U.S. Institute of Peace Press.

Lessa, Francesca, Tricia D. Olsen, Leigh A. Payne, Gabriel Pereira and Andrew G. Reiter. 2014. 'Overcoming Impunity: Pathways to Accountability in Latin America'. *The International Journal of Transitional Justice* 8 (1): 75–98. doi.org/10.1093/ijtj/ijt031.

Long, William J. and Peter Brecke. 2003. *War and Reconciliation: Reason and Emotion in Conflict Resolution.* Cambridge: MIT Press. doi.org/10.7551/mitpress/7154.001.0001.

Loveman, Mara. 1998. 'High-Risk Collective Action: Defending Human Rights in Chile, Uruguay, and Argentina'. *American Journal of Sociology* 104 (2): 477–525. doi.org/10.1086/210045.

Mallinder, Louise. 2007. 'Can Amnesties and International Justice be Reconciled?'. *The International Journal of Transitional Justice* 1 (2): 208–230. doi.org/10.1093/ijtj/ijm020.

Masono, Raymond. 2006. *Government Capacity and Citizen Expectations in Bougainville: The Impact of Political Autonomy.* Crawford School of Economics and Government Discussion Paper 06–08. Canberra: The Australian National University.

McEvoy, Kieran. 2007. 'Beyond Legalism: Towards a Thicker Understanding of Transitional Justice'. *Journal of Law and Society* 34 (4): 411–440. doi.org/10.1111/j.1467-6478.2007.00399.x.

McGovern, James and Monica Taga. 2009. *Review of the Bougainville Community Police Project (Phase 4): BCCP Review Report.* www.aid.govt.nz/about-aid-programme/measuring-results/evaluation/activity-reports/2010-review-and-evaluation-reports/bougainville-com (accessed 10 October 2013, site discontinued).

McSherry, J. P. and Raul Molina Mejia. 1992. 'Confronting the Question of Justice in Guatemala'. *Social Justice* 19 (3): 1–28.

Molina Mejia, Raul. 1999. 'The Struggle against Impunity in Guatemala'. *Social Justice* 26 (4): 55–83.

Nisira, Patrick. 2010. Speaking at 'Elections in Bougainville and Solomon Islands', State, Society and Governance in Melanesia Conference, The Australian National University, Canberra, 3 November 2010.

OHCHR (Office of the United Nations High Commissioner for Human Rights). 2006. *Rule-of-Law Tools for Post-Conflict States – Amnesties*. New York: United Nations.

Olsen, Tricia D., Leigh A. Payne, Andrew G. Reiter and Eric Wiebelhaus-Brahm. 2010. 'When Truth Commissions Improve Human Rights'. *The International Journal of Transitional Justice* 4 (3): 457–476. doi.org/10.1093/ijtj/ijq021.

Opotow, Susan. 2001. 'Reconciliation in Times of Impunity: Challenges for Social Justice'. *Social Justice Research* 14 (2): 149–170. doi.org/10.1023/A:1012888902705.

Orentlicher, Diane F. 1991. 'Settling Accounts: The Duty to Prosecute Human Rights Violations of a Prior Regime'. *Yale Law Journal* 100 (8): 2537–2615. doi.org/10.2307/796903.

Paz, Rojas B. 1999. 'Impunity and the Inner History of Life'. *Social Justice* 26 (4): 13–30.

Penrose, Mary Margaret. 1999. 'Impunity – Inertia, Inaction, and Invalidity: A Literature Review'. *Boston University International Law Journal* 17: 269–310.

Pham, Phuong and Patrick Vinck. 2007. 'Empirical Research and the Development and Assessment of Transitional Justice Mechanisms'. *The International Journal of Transitional Justice* 1 (2): 231–248. doi.org/10.1093/ijtj/ijm017.

Philpott, Daniel. 2006. *The Politics of Past Evil: Religion, Reconciliation and Transitional Justice*. Notre Dame: University of Notre Dame Press.

Rawls, John. 1958. 'Justice as Fairness'. *The Philosophical Review* 67 (2): 164–194. doi.org/10.2307/2182612.

Regan, Anthony J. 2001. 'Why a Neutral Peace Monitoring Force? The Bougainville Conflict and the Peace Process'. In *Without a Gun: Australia's Experiences Monitoring Peace in Bougainville, 1997–2001*, edited by Monica Wehner and Donald Denoon, 1–18. Canberra: Pandanus Books.

Regan, Anthony J. 2003. 'An Outcomes Perspective on Civil Society in Melanesia: Reflections on Experience from Bougainville'. Paper presented at the Fourth Plenary: Governance and Civil Society, State, Society and Governance in Melanesia Project, The Australian National University, Canberra, 1 October 2003.

Regan, Anthony J. 2005. 'Identities among Bougainvilleans'. In *Bougainville Before the Conflict*, edited by Anthony J. Regan and Helga M. Griffin, 418–446. Canberra: Pandanus Books.

Regan, Anthony J. 2009. 'Bougainville's New Directions: Presidential By-Election, Forming a New Ministry, and First Steps of the New Leadership'. State, Society and Governance in Melanesian Seminar, The Australian National University, Canberra.

Regan, Anthony J. 2010a. *Light Intervention: Lessons from Bougainville*. Washington: U.S. Institute of Peace Press.

Regan Anthony J. 2010b. Speaking at 'Elections in Bougainville and Solomon Islands', State, Society and Governance in Melanesia Conference, The Australian National University, Canberra, 3 November.

Richmond, Oliver P. 2009. 'Becoming Liberal, Unbecoming Liberalism: Liberal-Local Hybridity via the Everyday as a Response to the Paradoxes of Liberal Peacebuilding'. *Journal of Intervention and Statebuilding* 3 (3): 324–344. doi.org/10.1080/17502970903086719.

Roht-Arriaza, Naomi. 1996. 'Combating Impunity: Some Thoughts on the Way Forward'. *Law and Contemporary Problems* 59 (4): 93–102. doi.org/10.2307/1192193.

Roht-Arriaza, Naomi. 2006. 'The New Landscape of Transitional Justice'. In *Transitional Justice in the Twenty-First Century: Beyond Truth Versus Justice*, edited by Naomi Roht-Arriaza and Javier Mariezcurrena, 1–16. Cambridge: Cambridge University Press. doi.org/10.1017/CBO9780511617911.

Sanford, Victoria and Martha Lincoln. 2011. 'Body of Evidence: Feminicide, Local Justice, and Rule of Law in "Peacetime" Guatemala'. In *Transitional Justice: Global Mechanisms and Local Realities after Genocide and Mass Violence*, edited by Alexander Laban Hinton, 67–93. New Brunswick: Rutgers University Press.

Sasa, C. L. 2013. 'Local Government Accountability in Bougainville'. Masters of Philosophy thesis, Massey University.

Sikkink, Kathryn and Carrie Booth Walling. 2007. 'The Impact of Human Rights Trials in Latin America'. *Journal of Peace Research* 44 (4): 427–445. doi.org/10.1177/0022343307078953.

Sirivi, Josephine Tankunanu and Marilyn Taleo Havini, eds. 2004. *… As Mothers of the Land: The birth of the Bougainville Women for Peace and Freedom.* Canberra: Pandanus Books.

Tamanaha, B. Z. 2004. *On the Rule of Law: History, Politics, Theory.* Cambridge: Cambridge University Press. doi.org/10.1017/CBO9780511812378.

Thompson, L., prod. 2002. *Breaking Bows and Arrows: Bougainville.* Television broadcast, SBS Television Australia, 22 March 2002.

Thoms, Oskar N. T., James Ron and Roland Paris. 2010. 'State-Level Effects of Transitional Justice: What Do We Know?'. *The International Journal of Transitional Justice* 4 (3): 329–354. doi.org/10.1093/ijtj/ijq012.

United Nations General Assembly 2005. *Basic Principles and Guidelines on the Right to a Remedy and Reparation for Victims of Gross Violations of International Human Rights Law and Serious Violations of International Humanitarian Law.* UN Doc. A/RES/60/147 (16 November 2005).

Wallis, Joanne. 2014. *Constitution Making during State Building.* New York: Cambridge University Press. doi.org/10.1017/CBO9781107587700.

Weah, Aaron. 2012. 'Hopes and Uncertainties: Liberia's Journey to End Impunity'. *The International Journal of Transitional Justice* 6 (2): 331–343. doi.org/10.1093/ijtj/ijs007.

Weinstein, Harvey M. 2011. 'Editorial Note: The Myth of Closure, the Illusion of Reconciliation: Final Thoughts on Five Years as Co-Editor-in-Chief'. *The International Journal of Transitional Justice* 5 (1): 1–10. doi.org/10.1093/ijtj/ijr002.

8

Between *kastom*, church and commercialisation: Reconciliations on Bougainville as a form of 'transitional justice'?

Volker Boege

Peacebuilding on Bougainville is entering a decisive phase. A referendum on the future political status of the island, which is currently an autonomous region within Papua New Guinea (PNG), is scheduled for November 2019. According to the Bougainville Peace Agreement (BPA) of August 2001, the referendum has to include independence as one option. It can be argued that only with the referendum and the peaceful implementation of its result will peacebuilding have reached a satisfactory conclusion.

Reconciliations are seen by Bougainvilleans as an indispensable ingredient of peacebuilding. Countless reconciliations have been carried out already, and there are more to come. Efforts to speed up and complete reconciliations are currently increasing, because unfinished reconciliations are seen as a major obstacle to the conduct of a free and fair referendum.

While reconciliations are usually presented as the 'traditional' Bougainville approach to conflict resolution and justice, there are now many different types of reconciliations: reconciliations within and between families, clans and villages; between former conflict parties; at the political level in Bougainville; and in national and international politics. Concerns are growing about reconciliations losing their 'traditional' meaning, becoming superficial, tokenistic and commercialised, and thus less effective and legitimate. This could have serious negative impacts on peacebuilding, especially since more formal transitional justice mechanisms are of only minor significance. The BPA granted amnesty and pardon for offences arising out of the violent conflict. In marked contrast to other post-conflict political settlements, no provisions for a truth and reconciliation commission (TRC) were put in place. Moreover, the formal court system is underdeveloped in post-conflict Bougainville.

Without a realistic option to take cases to the courts, without a TRC, and with immunity provisions in place, *kastom* reconciliation became the main avenue for transitional justice. Secular civil society actors, who elsewhere are prominent agents in the transitional justice discourse, are still quite weak in Bougainville. Moreover, they decided to also focus on reconciliations. Finally, the churches, which are by far the most influential civil society institutions on the ground, are deeply involved in reconciliation processes – in fact, *kastom* reconciliation usually entails Christian principles and practices.

In the following, I will explore the understanding(s) of reconciliation(s) in the local Bougainville context, the current state of reconciliations and their significance as an indigenous means of transitional justice. It will become clear that reconciliations in Bougainville are a long way from the Western transitional justice discourse. There is a tension between Bougainville-style reconciliation(s) and the concept of reconciliation as promoted at the international level and pursued in peace interventions that follow the Western liberal peace and transitional justice approach.

Reconciliation(s) Bougainville-style

The ideal type of Bougainville reconciliation aims at the restoration of social harmony within and between communities and of social relationships between conflict parties (Boege and Garasu 2004; 2011). Reconciliation Bougainville-style is a concept that includes both Christian and *kastom* elements (Garasu 2002; Howley 2002); it is a term deeply rooted in the Christian faith, and at the same time it captures the Bougainville *kastom* approach to conflict resolution.[1]

Reconciliation is a long-term, complex and complicated multifaceted process in which the wrongs of the past are acknowledged, responsibility is accepted and shared, and the basis for a common future is created. Reconciliation breaks the cycle of pay-back (retribution), reconstructing relations and trust.

It basically comprises the following stages:

> first of all, an agreement between the two sides to reconcile, followed by a meeting with an exchange of gifts to show that peace has been restored and a first public reconciliation has taken place. Later, there will be further reconciliations and, finally much later, the offenders will very likely meet face to face with the victims and/or their relatives, admit their guilt, express sorrow and will be forgiven. (Howley 2002, 109)[2]

Often there is no clear-cut boundary between victims and perpetrators. The victims of today might have been the perpetrators in the past, and vice versa. In a war like the one fought in Bougainville, the phenomenon of victims-turned-perpetrators and perpetrators-turned-victims is quite common. And these victim-perpetrators have to live together again and to build a shared future in closely knit communities.

The conflict parties striving for reconciliation usually invite a neutral third party to steer the process, mostly respected community leaders who are highly esteemed for their knowledge of *kastom*, the history of communities and relationships of the parties in conflict, of kinship ties and of social circumstances prevailing in the conflict setting. As Bougainville has an oral culture, their knowledge of stories and their skills in storytelling are

---

1   *Kastom*, a Pidgin derivative of the English 'custom', is referred to by both politicians and grassroots people in Melanesia today in order to stress their cultural heritage and the difference between their own ways and foreign ways of governance, often depicting *kastom* as rooted in ancient pre-colonial traditions, a set of rules developed by the ancestors (Keesing 1993, 589). *Kastom* governance is thus presented as the other of, or even alternative to, introduced state-based institutions and forms of governance. At the same time, *kastom* is different from the customs of the pre-contact past. It has developed since the times of first contact and colonisation in the course of interaction and exchange of pre-contact custom and various external influences – Christian missions, colonial administrations, institutions of the nation state and the market economy. Hence *kastom* is not anachronistic, fixed and static, it continually changes in the course of dealing with new challenges.

2   For an ideal typical traditional reconciliation process, see Tanis (2002).

important for the process. Their rich experience, their skills in setting (and interpreting) signs of reconciliation enable them to reach a resolution that is acceptable to all sides.

In the process, a common understanding of the causes and the history of the conflict has to be developed. Conflict parties have to negotiate a consensus regarding the interpretation of the past. Only once such a consensus has been achieved can reconciliation take its course. Perpetrators are helped to see their roles in the conflict more clearly, retrace their steps, acknowledge that they have disrupted social networks and even caused violence. This is the foundation for taking responsibility for their wrongdoings and for admitting guilt. Perpetrators then have to apologise to the ones they wronged and ask for forgiveness. Victims must develop a willingness to accept the apologies and forgive. Heartfelt repentance and confession on the part of the offenders and heartfelt forgiveness on the part of the victims are the building blocks of reconciliation. Reconciliation is not 'forgive and forget', but to remember without feelings of hatred and desire for revenge.

This kind of reconciliation is not a one-off event or a quick fix. It needs time. Slowness, breaks and 'time outs' are deliberately built into reconciliation processes to give parties time to calm down, assess the state of the process so far, reformulate their position and to prepare themselves spiritually and emotionally for a resolution.

Once solutions are found, they are ratified in highly ritual forms. Ceremonies mark the culminating points of the reconciliation process. Usually there is not one reconciliation ceremony, but a series of ceremonies, according to the progress of reconciliation. The ceremonies vary from area to area,[3] but generally they encompass rituals such as breaking spears and arrows, drinking and eating together from the same dish, singing and dancing together or chewing betelnut together. These symbolic activities are expressions of commitment and trust and are more powerful than mere spoken or written words. Finally, gifts are exchanged (pigs, shell money, food, cash or a combination of all these items).

---

3   In some places, for instance, people bury large stones. 'The significance of the stone is that it is heavy and it does not move and it gives a sign of strong and unchanging reconciliation between the people' (Howley 2002, 111). In other places the parties 'would plant tangget plants on stone. This symbolised their promise to forget the past and remain as silent as stone. Anyone who violated this agreement would be cursed by the stone and any talebearer would be punished by its strength' (Tanis 2002, 59).

The whole community participates. Church services and prayers are usually an integral part of these activities, as 'Christian principles of reconciliation have conveniently found their place in the culture and have, indeed, added a great deal to the process, through the incorporation of prayers and public acknowledgements by priests and church ministers' (Tanis 2002, 60).[4] Church leaders were and are particularly active in initiating and stabilising reconciliation processes. There are reconciliations that are carried out in the church context only. They are cheaper (no compensation has to be paid), but often also lack legitimacy because the *kastom* dimension is missing. They tend to be seen as a kind of 'second class' reconciliation, although for strong Christian believers they can be the 'real' reconciliations. The involvement of the churches is the most significant and visible expression of 'civil society' participation in reconciliation processes, although the people who participate in these reconciliations hardly think of the churches as civil society actors in the Western liberal sense of the term.

Reconciliation ceremonies are loaded with spiritual meaning. Ceremony is an important vehicle for cleansing and purification. Mental healing is an important aspect of reconciliation. Reconciliation is not only an issue of reason and the intellect. It is a deeply emotional and spiritual experience. Reconciliation is about deeply felt remorse, shame and the desire for forgiveness. It is about deeply felt grief, anger and sorrow and the desire to forgive. It is about mending hearts.[5] It is about repairing broken relationships and restoring harmony so that people can live in peace not only with each other, but also with God and the spirits of the dead. God is present in reconciliation, and so are the spirits of the dead.[6] Social relations are guarded by the spirit world. Whenever social relations break down, the spirit world is affected. The worlds of the living and the dead are closely interconnected. Conflicts also play out in the spirit world. This is why cleansing rituals that appease the spirits are linked to reconciliation. If such cleansing rituals are not performed, the spirits of the fallen will not rest but come back and haunt the living. If the spirits of the dead cannot be appeased, all kinds of misfortune will befall

---

4   This is very similar to the relationship between *kastom* and Christianity in the Solomon Islands, see Jeffery (2013, 213).

5   See the title of Pat Howley's highly informative and moving book: *Breaking Spears and Mending Hearts* (Howley 2002).

6   Most Bougainvilleans are devout Christians, but this does not replace belief in the spirit world. Rather, this goes together; there is mixing and blending.

the communities – illness, accidents, madness, death. So in the course of a reconciliation process the spirits will be called on to remove any illness that has befallen the community because of the conflict and bring back healing to the sick and the community at large.

Proper burials of the dead are highly important. In fact, one major problem for reconciliation after the war was, and still is today, that many people who were killed have not been buried in a culturally appropriate manner. Relatives do not know where the remains of their kin are, or there are graves with bones that have not been identified. In order to find peace and to reconcile, the dead have to be given a proper burial (UNDP 2014, 12, 32). The unburied dead have an influence on the lives of the living, both the perpetrators and the relatives of the victims. Therefore, finding and bringing home the bodies, burying them properly and grieving at their graves is an indispensable dimension of reconciliation. This is why the topic of 'missing persons' looms large in the current stage of peacebuilding on Bougainville.[7]

With reconciliation at the heart of peacebuilding, justice is restorative rather than punitive (although punitive/retributive elements can be part of *kastom* conflict settlements). On Bougainville today there is much talk about restorative justice. This modern term mirrors the approaches to justice that were and are an integral part of Bougainville customary conflict resolution (Braithwaite, Charlesworth, Reddy and Dunn 2010, 122–124). As a Bougainville chief states: 'Restorative justice is not a new method in our societies. It is what our ancestors used for thousands of years to resolve minor and major disputes, up until colonial times' (Tombot 2003: 259). It is grounded in a fundamentally relational understanding of people and society – an understanding that necessitates and enables justice to be pursued as a way of restoring relationships that were severed,

---

7   Similar beliefs can be found in other post-conflict societies in the Global South. For East Timor, for example, Robins reports that a central need of victims 'was the performance of rituals that would permit the spirits of the dead to rest in peace, and this was emphasized in Timor where the consequences of not performing rituals for the dead were believed to be the potential sickness and death of family members' (Robins 2013, 53). 'For Timorese families a malign spirit is the most negative potential impact of a missing relative; addressing the issue of those who died in the conflict means not only addressing the needs of their families but also the demands of the spirits … the peace of the nation is dependent upon this, with recent violence perceived as arising from the many spirits of the conflict dead still not at rest' (Robins 2013, 54; see also Grenfell, Chapter 2, this volume).

disrupted or destroyed by violence and wrongdoing.[8] Priority is given not to the punishment of individual offenders, but to the restoration of social harmony within and between communities and the restoration of relationships between the communities of offenders and victims. In Bougainville, reconciliation and restorative justice are 'twin frameworks for peacebuilding' (Llewellyn and Philpott 2014, 14).

For restorative justice and reconciliation, the exchange of gifts plays an important role. Gifts to compensate for damage done and wrongs committed serve to cement reconciliation. Reconciliations thus do not only aim at spiritual and emotional healing, but they also have a material side. Reparations are signs for and part of restoring relationships. Traditionally, gifts were items held precious by the communities such as shell money, pigs, mats and food. Nowadays cash and modern goods are also exchanged. Gifts are exchanged as a symbol of the restoration of relationships. The exchange is an outward sign of reconciliation. Its purpose is to 'wash away the tears'. A Bougainville elder explains:

> When we make peace, it is not the food and it is not the pigs and it is not the speeches. It is the people saying 'I forgive you. You forgive me. Let us get on with our lives'. All the rest – the pigs, and the food and the speeches – are just the outwards signs of our peace making. The shell-money is something that people see and they can put their mind on as the sign of our making peace. (Peter Mekea, quoted from Howley 2002, 103)

Pat Howley makes a clear distinction between such an exchange of gifts and compensation, and he explains the difference as follows:

> Gifts – yes, restitution for damages such as burned houses – yes, but no compensation. A gift is to wash away the tears; it in no way is a payment for the loss incurred. Compensation is for gain and is equivalent to setting a value on the life of a loved one. With a gift, one asks for forgiveness; with compensation, there is no forgiveness and the person is attempting something which is impossible, that is putting a value on something that cannot be bought or paid for. (Howley 2002, 126)

---

8   On restorative justice and reconciliation as relational conceptions of justice as opposed to a liberal individualist notion with its focus on individual offenders and their punishment, see Llewellyn and Philpott (2014).

In reality, however, this distinction, with the giving of gifts as an integral part of *kastom* reconciliation, and compensation (meaning in particular the payment of cash) as a deviation from *kastom*, is becoming more and more blurred. People complain that the 'true' customary meaning of the exchange of material goods in the context of reconciliation processes is being lost. There are indeed people who try to instrumentalise reconciliation, including those who use reconciliation and accompanying compensation to make money (see below).

So let us have a closer look at the realities of reconciliation(s) on Bougainville today.

Reconciliations today – between *kastom* and commercialisation

Part of the post-conflict political settlement on Bougainville was the constitutional guarantee of immunity from prosecution in respect of offences arising from crisis-related activities. The Lincoln Agreement of January 1998, which terminated violent conflict, declaring a 'permanent and irrevocable ceasefire', as well as the BPA-granted amnesty and pardon 'for all persons involved in crisis related activities or convicted of offences arising out of crisis related activities' (BPA, clause 33).[9] Immunity regulations were incorporated into the PNG and Bougainville constitutions. They covered a broad range of issues and in general applied to the time period between 1 October 1988 and 30 August 2001 (signing of the BPA).[10]

The amnesty and pardon regulations were complemented by the decision to deal with human rights abuses and other wrongs committed during the war through *kastom* reconciliation. The Bougainville Constitutional Commission (BCC) in its final 2004 report recommended that 'as far as possible … Bougainville kastom' should be used 'when dealing with human rights abuses and pursuing reconciliation' (BCC 2004, 199); and

---

9   The BPA states that 'the arrangements for pardon and amnesty are intended to reduce tensions and divisions that could continue to flow from the conflict' (BPA, clause 341(d)). See also clause 10 (Amnesty and Pardon) of the 'Lincoln Agreement on Peace, Security and Development on Bougainville', 23 January 1998.

10   See Constitution of the Autonomous Region of Bougainville, Schedule 6.1 and 6.2. Declaration in respect of immunity (pp. 159–160). There are exceptions for which other dates were set, in particular with regard to the possession, ownership and control of firearms.

in cases where the courts would become involved, they would have to 'take any customary settlements of matters before them into account' (ibid.).[11] Clause 185 in the Bougainville Constitution allows for the establishment of 'a special human rights enforcement body' with powers to 'encourage reconciliation among parties involved in abuses or infringement of human rights (including all parties in the Bougainville conflict)', and clause 186 stipulates that 'customary methods of dealing with such abuses [of human rights] should be utilized wherever possible'. Such a 'special human rights enforcement body' has not been set up. No truce and reconciliation commission was established. Whether to have one or not was discussed, but no consensus could be reached (Wallis 2014, 294), and the debate about pros and cons of a TRC is ongoing even today.[12]

With the immunity provisions in place, without a realistic option to take cases to the courts and without a TRC, *kastom* reconciliation in fact became the main avenue for transitional justice. And in general it has worked well.

There is no doubt about the importance of *kastom* reconciliation for peacebuilding on Bougainville (Braithwaite, Charlesworth, Reddy and Dunn 2010, 67–76). As the war was not only waged between the government of PNG and its Bougainvillean allies on the one hand and the secessionist Bougainville Revolutionary Army (BRA) on the other, but a complex mixture of this 'big' war and a host of 'mini wars' that were fought under the umbrella of the 'big' war in various local contexts, it was not sufficient to merely end the war of secession by political negotiations, it was also necessary to terminate the 'mini wars' and build peace at the local level. The parties fighting each other were not anonymous mass armies but mostly people who knew each other – they were 'intimate enemies' (Theidon 2006). Building peace between them was done by drawing on *kastom* ways of conflict resolution and reconciliation. This happened in many places all over Bougainville over the last two decades, and it continues today. These 'local reconciliation efforts have done more to consolidate popular commitment to peace than any other aspect of the process' (Regan 2001, 15). They were the means to restore social networks and relations that had broken down during the war, and to restore social trust and a sense of moral order. Secular

---

11   See Constitution of the Autonomous Region of Bougainville, clauses 185 and 186.
12   In neighbouring Solomon Islands a different path was taken, with mixed results. See Jeffery 2013; Cronin, Chapter 10, this volume.

civil society organisations were involved to a certain extent. Oftentimes supported by international partners like Care Australia, Save the Children or the International Committee of the Red Cross/Red Crescent, local NGOs (for example, the Nazareth Centre for Rehabilitation, Nasioi Peacebuilding Association, Bougainville Indigenous Dialogue or the Bougainville Healthy Communities Program) carried out specific peace projects that initiated or contributed to reconciliations. Even more important, however, were the churches, given their local embeddedness in each and every place in Bougainville.

The processes at the grassroots level were of decisive importance for the stabilisation of the overall peace and the success of peacebuilding at the 'higher' political levels. While in conventional Western academic and political thinking 'the top-down story is the master narrative and the bottom-up reconciliations are subsidiary', in the Bougainville case 'in important ways the bottom-up micro narratives subsume and infuse the top-down peace' (Braithwaite 2011, 140). While secular civil society organisations have only played minor roles, the churches, embedded as they are in the local context, have managed to substantially influence and shape these 'micro narratives'.

There are problems, however. Some reconciliation processes have been dragging on for a long time, and others have not yet started. Particularly in light of the November 2019 referendum there is a growing sense of urgency with regard to outstanding or unfinished reconciliations, and efforts to speed up reconciliations are intensifying. In recent times, so-called 'mass reconciliations' have gained prominence. In these 'mass reconciliations' a number of diverse cases in one region are lumped together and dealt with in one process. The last phase before the referendum, from mid-2018 onwards, saw a marked increase in the numbers of mass reconciliations dealing with crisis-related issues. They often were organised by District Peace and Security Committees (formal governance institutions). They have taken place in various regions of Bougainville, even in areas where current non-crisis-related divisions run deep (e.g. in the Panguna mine area). Mass reconciliations draw wide public attention, and they are propagated by the political elite as the means to finally wrap up the reconciliation business. It is not clear how effective and legitimate these mass reconciliations will be in the longer term. They clearly represent a deviation from what so far has been seen as *kastom* reconciliation. Such mass reconciliations serve a political purpose, which is important but can leave wounds open at the interpersonal level. In general, people approve of mass reconciliations because they see the need to speed up reconciliation processes in view of the upcoming referendum, but they also insist on the significance of more intimate clan-, family- and group-based reconciliations. Often these 'small' reconciliations are perceived as stepping stones towards mass reconciliations. One view is that the small 'clan' or 'ward' reconciliations have to come first, and the bigger 'community' or 'mass' reconciliations later. Others, however, hold the view that initial more symbolic mass reconciliations can serve as the starting point for more meaningful and effective 'small' reconciliations.

Then there is the issue of money. Reconciliations are costly, and they can be used as a money-making device. Bringing people together for reconciliation ceremonies and feeding them, and providing the gifts/compensation items, often costs a lot of money. This is why parties who want to reconcile increasingly ask for outside assistance, mainly in the form of cash. Such outside assistance started in the times of the Peace Monitoring Group (PMG) and the United Nations Observer Mission on Bougainville (UNOMB) immediately after the war. Over time it became more and more normal that outsiders would provide the resources that make reconciliations possible, and for conflict parties to demand such outside support (UNDP 2014, 12). Today, for example, the Australian-funded Bougainville Peacebuilding Program pays for reconciliations. Sometimes this even goes as far as parties demanding the money they have to pay as compensation from outside sources. In fact, compensation is increasingly in the form of cash – in addition to or instead of traditional items such as pigs or shell money. Reconciliations today can be a means to make money. Moreover, many reconciliations today are not crisis-related any more, but deal with post-crisis or current issues, and sometimes one gets the impression that conflicts are incited in order to make money out of the ensuing reconciliations.

Bougainvilleans have a tendency to blame outsiders for the commercialisation/monetisation/commodification of reconciliations – these outsiders brought the money in and thus distorted the true meaning of Bougainville customary reconciliation, undermining its legitimacy. Over and over again you can hear the complaint that 'it is all about money'. But at the same time, many Bougainvilleans also complain about the cost of reconciliations and say that they therefore need the money from outside sources.

Despite this trend, many of today's reconciliations are not commercialised, with conflict parties deliberately abstaining from compensation in the form of money (or with money only as a minor element in the mix of gifts exchanged), and the parties themselves providing the food, covering the costs of transport and so on. People are very proud of these – as they see them – 'true' reconciliations, contrasting them with what they call phoney reconciliations. Phoney reconciliation is superficial, hollow tokenism or a way to make money. A report about such a phoney reconciliation says that it 'meant nothing because the organisers used government money and the preparation and the discussion essential to any genuine reconciliation did not take place' (Howley 2002, 17). This kind of phoney reconciliation is in itself a cause of conflict, because people 'are angry because the value of the traditional form has been debased by people in high places' (Howley 2002, 117) who make 'reconciliation' 'a sham' (ibid., 118).

This criticism often is applied to reconciliation efforts in the political realm. When it comes to reconciliation in the context of politics, things become difficult indeed. Reconciliation at the interpersonal level is a painful and complicated emotional and spiritual process, and these dimensions are usually excluded from the political sphere. Nonetheless, people expect that their leaders who deal with the high-level political processes also pay due attention to the necessities of reconciliation, but then often criticise as hollow tokenism the inclusion of gestures of reconciliation into political negotiations and agreements. Nevertheless, paying tribute to customary and Christian symbols of reconciliation in the high-level political context has contributed to peacebuilding. It is of importance for the people to see their leaders adhere to *kastom* reconciliation, even if political reconciliations are of another quality than the interpersonal customary community reconciliations described above (Tanis 2002).[13]

There is a lot of talk about the need to reconcile with 'Papua New Guinea', or with 'Australia', or with the 'Papua New Guinea Defence Force' (PNGDF). On the other hand, there is a lot of uncertainty about what this could look like. National or international reconciliation is obviously different from reconciliation in the local interpersonal context. Attempts for reconciliations with the PNG Government and the

---

13   On the relation between 'bottom-up interpersonal reconciliation' and 'top-down political reconciliation on the grand scale' see Bloomfield (2006, 27–28).

PNGDF that so far have been made are generally seen as unsatisfactory, and political leaders are blamed for that. Almost the same difficulty arises with regard to reconciliations between the political leaders of various Bougainville factions – for example, between the Autonomous Bougainville Government (ABG) and the Meekamui movement, or between the various factions of Meekamui.[14] The big question is how to upscale or transfer an approach that works in the local community context to other contexts, without that approach being instrumentalised and thus losing legitimacy and effectiveness.

This is a fundamental question, which points to the limits of customary reconciliation. From what has been said so far, it should have become clear that customary reconciliation hinges on the existence of a community of relationships and values that are rooted in a common view of the world and a shared acknowledgement of customary institutions. It works within and between relatively small communities in the local context. Conflicts among the members of the 'we-group' of the community can be addressed and solved this way. Conflicts between neighbouring local communities pose relatively small problems, because some overarching customary principles can usually be developed and applied that allow for the creation of common ground. In other words: *kastom* reconciliation works for 'intimate enemies' (Theidon 2006), people who are bound by some kind of relationships, a shared worldview and shared norms. Dealing with outsiders is much more difficult. Conflicts between 'us' and 'them', who do not share our culture, are much more difficult to tackle. If 'they' do not understand, do not respect, or are unwilling to be included in 'our' ways of conflict resolution, reconciliation becomes very difficult or even impossible (Boege 2006).

---

14   The Meekamui movement emerged from the BRA. It comprises those ex-BRAs who have not joined the peace process officially, but also do not disrupt it. Meekamui is still in control of the area around the Panguna mine in central Bougainville and pockets of territory in South Bougainville. The Meekamuis have their own structures of governance, but also cooperate with the ABG. The 'border' between the Meekamui-controlled areas and the rest of Bougainville is rather porous, and there is considerable exchange. Over the years, the Meekamui movement has split into several factions. At present, complicated processes of rapprochement between the ABG and Meekamui, between the different Meekamui factions, and between the Meekamuis and their former comrades from the BRA, are underway, which might lead to some kind of 'reunification' in the future. In light of the upcoming referendum on independence, there is general agreement that 'unity' of all Bougainville political factions is urgently needed, and efforts have intensified to achieve that unity. In 2016 and 2017 several important reconciliations between these political factions have taken place.

This problem became obvious in the attempts to reconcile with Rio Tinto/Bougainville Copper Limited (BCL), the company that operated the Panguna mine and that by many Bougainvilleans is seen as the main culprit in the Bougainville saga.[15] There is general acknowledgement that there has to be reconciliation with Rio Tinto/BCL and, over the last years, BCL had indicated that it was willing to come in for reconciliation. A lot of thought and effort from various sides was put into making 'bel kol' possible (McKenna 2015). Bel kol (cooling of the heart) is the very first symbolic step in a longer reconciliation process, a gesture of willingness to start reconciliation. Various dates for a bel kol ceremony were announced, but the ceremony had to be postponed again and again. Stakeholders could not agree on the content, form and meaning of bel kol, and some stakeholders remained opposed to it. The consensus necessary for reconciliation could not be reached. There were some who said that bel kol, as planned, would not be genuine reconciliation, but only about money. And there were others who obviously were interested in just that: money, who wanted to make more money out of bel kol. Now that the BCL majority shareholder Rio Tinto has walked away from BCL and the Panguna mine, most probably there will be no bel kol in the forseeable future.

Another fundamental question concerns the relationship between kastom reconciliation and human rights, and women's rights in particular.[16] Whether serious human rights violations and crimes such as torture or pack rape that were committed during the war can appropriately be dealt with in the frame of kastom reconciliation is questionable. There was considerable sexual violence against women during the Bougainville war, which is difficult to discuss in public.[17] Here the question arises as to whether 'traditional' kastom reconciliation is adequate to deal with 'modern' forms of violence that had not been part of traditional societal life and conflict. In other words, kastom reconciliation is not a panacea for all ills. Joanne Wallis rightly makes the point that 'the decision to prioritise local customary reconciliation over prosecution in formal justice institutions for crimes committed during the crisis, and the resulting

---

15   Bougainville Copper Limited (BCL) was majority owned by Rio Tinto (previously Conzinc Riotinto of Australia (CRA)). In 2016, Rio Tinto withdrew from BCL and transferred its shares in the company to the ABG and the PNG Government.
16   See Wallis, Chapter 7, this volume; George 2016.
17   This is similar to Solomon Islands or East Timor. For those cases, see Guthrey (2016) and Vella (2014a, 2014b). On the 'perceived incompatibility between cultural norms and publicly airing sensitive stories' (Guthrey 2015, 5), see Guthrey (2015, 161–162).

developing culture of impunity, highlights the challenge of achieving a balance between liberal and local customary practices' (Wallis 2014, 296; see also Wallis, Jeffery and Kent 2016, 174).

Finally, there is the question of power relations. Power is not absent from reconciliation. Who is in a position to determine the need for reconciliation in a specific case? Whose interests are served, and whose not? How do power imbalances play out in reconciliation processes?

Imbalances with regard to age, kinship networks or resourcefulness play a role, but the most prominent imbalance is gender related; with regard to 'asymmetries in power structures, gender relations and gender-specific experiences of violence need to be considered' (Fischer 2011, 423). Although it would be misleading to think of women in Bougainville as generally powerless or less powerful than men,[18] in certain contexts gendered power relations are significant, and this can affect the position of women in reconciliations. Furthermore, young people generally have a lesser status in communities than older people. The very old, old widows in particular can also be powerless (if they lack family support), and there are clans or extended families that are more powerful than others. These power asymmetries can all affect reconciliations.[19]

Conclusions

Reconciliations in Bougainville have not much to do with the Western reconciliation and transitional justice discourse. That discourse does not pay much attention to historical, social and cultural contexts. In fact, as 'a highly normative formula with universalist claims, the reconciliation discourse tends to make context a blind spot' (Eastmond 2010, 5). Or, as Erin Baines put it: 'International and national policy makers have imposed a uniform approach on justice after conflict, ignoring the complex local dynamics that are most relevant to people's lives' (Baines 2010, 415).

---

18   Most communities in Bougainville are matrilineal, with a relatively strong position of women in the customary social context. Bougainville women were highly influential actors in peacebuilding (Havini and Sirivi 2004; King 2009).

19   For a critique of 'ethnojustice', including customary reconciliation, see Branch (2014), who argues that this type of justice consolidates 'a patriarchal, gerontocratic order' (p. 616) and 'empowers older men at the expense of youth and women' (p. 619).

Reconciliations in Bougainville are indeed highly context-specific, and the term has to be understood in this specific context. Bougainville reconciliations serve communities for which the maintenance of social relationships is essential to their members' material and spiritual wellbeing and security. They are geared towards the restoration of relationships between 'intimate enemies' after violent conflict, including the restoration of relationships with the spirit world and God. They do not necessarily lead from point A – violence, conflict – to point B – conflict resolution, harmony – in a linear way. They are complex and open-ended; 'final settlements' are not 'final' at all, but are open to renegotiation at some time in the future. The past is not past: it can resurface (or be made to resurface) at any time; 'resolutions' therefore are not really 'resolutions'. Accordingly, reconciliation 'describes a process rather than an end state or outcome' (Fischer 2011, 415). This does not fit well with the conventional mainstream understanding of transitional justice in the Western-dominated international discourse.

Reconciliations are embedded in the everyday life of communities as merely one aspect. People want to get on with their 'normal lives', and reconciliations matter only inasmuch as they (hold the promise to) make this possible. This pragmatic approach to reconciliation pays attention to restorative justice and material reparation, at the same time though it is not in contrast to the emotional and spiritual importance of reconciliation; rather, the material and the spiritual elements go hand in hand, given that everyday life is imbued with spirituality and emotions. Reconciliations that are motivated by pragmatic considerations do not pay much attention to legal concerns. They are definitely not the functional equivalent of legal procedures.[20] Legal, normative and institutional questions are of little relevance to these reconciliations, which are embedded in specific worldviews and cosmologies, from which they draw their meaning and moral might. Furthermore, Bougainville reconciliations connect reason and emotion. While in Western concepts, peacebuilding is (or is presented as being) very much an issue of reason, rational procedures and rational politics, for Bougainville reconciliations, feelings and spirituality are crucial. Rational elements play a role, but peace cannot be built, and justice cannot be restored, without addressing people's emotions and spirituality. This is why the churches have

---

20   It is a common misunderstanding that 'customary law', 'traditional courts' and 'customary conflict resolution' are functional equivalents of, and can operate like, statutory law, state courts and alternative dispute resolution, filling the gaps if the latter are absent.

a prominent place in Bougainville reconciliations, in contrast to secular civil society organisations that are bound to Western understandings of transitional justice.

Finally, one significant advantage of reconciliations of the Bougainville type is that people can implement them themselves: they have agency, they are in control, they have voice. Reconciliations are sociocultural mechanisms at people's immediate disposal, they are familiar with the process and they know what outcomes can be expected. This marks an important difference to TRCs, trials and other mechanisms of transitional justice; these are not at the disposal of and under the control of ordinary community members, they lack clarity of process and outcomes for the community, and in them victims and perpetrators are largely objects of external mechanisms (Guthrey 2015, 2016). This is not to say that TRCs and so forth cannot be valuable and necessary. What I tried to say in this chapter is that context-specific, locally grounded reconciliation can make a decisive contribution to peacebuilding. This, at least, is the case in Bougainville, and perhaps this type of reconciliation *is* actually transitional justice.

Bibliography

Baines, Erin. 2010. 'Spirits and Social Reconstruction after Mass Violence: Rethinking Transitional Justice'. *African Affairs* 109 (436): 409–430. doi.org/10.1093/afraf/adq023.

BCC (Bougainville Constitutional Commission). 2004. *Report of the Bougainville Constitutional Commission. Report on the Third and Final Draft of the Bougainville Constitution.* Arawa and Buka: Bougainville Constitutional Commission.

Bloomfield, David. 2006. *On Good Terms: Clarifying Reconciliation.* Berghof Report no. 14. Berlin: Berghof Research Center for Constructive Conflict Management.

Boege, Volker. 2006. *Traditional Approaches to Conflict Transformation – Potentials and Limits.* Berghof Handbook for Conflict Transformation. Berlin: Berghof Research Center for Constructive Conflict Management.

Boege, Volker and Lorraine Garasu. 2004. 'Papua New Guinea: A Success Story of Postconflict Peacebuilding in Bougainville'. In *Searching for Peace in Asia Pacific: An Overview of Conflict Prevention and Peacebuilding Activities*, edited by Annelies Heijmans, Nicola Simmonds and Hans van de Veen, 564–580. Boulder and London: Lynne Rienner.

Boege, Volker and Lorraine Garasu. 2011. 'Bougainville: A Source of Inspiration for Conflict Resolution'. In *Mediating across Difference. Oceanic and Asian Approaches to Conflict Resolution*, edited by Morgan Brigg and Roland Bleiker, 163–182. Honolulu: University of Hawai'i Press. doi.org/10.21313/hawaii/9780824834593.003.0009.

Braithwaite, John. 2011. 'Partial Truth and Reconciliation in the *Long Durée*'. *Contemporary Social Science* 6 (1): 129–146. doi.org/10.1080/17450144.2010. 534498.

Braithwaite, John, Hilary Charlesworth, Peter Reddy and Leah Dunn. 2010. *Reconciliation and Architectures of Commitment: Sequencing Peace in Bougainville*. Canberra: ANU E Press. doi.org/10.22459/RAC.09.2010.

Branch, Adam. 2014. 'The Violence of Peace: Ethnojustice in Northern Uganda'. *Development and Change* 45 (3): 608–630. doi.org/10.1111/dech.12094.

Constitution of the Autonomous Region of Bougainville. 2005. Buka: Autonomous Bougainville Government.

Eastmond, Marita. 2010. 'Introduction: Reconciliation, Reconstruction, and Everyday Life in War-Torn Societies'. *Focaal – Journal of Global and Historical Anthropology* 57: 3–16. doi.org/10.3167/fcl.2010.570101.

Fischer, Martina. 2011. 'Transitional Justice and Reconciliation: Theory and Practice'. In *Advancing Conflict Transformation. The Berghof Handbook II*, edited by Beatrix Austin, Martina Fischer and Hans-Joachim Giessmann, 405–430. Opladen: Barbara Budrich Verlag.

Garasu, Lorraine. 2002. 'Women Promoting Peace and Reconciliation'. In *Weaving Consensus – The Papua New Guinea–Bougainville Peace Process*, edited by Andy Carl and Lorraine Garasu, 28–31. Conciliation Resources Accord Issue 12/2002. London: Conciliation Resources.

George, Nicole. 2016. 'Light, Heat and Shadows: Women's Reflections on Peacebuilding in Post-Conflict Bougainville'. *Peacebuilding* 4 (2): 166–179. doi.org/10.1080/21647259.2016.1192241.

Guthrey, Holly L. 2015. *Victim Healing and Truth Commissions: Transforming Pain through Voice in Solomon Islands and Timor-Leste*. New York and London: Springer. doi.org/10.1007/978-3-319-12487-2.

Guthrey, Holly L. 2016. 'Local Norms and Truth Telling: Examining Experienced Incompatibilities within Truth Commissions of Solomon Islands and Timor Leste'. *The Contemporary Pacific* 28 (1): 1–29. doi.org/10.1353/cp.2016.0009.

Havini, Marilyn T. and Josephine Tankunani Sirivi, eds. 2004. ... *As Mothers of the Land: The Birth of the Bougainville Women for Peace and Freedom*. Canberra: Pandanus Books.

Howley, Pat. 2002. *Breaking Spears and Mending Hearts: Peacemakers and Restorative Justice in Bougainville*. London – Annandale: Zed Books – The Federation Press.

Jeffery, Renée. 2013. 'Reconciliation and the Rule of Law in the Solomon Islands'. In *Transitional Justice in the Asia Pacific*, edited by Renée Jeffery and Hun Joon Kim, 195–227. Cambridge: Cambridge University Press. doi.org/10.1017/CBO9781139628914.007.

Keesing, Roger M. 1993. 'Kastom Re-examined', *Anthropological Forum* 6 (4): 587–596. doi.org/10.1080/00664677.1993.9967434.

King, Barbara. 2009. 'Women and Peacebuilding: A Feminist Study of Contemporary Bougainville'. PhD thesis, University of Queensland.

Llewellyn, Jennifer J. and Daniel Philpott. 2014. 'Restorative Justice and Reconciliation: Twin Frameworks for Peacebuilding'. In *Restorative Justice, Reconciliation, and Peacebuilding*, edited by Jennifer J. Llewellyn and Daniel Philpott, 14–34. Oxford: Oxford University Press. doi.org/10.1093/acprof:oso/9780199364862.003.0002.

McKenna, Kylie. 2015. 'Mining and Reconciliation: Negotiating the Future of the Panguna Mine in Bougainville'. *SSGM In Brief* 2015/35. Canberra: ANU.

Regan, Anthony. 2001. 'Why a Neutral Peace Monitoring Force? The Bougainville Conflict and the Peace Process'. In *Without a Gun: Australians' Experiences Monitoring Peace in Bougainville, 1997–2001*, edited by Monica Wehner and Donald Denoon, 1–18. Canberra: Pandanus Books.

Robins, Simon. 2013. 'An Empirical Approach to Post-Conflict Legitimacy: Victims' Needs and the Everyday'. *Journal of Intervention and Statebuilding* 7 (1): 45–64. doi.org/10.1080/17502977.2012.655618.

Tanis, James. 2002. 'Reconciliation: My Side of the Island'. In *Weaving Consensus: The Papua New Guinea–Bougainville Peace Process*, edited by Andy Carl and Lorraine Garasu, 58–61. Conciliation Resources Accord Issue 12/2002. London: Conciliation Resources.

Theidon, Kimberly. 2006. 'Justice in Transition: The Micro-Politics of Reconciliation in Postwar Peru'. *Journal of Conflict Resolution* 50 (3): 433–457. doi.org/10.1177/0022002706286954.

Tombot, John. 2003. 'A Marriage of Custom and Introduced Skills: Restorative Justice Bougainville Style'. In *A Kind of Mending: Restorative Justice in the Pacific Islands*, edited by Sinclair Dinnen, 255–264. Canberra: Pandanus Books.

UNDP (United Nations Development Programme). 2014. *Peace and Development Analysis: Findings and Emerging Priorities.* Port Moresby: United Nations Development Programme Papua New Guinea Country Office.

Vella, Louise. 2014a. 'What Will You Do with Our Stories?' Truth and Reconciliation in the Solomon Islands'. *International Journal of Conflict and Violence* 8 (1): 91–103.

Vella, Louise. 2014b. 'Translating Transitional Justice: The Solomon Islands Truth and Reconciliation Commission'. *SSGM Discussion Paper* 2014/2. Canberra: ANU.

Wallis, Joanne. 2014. *Constitution Making during State Building.* New York: Cambridge University Press. doi.org/10.1017/CBO9781107587700.

Wallis, Joanne, Renée Jeffery and Lia Kent. 2016. 'Political Reconciliation in Timor Leste, Solomon Islands and Bougainville: The Dark Side of Hybridity'. *Australian Journal of International Affairs* 70 (2): 159–178. doi.org/10.1080/10357718.2015.1113231.

9

Vernacularising 'child rights' in Melanesian secondary schools: Implications for transitional justice

David Oakeshott[1]

As the linkages between education and transitional justice have become more explicit in the last decade (Cole 2007; Ramírez-Barat and Duthie 2015), attention has centred overwhelmingly on the role of the state in those linkages. Cole and Murphy (2009, 3) have framed education as a justice institution where 'students first come into contact with official structures of their society'. Paulson (2009, 10) has argued that post-conflict investment in education could signal to citizens their government's commitment to peace. And Cole (2007, 123) argues that for transitional justice, education can 'potentially function as a secondary phase (after trials and truth commissions) that reflects the state's commitment to institutionalising transitional justice'. Even at the school level, King (2014), McCully (2012) and Quaynor (2012) have argued that pedagogical reform to promote critical thinking and open dialogue among students models democratic politics far better than the rote memorisation of curricular content.

1   The author's research is supported by an Australian Government Research Training Program (RTP) Scholarship. Dr John Cox, La Trobe University, and the editors of this volume deserve special thanks for their commentary on earlier drafts of this paper.

Human rights education is one way to model democratic politics. It has itself been a recent addition to thinking about the role of education in transitional justice (Bellino 2014b; Davies 2017a, 2017b), and has been included in the recommendations of several truth commissions (Paulson and Bellino 2017, 351). It is tied closely to the topic of pedagogical reform, given that such changes, it is argued, should take place within a broader school culture of non-violence and respect for the rights of children (Davies 2017a, 339–340). In this way, teaching human rights consciousness could be the conduit through which teachers and students from all parties to a conflict learn to live together again; it will teach them to see each other as equals in rights (Davies 2017b, 11). However, non-violent school cultures can be hard to find in post-conflict societies. Davies's own evidence from Sri Lanka found that, despite government efforts at pedagogical reform, school violence was rising in areas where violence was particularly prevalent in life outside school (Davies 2017a, 343). Likewise, Bellino (2014b) showed that young Guatemalans' rights consciousness was shaped by both school and their lives outside it.

The role of civil society in scholarship on education and transitional justice has been understood within state-centric frameworks of analysis. In circumstances where transitional justice mechanisms have been disbanded but the state is unable or refuses to commit to transitional justice, civil society can step in to fill the void (Bellino 2014a, 142; Cole 2017, 16–18; Ramírez-Barat and Duthie 2015, 25–27).

In this context, I consider the 'Child Rights Network' at two Catholic secondary boarding schools, St Joseph's College, Mabiri (in Bougainville), and St Joseph's National Secondary School, Tenaru (in Solomon Islands).[2] The Child Rights Network was designed by the Marist Brothers District of Melanesia to introduce the United Nations Convention on the Rights of the Child (UNCRC) into the daily lives of teachers and students at its schools. Critically also, the Marist Brothers ran the schools themselves. Churches are highly regarded and influential throughout Melanesia (Monson 2013; Tomlinson and McDougall 2013, 2). Moreover, they have historically performed governance functions that a classical Weberian understanding of the state (as distinct from civil society) would view as state prerogatives (Eriksen 2013; McDougall 2008). They have dominated

---

2   This paper is based on findings from 10 months of PhD field research using semi-structured interviews and ethnographic observations in Solomon Islands and Bougainville from mid-2015 to mid-2016.

in the provision of education, for example (Laracy 1976, 22; Oakeshott and Allen 2015, 6; Palmer 1980, 40). This intensified in the wake of the civil conflicts in Bougainville and Solomon Islands as policymakers and donors looked increasingly to churches to provide governance in the absence of functioning states (McDougall 2008, 1). Nevertheless, although their functions overlap with the state's, churches are still touted as the most active and persuasive components of civil society in Melanesia (Richmond 2011, 128; Dinnen 2001, 100).

In this chapter, I critically discuss the 'vernacularisation' (Merry 2006a) of human rights at Mabiri and Tenaru, and argue that it addresses some conflict legacies without fundamentally altering the nature of everyday life at school. In the first section, I show that although Merry's concept of vernacularisation helps us move our analyses beyond simply perceived incompatibilities between rights and indigenous culture, vernacularisation in Bougainville and Solomon Islands is complicated by legacies of their respective civil conflicts, such as the further entrenchment of corporal punishment and breakdown of customary authority. In the second section, I establish that resistance from teachers to the Child Rights Network did indeed revolve around the issue of corporal punishment (as well as students' manual labour). Third, I demonstrate that even though participants vernacularised rights in different ways, little about the ideal citizen into which the schools hoped to form their students was changed. Finally, I explain how those who engaged critically with the concept and vocabulary of rights also learned how to identify and respond to justice issues at school.

Vernacularisation in Melanesia and post-conflict schooling

Pacific Island countries have been slow to incorporate human rights treaties into their domestic legal systems and regularly fail to meet the reporting requirements in those conventions (Farran 2012, 200). Papua New Guinea ratified the UNCRC in 1993 but only provided its first report in 2000, for example (ibid., note 5). In Solomon Islands, where corporal punishment and physical violence against children are common (Evans 2016, 73–74), the rights discourse is not widely tolerated by large segments of the adult population either (ibid., 81).

Popular resistance to human rights in Melanesia is often based on a perceived incompatibility with indigenous *kastom* (Evans 2016; Soaki 2017). However, while this resistance might suggest that *kastom* is a fixed set of traditional practices, recognising the contemporary influences on, and uses of, *kastom* shows that it and human rights need not be viewed as irreconcilable opposites. *Kastom* has always been changing and thus has become infused with elements of indigenous cultures, colonialism, Christianity and modern-day politics (Akin 2013). Contemporary *kastom* ideology among people from the island of Malaita, for example, was born in their resistance to British colonial rule (Akin 2013). Malaitan *kastom* has become a marker of contemporary island/provincial identity for Malaitans and also an 'other' from which Solomon Islanders from other provinces form their own provincial/island identities (Cox 2017, 81). As *kastom* is continuously reinterpreted when it is used to respond to new ideas and institutions, it is little wonder that Cox found a kindergarten principal in a conservative village of Western Province who had abandoned corporal punishment in favour of a human rights–centred approach to discipline. The principal now favours dialogue between teachers, students and parents. *Kastom* and human rights were not 'two incompatible cultural domains' for this principal (Cox 2017, 84).

Nevertheless, overall, human rights remains an uncomfortable fit in the Pacific, which Sally Engle Merry's (2006a) concept of 'vernacularisation' helps us understand. The concept describes the ways local cultural concepts are appropriated by civil society to spread the human rights regime. In using vernacularisation to analyse gender violence in the Pacific, Biersack and Macintyre (2016, 4) have shown that human rights is itself an ideology that merely 'alleges universality' and one that 'views any doctrine that deviates from it as merely "local" and aberrant' (ibid., 5). Indeed, Taylor (2008, 166) argues that the image of the 'human' in the human rights regime actually originates in forms of individual personhood more common in the West, which is often contrasted with more collectivist understandings of personhood in non-Western contexts (Jolly 2016, 345). The 'intermediaries' (Merry 2006b, 39) who champion (vernacularise) human rights for local populations are members of civil society because, as the local elites of their societies, they can speak the international language of human rights to people in their local context (Biersack and Macintyre 2016, 13).

Although flows of cultural change brought by human rights are typically directed from the Western human rights discourse at the top, down to the recipient context below, in some instances the meaning of 'rights' changes considerably when they are rendered in ways that make sense locally (Biersack and Macintyre 2016, 11–12; Jolly 2016, 355). Hermkens's (2013) thought-provoking ethnographic research with the Mbirau people of Marau Sound, on Guadalcanal, Solomon Islands, is a noteworthy example. She found that when foreign organisations and non-governmental organisations (NGOs) deliver human rights, they construe local social realities and cultures simply as problems to be overcome in the empowerment of women (see also Cox 2017, 69). But Hermkens shows that the Mbirau women with whom she worked 'translate rights as duties towards one's family, or as bringing awareness of Women's responsibility to get involved in local politics in order to improve their tribe's future' (Hermkens 2013, para. 36). Importantly, the responsibility her participants described was not a result of their claim to a universal, and individual, right as defined by the international human rights regime, but was rather understood relationally, in terms of 'the moral framework in which relationships are embedded' (ibid., para. 37). Hermkens's ethnography showed how human rights can be vernacularised as responsibilities in a way that reinforces the duties women have towards the men in their lives.

Vernacularisation at the Mabiri and Tenaru schools has been directed through the Child Rights Network, which the Marist Brothers District of Melanesia established at all their schools in Melanesia in the mid-2000s. Then District Leader Br Ken McDonald recalled that the district's engagement with rights began when it assisted with Vanuatu's 'universal periodic review' of the UNCRC (interview with Br Ken McDonald, 26 April 2017). The district's commitment to child protection through a rights-based framework deepened thereafter and eventually saw it employ a Child Advocacy Officer, Chris Beatus, who began implementing the Child Rights Network through biannual workshops at all Marist schools in the district (ibid.). The workshops I observed at Mabiri in 2016 connected the principles of the Marist charism to the rights provisions in the UNCRC and Papua New Guinea's Lukautim Pikinini Act passed in 2009.

However, conflict legacies have made the task for the Child Rights Network more difficult at Mabiri and Tenaru. One legacy has been the further legitimisation of corporal punishment. Participant A, in Bougainville, told me how after the Bougainville 'Crisis', one of her close relatives could never overcome his anger when he returned to teaching. He became physically abusive towards his students, particularly to the children of the combatants who killed his father. In the end the pain was too much. He left teaching, and formal employment entirely (confidential interview, 17 September 2015). Several members of the Catholic education system also acknowledged that the Crisis further normalised physical abuse of students (confidential interview with Participant B, 7 February 2016; interview with Chris Beatus, 13 September 2015).

Another conflict legacy in Bougainville arises from the damage done to customary forms of authority during the Crisis. The Crisis started in mid-1988, and was chiefly a war between the Papua New Guinea Defence Force and Bougainville Revolutionary Army (BRA) until armed (Bougainvillean) opposition to the BRA formed in 1990 (Regan 1998, 279). Beneath the anti-PNG dimensions were atrocities committed within cultural, language and even family groups that broke down mechanisms of customary authority. In the end, violence gained considerable popular legitimacy as a means to solve disputes (ibid.). Young people now grow up in this environment (Kent and Barnett 2012), and the continued antisocial behaviour of boys in particular, which older Bougainvilleans describe as 'acting BRA', has become a particular challenge for educators. Ultimately, because of the Crisis, students are more likely to challenge authority figures and misbehave and teachers are less likely to show restraint in disciplining their students harshly.

Corporal punishment occurs in Solomon Islands schools too (Cox 2017), and its civil conflict, known as the 'Tension' or 'Ethnic Tension', certainly called into question Solomon Islanders' capacity to live together peacefully. The Tension began in 1998 when local militia on Guadalcanal began violently evicting settlers (predominantly from the neighbouring island of Malaita) from the rural and peri-urban areas around the capital, Honiara.[3] A rival militia then formed to protect the Malaitan evictees who had taken refuge in Honiara. The town became a Malaitan enclave and violent confrontations between the Malaitan and Guadalcanal militias intensified on the outskirts (Dinnen 2002, 287). The rest of the country was relatively free of widespread violence, but was directly affected by the near total collapse of the Solomon Islands state. Although the signing

---

3   The underlying causes of the Tension have been discussed in depth elsewhere (Fraenkel 2004; Moore 2004; Allen 2013).

of the Townsville Peace Agreement (TPA) in October 2000 effectively ended the warfare between the two groups (McDougall 2016, 18), the Tension continued until 2003. Just as localised fighting was common in Bougainville, so too was violence common not only between, but also within, Malaitan and Guadalcanal groups post-2000.

In these contexts, and because the formal instruction of the Child Rights Network is largely limited to biannual workshops, teachers and students at Mabiri and Tenaru largely perform the roles of intermediaries themselves. Much of the vernacularisation, therefore, happens on playgrounds, in dormitories and dining halls, and in other extracurricular activities in which students spend most of their time. In these spaces outside the classroom, 'child rights' – which is the term participants use to describe human rights discourses, practices and their Child Rights Network – pervade debates about the structures of schooling that shape their daily lives and address legacies of the Crisis and the Tension.

Rights discourse and the structures of schooling

Child rights were part of a challenge to two structures of schooling – discipline protocols and manual labour – that upset the authority of teachers over their students. This authority was based on a strict power imbalance between teachers and students, which Teacher B, at Mabiri, summarised:

> I know that there are still teachers who are not very comfortable with child rights. And I know that there are teachers who still would prefer to give students a smack or two for not doing homework or something. To them they think that is the way to do it, just because [they say] 'that's the way my teachers taught me in the past' (confidential interview, 18 February 2016).

And Teacher S at Tenaru explained that students learn from this teacher–student relationship that they should follow the orders of authority figures unquestioningly rather than form opinions themselves (confidential interview, 13 August 2015). She said teachers were struggling with the notion that students should be 'saying what they think' (confidential interview, 13 August 2015).

The scale of the challenge that the rights discourse posed became clear when teachers at both schools considered their discipline protocols. Teacher V and several of his colleagues at Tenaru have observed a shift towards 'pastoral care' in the last five years, which is informed by child rights and the Marist charism described below. Rather than strict enforcement of the rules, the school's pastoral care process aims to develop students' decision-making capacities by showing them leniency when they make mistakes (confidential interview with Teacher Y, 29 November 2015). In this reformulation of discipline practices, recidivist students should be counselled long before any serious disciplinary measures are taken, and the language of 'punishment' has been replaced with that of 'community service'. However, this change has left several teachers uncertain of how to react to students they catch breaking the rules. Teacher V confessed he could see no basis in the school rules for the new discipline decisions the administration was making and wondered aloud if he was supposed to follow the discipline procedures set out in the rules, or if human rights had become a hidden rule (confidential interview, 10 September 2015). Teacher U also blamed child rights specifically for the rights/rules confusion (confidential interview, 1 December 2015).

Teachers would often measure these changes to discipline and child rights against their compatibility with *kastom*, which included showing deference to authority.[4] At Tenaru, Teacher S noted that students' focus on the rules and on rights language only confuses them:

> [B]ecause that is how the society is; authority and rules speaks [sic] for the authority. And um responsibility, when we were growing up, responsibility, you do what your mother and father tells you or what the tribe expects out of you and not so much of thinking for yourself (confidential interview, 1 December 2015).

This apparent rights/rules clash in both teachers' and students' images of Melanesian culture also emerged in discussions of the manual labour that both schools make students undertake. Most schools in Solomon Islands and Bougainville rely on student labour to grow food and maintain school infrastructure, although the actual time spent working varies

---

4   Melanesia is famed for its cultural diversity. Understandings of the role of children in society and the socialisation of young people thus vary widely and are constantly changing (Herdt and Leavitt 1998). Nevertheless, at school, and certainly in conversations with me, teachers and students would often refer to an image of a Bougainvillean, Solomon Islander or pan-Melanesian *kastom* when discussing the Child Rights Network.

from school to school. Teacher B, at Mabiri, outlined the argument the child rights sceptics often make: they emphasise that in Bougainvillean society young people must work hard to survive. Child rights discourse clashes with this articulation of social order because it limits the work students can do if too much is considered abuse (confidential interview, 16 February 2016). Another teacher at Mabiri, Teacher C, added that child rights were also a challenge to one of the tenets of Marist education, 'love of work', which could be seen as abuse even though it is intended to teach youth that diligent effort breeds success (confidential interview with Teacher C, 21 February 2016; Institute of the Marist Brothers of the Schools 1988, 36).

In sum, at first glance the Child Rights Network clashed with some well-established structures of schooling, including the strict power imbalance of the teacher–student relationship that, as we saw above, the Crisis and the Tension had intensified. However, resistance to change was not the position for all teachers and students by any means. The next section shows that productive engagement with rights was achieved through its incorporation into the structures of schooling, but not in a way that changed how participants understood the fundamental purpose of Catholic education.

Vernacularising rights within Marist charism

Despite the scepticism noted above, advocates typically framed the child rights approach as a complement to local cultures and Christianity to convince sceptical teachers to adopt them. In respect of discipline and pastoral care, for instance, child rights provided a vocabulary used to support the Marist charism, and that charism was itself a way to enact child rights principles. At Mabiri, Teacher B noted that the school cannot afford to employ a counsellor, nor does the administration have anywhere they can refer students in need of support. They are faced with a choice between expelling a problematic student or counselling that student themselves. Several students were in this position in the first semester of 2016, either through violent behaviour or drug offences. While most teachers were sceptical and favoured expelling students, the administration argued that Marist schools are supposed to work with young people, in Br McDonald's terms, 'on the edge' (interview, 26 April 2017). Thus, abandoning the students would contradict their core principles. Teacher B explained it to his colleagues in precisely these terms:

> [W]hat I used was this idea of this is a Marist school and it's supposed to help the young people. And if I decide to terminate the child from the beginning because the school rules say so, then I live with the fact that I sent someone who is very young home and now he is living at home [and] he hasn't completed his schooling. So to me, that's not very, I think I have failed morally or something, my moral responsibility over the child (confidential interview, 6 June 2016).

There was thus a tension between the application of the school rules, which impose the strict power imbalance between teachers and students and leave several teachers confused (as we saw above), and Teacher B's moral duties to the students in his care. In similar vein, Teacher X pointed out that the Marist charism emphasises constant 'presence' with students, just as child rights have encouraged teachers to be approachable and available to students to support their learning (confidential interview, 6 December 15).

An incident at Tenaru demonstrates that the moral obligation Teacher B described is tied directly to child rights and extends beyond immediate teacher–student relationships. A few years ago the school administration transferred to another school a teacher who was persistently drunk and physically abusive towards his family. When I asked Teacher B what he would have done, he replied:

> I think with the establishment of the, what, child rights and those kind of things … before you send them away make sure you at least you should have tried something to help the teacher before he goes to the new school. Otherwise you send [away] someone who is going to repeat the same problems and you don't want that, to send someone to a community and then he'll just become the same person again (confidential interview, 18 February 2016).

And this is exactly what the administration at Tenaru had done. The troubled teacher was counselled by the Marist Brothers and the school's headmaster (formal counselling services were not accessible) before being transferred. In this instance, the school had deployed child rights principles and the Marist ethos to address conflict-related behaviours in exactly the way the district administration had hoped they would when it established Child Rights Network.

Interestingly also, Teacher B appeared to hold a similar opinion of human rights to the kindergarten teacher who Cox (2017) interviewed; rights were distinct from culture, but still compatible. Teacher B had observed that in resisting child rights some teachers had themselves forgotten that rights do not overrule responsibilities to society:

> [O]ne of the misunderstandings that I think people get is that people got so involved with rights that they forgot the other aspect of rights, and that was the responsibilities that children have in our society. And even to the extent that students were actually [saying] 'I have a right to this, and I have a right to this' and that's because they were not being taught that they also have responsibilities to go in line with that. So to me that's probably one reason why people didn't accept it so easily (confidential interview, 18 February 2016).

In this case, Teacher B appeared to keep the concept of rights distinct from 'the moral framework in which relationships are embedded' (Hermkens 2013, para. 37) because those frameworks were located in the responsibilities of young people in society. Rights, then, were only useful in so much as they could be a tool teachers could deploy when forming students into the (relational) citizens they desire them to be.

This was also borne out in the debate noted above about manual labour. Learning to love work – one of the pillars of the Marist charism – was essential if students were to become good members of their society. Indeed, Teacher B became uncharacteristically intolerant of anyone who did not love working:

> But if you feel that it is not satisfying to you then probably you stop doing it and look for somewhere else where you just sit down … and just wait for something to come to you … So our place is better for people who really work hard in order to survive. So for you to stop someone from really working then I don't think it's probably right (confidential interview, 18 February 2016).

For Teacher B, students must learn to love work because somebody who does not love work does not fit in. And Teacher B told his colleagues that students would learn to love work through the satisfaction they will feel from meeting their responsibilities to the school community.

Child rights could be applied to prevent teachers from working students too hard, but they were not a justification for halting all manual labour. There remained a conceptual distinction between a productive (relational) citizen cognisant of their responsibilities to others, on the one hand, and a rights-holding individual, on the other.

For other teachers and students, however, rights were vernacularised in relational terms in the way Hermkens (2013) described above. Teacher Y argued child rights were a vehicle to teach about obligations to the school community. Rather than scolding a child for doing the wrong thing, she said teachers could talk about how students have the right to make decisions, but are personally responsible for their actions (confidential interview, 4 December 2015). Similarly, despite admitting it confused some students, Teacher S at Tenaru noted how the rights discourse has changed the language she uses when disciplining students: 'when you talk the language you use, not so much as rule, but saying it's your responsibility to attend classes, to be on time, to be in the dining hall' (confidential interview, 1 December 2015).

Occasionally also, teachers would say they had seen evidence of students who understood child rights properly, meaning relationally. For example, Teacher Z remembered asking a male senior student why he never chewed betelnut at school. The boy replied that he had considered it, and ultimately concluded that although he had the right to chew betelnut he respected the school rules (that ban it) first of all (confidential interview, 4 December 2016). To Teacher Z, this response meant that the boy understood 'what is called respect in the village. Because that respect in the village, in our society here, that is the foundation of child rights. He might think he [could] do something, but he has to think [about the consequences of] the action' (ibid.). Thus, Teacher Z argued the boy had understood rights properly because he had fitted them into the 'moral framework in which relationships are embedded' (Hermkens 2013, para. 37).

It is noteworthy here that students and teachers at Tenaru had far more opportunity to adopt the discourse and practice of child rights than those at Mabiri. Mabiri is an all-boys boarding school that only offers two years of schooling (grades 9 and 10 or two years of vocational education), whereas Tenaru, a coeducational boarding school, offers grades 7 to 12. Additionally, Tenaru's workshops themselves better facilitate engagement with child rights. The students' child rights workshops I observed at Mabiri in 2016 were conducted at night with groups of at least 80 students and were condensed to fit the limited time that the school had electricity in the evenings. By contrast, at Tenaru the 24-hour power supply allowed Chris Beatus to teach more creatively to smaller groups of students (interview with Chris Beatus, 13 September 2015). Moreover, Tenaru's teachers had been at the school several years and were familiar with child rights concepts, whereas most of Mabiri's teaching staff had transferred from other non-Marist schools that year and had little prior experience with child rights.

Nevertheless, following sustained critical engagement with child rights and the Marist ethos, some participants described profound changes to their daily lives. Teacher Y, at Tenaru, who had hospitalised a student with his violence during the Tension, told me child rights had helped him temper his disciplinary actions dramatically and embrace pastoral care (confidential interview, 4 December 2015). Teachers S and R were even changing their own parenting, preferring to reason and persuade rather than scold their children (confidential interviews, 14 November and 1 December 2015).

We have seen that this vernacularisation of child rights framed them as either distinct from or part of 'the moral framework in which relationships are embedded' (Hermkens 2013, para. 37). Either way, however, rights language was useful only insofar as it reinforced the image of the citizen into whom the schools aimed to form their students: a Christian and relational person willing to respect authority by showing deference to it. The success of this vernacularisation notwithstanding, the process itself would seem significant for transitional justice because it directly addressed the breakdown of customary authority the Crisis and the Tension brought about.

Learning about justice

The Child Rights Network also gave students and teachers a framework they could use to articulate and address justice issues at school. For example, Teacher R at Tenaru remembered an occasion in which the students of one Grade 9 class confronted one of their teachers about that teacher's ongoing absence from class and failure to hold tests at scheduled times. After the incident the teacher in question felt disrespected and even less committed to teaching, effectively making the situation worse. Although Teacher R admitted that this newfound assertiveness from students made most teachers uncomfortable, he had decided the students had the right to complain if their right to education had been violated (confidential interview, 14 November 2015). Teacher R and this Grade 9 class recognised an injustice in their school and rights discourse gave them a framework in which to respond to it.

Although the students in the example above appeared to make their situation worse, such an outcome was not inevitable, which an episode during my interview with Teacher X at Tenaru demonstrates. It was just before lunchtime on a school day, and we were interrupted by a knock on the door of his house. Two girls in Grade 8, who had just finished their physical education lesson, asked for a drink of water. Teacher X was happy to oblige, and we joined them on the veranda. Technically, the students were out of bounds, but nobody cared. Shortly after, two of their classmates appeared. One was carrying a plastic bag full of vegetables and, once she saw Teacher X, made a false show of hiding it. Everyone laughed, and in doing so we all tacitly acknowledged that their rule-breaking would have no consequences. The girls let us in on their plan for the afternoon. They had left campus to collect the vegetables from a relative of one of the girls living in a nearby village. They would take rice from the dining hall at lunch, then take everything to the kitchen of another staff member to cook there, effectively abstaining from the school's afternoon program. In an effort to dissuade them, Teacher X led a discussion about the decisions they were making, but when they left he was sure they would proceed with their plan. Far from making their situation worse, rights discourse was the framework through which the students were allowed to introduce some diversity into their diet.

Indeed, Teacher X understood this episode in the broader context of child rights and pastoral care. He talked to them about the decisions they were making but did not ultimately enforce the school rules. Moreover, Teacher X was a member of the school's pastoral care committee, which evaluates physical, spiritual and academic life at the school (confidential interview with Teacher S, 13 August 2015). In 2015, the committee had been particularly worried about deficiencies in the students' diet. Teacher X reasoned that if teachers were eating well in their own homes, he had no right to deprive students of variation in their own diet (confidential interview, 15 October 2016). Therefore Teacher X's reaction to the girls' plan was not seen through an authoritarian lens, but through child rights and the Marist charism, which led him to frame the episode as one about the justice of the students' (dietary) situation.

In fact, the teacher–student relationship was rendered largely informal for the hungry students – they knew they could break some rules with impunity. Informal teacher–student relationships were typical of the schools I visited, and this was widely attributed to the hospitality of Melanesian cultures generally. But Teacher Z also explained that:

> They have the right to come and ask me for something that [would] help them … if somebody has missed out in dining hall, for the dinner, and comes to one of the teachers to help him or her with the cooking pot [because] she or he is quite hungry then though the school rule is there – it's late, don't move or do anything after late bell – but we have to make [the exception] because of the situation (confidential interview, 4 December 2016).

Teacher Z used rights language in support of the informality that led to a just outcome consistent with the hospitality of Melanesian sociality and the school's view of its duty of care.

However, Teacher B also identified new risks to the teachers that could arise from the combination of students' awareness of child rights and the informality of teacher–student relationships that allow students to visit teachers in their homes (confidential interview, 24 February 2016). In these circumstances, he worried that students armed with knowledge of rights might allege inappropriate behaviour from a teacher. As a compromise he encouraged teachers to only meet with students in public outside their houses. In this way, Teacher B found a level of formality in the teacher–student relationship that reconciled the rights of students, teachers and his image of Melanesian sociality.

Ironically, an unintended outcome of the articulation of justice issues at school within the frameworks established by child rights and Marist charism may be that it turns teachers away from the formal justice mechanisms of the state. In Bougainville in 2013 teachers at a non-Marist secondary school caught a student dealing drugs on campus. They turned him over to police but the student was murdered while in custody. Chris Beatus argued that if the teachers had respected the rights of the child and adhered to the 'Marist way' they would never have called the police (interview, 13 September 2015). Compare the decision to call the police to the attitude of Teacher B to his students:

> When students do something that's a little bit, ah, naughty. I'd rather talk to them about something that they are good at rather than talk to them about their negative behaviour … And I think to me, it will really save the child because all of a sudden he's going to realise that 'oh someone is noticing my goodness and not noticing my weaknesses all the time'. So to me that's probably the whole change of my outlook on the child too (confidential interview, 18 February 2016).

This change to his 'outlook on the child' came from the application of the Marist ethos which child rights reinforced. He was loath to ever call the police to follow up incidents in the school because he thought it would be too dangerous to leave a child in their care.

Conclusion

The Child Rights Network met with resistance from some teachers, in particular at Mabiri and Tenaru, for reasons entirely consistent with resistance to human rights in Bougainville and Solomon Islands more broadly. Protests that child rights fitted awkwardly with some central aspects of how Mabiri and Tenaru functioned, such as aspirations for strict discipline and the necessity of manual labour, were justified with their perceived incompatibilities with *kastom*. Combined with the more rebellious behaviour of young people (particularly in Bougainville) and the enhanced popular legitimacy of corporal punishment following the Crisis and the Tension, we might have expected that adopting child rights would lead to some fundamental changes to teacher–student relationships at school. This was true to an extent. Thus, although there was no single form of vernacularisation among teachers and students, the initiative brought child rights discourse and began a new regime of practice to the two schools. Child rights offered a vocabulary through which students could see themselves as equals in rights and therefore object to instances of everyday violence and abuse without 'acting BRA'.

Ultimately, however, the vernacularisations of rights at Tenaru and Mabiri changed little about the image of the person into whom teachers hoped to form students. This image was of a person able to fit comfortably within the existing moral frameworks of relationships in society, which implied a reassertion of frameworks of authority (requiring deference from young people) that broke down during the Crisis and Tension. Thus, while in their daily lives at school people interacted creatively with rights, they did so within the established structures of schooling.

Notably, the reassertion of deference to authority through the integration of child rights with the Marist charism is quite different from the role of human rights education envisioned in transitional justice. Human rights education encourages students to model democracy by questioning authority figures critically, but the data presented here suggests the application of transitional justice to education in Melanesia needs an understanding of what modelling democracy looks like locally.

We have also seen that learning to view rights relationally or to use them to identify justice issues is a long-term project because the learning happens in unplanned moments when incidents occur. We saw that teachers and senior students were much more experienced with child rights at Tenaru where the teaching staff was stable and students had up to six years to learn them. By contrast, Mabiri's teachers were mostly new to child rights and the students would have only two years at most to adopt them. Such structural limitations would no doubt limit any transitional justice initiative that other church or government schools would employ.

Finally, it is worth noting an inherent limitation of civil society's involvement in transitional justice through education in Melanesia. An important goal of transitional justice is the rebuilding of trust in democratic institutions. In Solomon Islands, for example, Dinnen (2012, 71) has noted that 'longer-term peace-building and nation-building agendas will require a much closer focus on strengthening the contract between the Solomon Islands state and its citizens'. In transitional justice, because education is considered a state institution, and one with which it is assumed almost all children and parents have contact, improvements in the delivery of education are seen as a way for the state to rebuild its reputation. But when in reality the church schools analysed here performed the education function widely considered a state responsibility, and vernacularisation of rights within their charism encouraged teachers to withdraw from the formal justice system in the name of child protection, civil society would appear to be at odds with the aim of transitional justice to build trust in the state over the longer term.

Bibliography

Akin, David. 2013. *Colonialism, Maasina Rule, and the Origins of Malaitan Kastom*. Centre for Pacific Island Studies. Honolulu: University of Hawai'i Press. doi.org/10.21313/hawaii/9780824838140.001.0001.

Allen, Matthew. 2013. *Greed and Grievance: Ex-Militants' Perspectives on the Conflict in Solomon Islands, 1998–2003*. Honolulu: University of Hawai'i Press. doi.org/10.21313/hawaii/9780824838546.001.0001.

Biersack, Aletta and Martha Macintyre. 2016. 'Introduction: Gender Violence and Human Rights in the Western Pacific'. In *Gender Violence and Human Rights: Seeking Justice in Fiji, Papua New Guinea and Vanuatu*, edited by Aletta Biersack, Margaret Jolly and Martha Macintyre, 1–45. Canberra: ANU Press. doi.org/10.22459/GVHR.12.2016.

Bellino, Michelle. 2014a. 'Whose Past, Whose Present? Historical Memory among the "Postwar" Generation in Guatemala'. In *(Re)Constructing Memory: School Textbooks and the Imagination of the Nation*, edited by James Williams, 131–151. Rotterdam: Sense Publishers. doi.org/10.1007/978-94-6209-656-1_7.

Bellino, Michelle. 2014b. 'Educating for Human Rights Consciousness'. *Listening: Journal of Communication Ethics, Religion, and Culture* Fall: 36–157.

Cole, Elizabeth. 2007. 'Transitional Justice and the Reform of History Education'. *The International Journal of Transitional Justice* 1 (1): 115–137. doi.org/10.1093/ijtj/ijm003.

Cole, Elizabeth. 2017. *No Legacy for Transitional Justice Efforts without Education: Education as an Outreach Partner for Transitional Justice*. New York: International Center for Transitional Justice. www.ictj.org/publication/no-legacy-transitional-justice-efforts-without-education (accessed 17 January 2019).

Cole, Elizabeth and Karen Murphy. 2009. 'History Education Reform, Transitional Justice and the Transformation of Identities'. *International Center for Transitional Justice Research Brief*, 1–4.

Cox, John. 2017. 'Kindy and Grassroots Gender Transformations in Solomon Islands'. In *Transformations of Gender in Melanesia*, edited by Martha Macintyre and Ceridwen Spark, 69–93. Canberra: ANU Press. doi.org/10.22459/TGM.02.2017.03.

Davies, Lynn. 2017a. 'Justice-Sensitive Education: The Implications of Transitional Justice Mechanisms for Teaching and Learning'. *Comparative Education* 53 (3): 333–350. doi.org/10.1080/03050068.2017.1317999.

Davies, Lynn. 2017b. *The Power of a Transitional Justice Approach to Education: Post-Conflict Education Reconstruction and Transitional Justice*. New York: International Center for Transitional Justice. www.ictj.org/publication/power-transitional-justice-approach-education (accessed 17 January 2019).

Dinnen, Sinclair. 2001. 'Restorative Justice and Civil Society in Melanesia: The Case of Papua New Guinea'. In *Restorative Justice and Civil Society*, edited by Heather Strang and John Braithwaite, 99–113. Cambridge: Cambridge University Press.

Dinnen, Sinclair. 2002. 'Winners and Losers: Politics of Disorder in the Solomon Islands 2000–2002'. *The Journal of Pacific History* 37 (3): 285–298. doi.org/10.1080/0022334022000047830.

Dinnen, Sinclair. 2012. 'The Solomon Islands – RAMSI, Transition and Future Prospects'. *Security Challenges* 8 (4): 61–71.

Eriksen, Annelin. 2013. 'Christian Politics in Vanuatu: Lay Priests and New State Forms'. In *Christian Politics in Oceania*, edited by Matt Tomlinson and Debra McDougall, 103–121. New York: Berghahn Books.

Evans, Daniel. 2016. 'Forgotten Voices in the Forgotten Conflict: The Role of Children in Post-Conflict Peacebuilding in Solomon Islands'. *International Journal of Children's Rights* 24 (1): 65–92. doi.org/10.1163/15718182-02304010.

Farran, Sue. 2012. 'Children of the Pacific: Giving Effect to Article 3 UNCRC in Small Island States'. *International Journal of Children's Rights* 20 (2): 199–223. doi.org/10.1163/157181812X622196.

Fraenkel, John. 2004. *The Manipulation of Custom: From Uprising to Intervention in the Solomon Islands*. Canberra: Pandanus Books.

Herdt, Gilbert and Stephen Leavitt. 1998. 'Introduction: Studying Adolescence in Contemporary Pacific Island Communities'. In *Adolescence in Pacific Island Societies*, edited by Gilbert Herdt and Stephen Leavitt, 3–26. Pittsburgh: University of Pittsburgh Press.

Hermkens, Anna-Karrina. 2013. '"Raits Blong Mere"? Framing Human Rights and Gender Relations in Solomon Islands'. In *Intersections: Gender and Sexuality in Asia and the Pacific*, 33 (December), intersections.anu.edu.au/issue33/hermkens.htm (accessed 25 January 2017).

Institute of the Marist Brothers of the Schools. 1988. *In the Footsteps of Marcellin: Marist Educators for Today*. Port Moresby: Institute of the Marist Brothers of the Schools.

Jolly, Margaret. 2016. '"When She Cries Oceans": Navigating Gender Violence in the Western Pacific'. In *Gender Violence and Human Rights: Seeking Justice in Fiji, Papua New Guinea and Vanuatu*, edited by Aletta Biersack, Margaret Jolly and Martha Macintyre, 341–380. Canberra: ANU Press. doi.org/10.22459/GVHR.12.2016.08.

Kent, Stuart and Jon Barnett. 2012. 'Localising Peace: The Young Men of Bougainville's "Crisis Generation"'. *Political Geography* 31 (1): 34–43. doi.org/10.1016/j.polgeo.2011.09.003.

King, Elizabeth. 2014. *From Classrooms to Conflict in Rwanda*. New York: Cambridge University Press. doi.org/10.1017/CBO9781139600217.

Laracy, Hugh. 1976. *Marists and Melanesians: A History of Catholic Missions in the Solomon Islands*. Canberra: Australian National University Press.

McCully, Alan. 2012. 'History Teaching, Conflict and the Legacy of the Past'. *Education, Citizenship and Social Justice* 7 (2): 145–159. doi.org/10.1177/1746197912440854.

McDougall, Debra. 2008. 'Religious Institutions as Alternative Structures in Post-Conflict Solomon Islands? Cases from Western Province'. *State, Society and Governance in Melanesia Discussion Paper* 2008/5. Canberra: ANU.

McDougall, Debra. 2016. *Engaging with Strangers: Love and Violence in Rural Solomon Islands*. New York: Berghan Books. doi.org/10.2307/j.ctvgs09mh.

Merry, Sally Engle. 2006a. *Human Rights and Gender Violence: Translating International Law into Local Justice*. Chicago: University of Chicago Press. doi.org/10.7208/chicago/9780226520759.001.0001.

Merry, Sally Engle. 2006b. 'Transnational Human Rights and Local Activism: Mapping the Middle'. *American Anthropologist* 108 (1): 38–51. doi.org/10.1525/aa.2006.108.1.38.

Monson, Rebecca. 2013. 'Vernacularising Political Participation: Strategies of Women Peace-Builders in Solomon Islands'. *Intersections: Gender and Sexuality in Asia and the Pacific*. 33 (December), intersections.anu.edu.au/issue33/monson.htm (accessed 25 January 2017).

Moore, Clive. 2004. *Happy Isles in Crisis: The Historical Causes for a Failing State in Solomon Islands, 1998–2004*. Canberra: Asia Pacific Press.

Oakeshott, David and Matthew Allen. 2015. 'Schooling as a "Stepping-Stone to National Consciousness" in Solomon Islands: The Last Twenty Years'. *SSGM Discussion Paper* 2015/8. Canberra: ANU.

Palmer, Bruce. 1980. 'Options for the Development of Education in the Solomon Islands: A Critical Analysis'. PhD thesis, University of New England.

Paulson, Julia. 2009. *(Re)creating Education in Postconflict Contexts: Transitional Justice, Education, and Human Development.* Research Report. New York: International Center for Transitional Justice.

Paulson, Julia and Michelle Bellino. 2017. 'Truth Commissions, Education, and Positive Peace: An Analysis of Truth Commission Final Reports (1980–2015)'. *Comparative Education* 53 (3): 351–378. doi.org/10.1080/0305006 8.2017.1334428.

Quaynor, Laura. 2012. 'Citizenship Education in Post-Conflict Contexts: A Review of the Literature'. *Education, Citizenship and Social Justice* 7 (1): 33–57. doi.org/10.1177/1746197911432593.

Ramírez-Barat, Clara and Roger Duthie. 2015. *Education and Transitional Justice: Opportunities and Challenges for Peacebuilding.* New York: International Center for Transitional Justice. www.ictj.org/sites/default/files/ICTJ-UNICEF-Report-EducationTJ-2015.pdf (accessed 14 August 2017).

Regan, Anthony. 1998. 'Causes and Course of the Bougainville Conflict'. *The Journal of Pacific History* 33 (3): 269–285. doi.org/10.1080/00223349808572878.

Richmond, Oliver. 2011. 'De-romanticising the Local, De-mystifying the International: Hybridity in Timor Leste and the Solomon Islands'. *The Pacific Review* 24 (1): 115–136. doi.org/10.1080/09512748.2010.546873.

Soaki, Pauline. 2017. 'Casting Her Vote: Women's Political Participation in Solomon Islands'. In *Transformations of gender in Melanesia*, edited by Martha Macintyre and Ceridwen Spark, 95–114. ANU Press: Canberra. doi.org/10.22459/TGM.02.2017.04.

Taylor, John. 2008. 'The Social Life of Rights: "Gender Antagonism", Modernity and *Raet* in Vanuatu'. *The Australian Journal of Anthropology* 19 (2): 165–178. doi.org/10.1111/j.1835-9310.2008.tb00120.x.

Tomlinson, Matt and Debra McDougall. 2013. 'Introduction: Christian Politics in Oceania'. In *Christian Politics in Oceania*, edited by Matt Tomlinson and Debra McDougall, 1–21. New York: Berghahn Books.

10

Mis-selling transitional justice: The confused role of faith-based actors and Christianity in Solomon Islands' Truth and Reconciliation Commission

Claire Cronin

In 2008, five years after the arrival of RAMSI (the Regional Assistance Mission to Solomon Islands), which ostensibly brought an end to the country's 'ethnic tensions', Solomon Islands established its Truth and Reconciliation Commission (TRC). The vocabulary and rhetoric of truth and reconciliation were first introduced in this post-conflict environment by faith-based organisation SICA (the Solomon Islands Christian Association) (TRC 2012, 9). The paradigm of transitional justice had been notably absent from the country's post-conflict discourse until this time, with previous peacebuilding work either having been informed by RAMSI's narrowly focused state-building agenda,[1] or taking the form of small-scale reconciliation projects spearheaded by *kastom*[2] and faith leaders.

---

1   RAMSI's work was informed by a three-'pillar' framework consisting of a focus on law and justice, economic governance and growth, and machinery of government. The machinery of government pillar focused on strengthening national accountability institutions, bolstering parliament and the electoral system and strengthening provincial systems of government. Some scholars claim that RAMSI's focus on policing and state-building came at the expense of delving into the underlying structural inequalities in the country that had led to the conflict in the first place (for more information, see Braithwaite et al. 2010).

2   The concept of *kastom* in Solomon Islands loosely corresponds to the concept of 'custom' or tradition, but is more nuanced, being closely tied to the country's complex colonial history. *Kastom*, as it

SICA proposed that a truth and reconciliation commission would provide a necessary opportunity for victims of the ethnic tensions to talk about their experiences, would assist in the fulfilment of the government's 'National Unity' agenda[3] and would be accepted as a morally legitimate institution, both by the Solomon Islands people and by the international community. Influenced by international media attention surrounding South Africa's Truth and Reconciliation Commission, the organisation proposed that the theological overtones of the South African truth commission would resonate with the country's 96 per cent Christian population. In this small Pacific Island country, civil society is overwhelmingly composed of faith-based actors and as such it is difficult to extrapolate faith-based organisations (FBOs) from a hypothetical secular civil society base – even a number of the international NGOs with bases in the country operate from within a faith-based perspective.[4] Solomon Islands' civil society, therefore, overwhelmingly grounds its understanding of morality and justice in biblical theology, and Christian subjectivities are integral to public understandings of both social justice and appropriate responses to injustice.

Being a transitional justice initiative, however, the TRC grounded its analysis of the violence that occurred during the ethnic tensions in the internationally normative, arguably secular,[5] framework of international human rights law, and the related fields of international humanitarian and criminal law. Transitional justice evolved alongside the international human rights system as a means of enabling nations to come to terms with the aftermath of mass human rights violations, crimes against

---

is currently understood, connotes a way of life and set of values distinguishable from that of outsiders, and an ideology that governs one's interactions with each other, God, the land and the ancestral spirits.

3   The concepts of 'national unity' and reconciliation have been pertinent in Solomon Islands' politics since before the ethnic tensions. From 1993 to 1997, for example, Mamaloni led the Group for National Unity and Reconciliation (GNUR), forming the leading government political party from 1994 to 1997. Following the Townsville Peace Agreement (TPA) in 2000, the government established the Ministry of National Unity, Reconciliation and Peace (MNURP) to oversee implementation of the TPA.

4   For example, World Vision has a main office in Honiara and regional offices through the country. As this chapter will describe, Caritas has a notable presence in Solomon Islands, particularly with regards to providing training for trauma counsellors.

5   I say 'arguably secular', as many scholars (see, for example, Moyn's discussion in *Christianity and Human Rights*, 2015) have located the origins of the modern human rights discourse in Christian moral traditions. Therefore, whilst the discourse today stands as a secular one, its origins may be traced to Christian theology.

humanity and genocide (Robertson 2012; Hayner 2010; Teitel 2002).[6] Although the international legal norms underpinning transitional justice were blended, seemingly successfully, with theological notions such as forgiveness and interpersonal reconciliation in post-apartheid South Africa (Tutu 2000; Shore 2008), from the outset of the Solomon Islands experience a disconnect was evident between the ideological framework through which the TRC would eventually operate (international, secular), and the framework through which the public expected the TRC to operate (local, faith-based). During my 16 months of doctoral fieldwork in Solomon Islands, I was consistently told that the TRC had failed 'to touch the heart of the people'. I propose that this failure to strike a chord with the sentiment of the local population may in part be due to a gulf between people's expectations of, and the realities of, the ideological underpinnings of the TRC's work.

This chapter analyses the way faith-based civil society in Solomon Islands 'sold' the concept of a truth commission to the Solomon Islands public. It argues that an overemphasis on the role that Christianity and the church might play in a future commission's work, and an underemphasis on the central role that the international human rights framework would play, was at least partially responsible for the groundswell in public support for the TRC's establishment. I draw upon Sally Engle Merry's concept of 'vernacularisation' to support this argument. The concept refers to the translation of transnational justice discourses into local settings, and the layering that occurs when the subjectivities associated with these discourses (for example, victims and perpetrators of human rights abuses) come into contact with local discourses and subjectivities. Merry writes that vernacularisation:

> … requires … changes in the form and presentation of human rights ideas and institutions. First, they need to be framed in images, symbols, narratives, and religious or secular language that resonate with the local community … Second, they need to be tailored to the structural conditions of the place where they are deployed, including its economic, political, and kinship systems (Merry 2006, 220).

---

6   Most scholars agree that the original transitional justice project was the Nuremberg Trials of war criminals following the Holocaust that gave way to the creation of the Universal Declaration of Human Rights (UDHR) and the International Genocide Convention. Eventually, these paved the way for the International Bill of Rights (the UDHR alongside the International Covenant of Civil and Political Rights (ICCPR) and the International Covenant on Economic, Social and Cultural Rights (ICESCR)) and the Rome Statute of the International Criminal Court (ICC).

Vernaculisation occurs along a continuum, with replication at one end and hybridisation at the other. With replication, '[t]he adaptation is superficial and primarily decorative' (Merry 2006, 220), whereas hybridisation occurs when there is a greater depth of assimilation between the various justice discourses that come together. This chapter asks the question: did the Solomon Islands TRC achieve hybridisation between human rights and local understandings of morality and justice rooted in Christianity and *kastom*, or was the human rights discourse merely 'superficial' and 'decorative'?

My analysis is based on the PhD fieldwork I conducted between 2012 and 2014, and my doctoral thesis that uses a post-colonial and post-conflict lens to scrutinise the success of the Solomon Islands TRC. My fieldwork consisted of ethnographic research spanning 16 months in Honiara (the largest city on Guadalcanal and also the nation's capital), Auki (the largest city on Malaita) and the Marau Sounds area on Guadalcanal's rural coastline. During this time, I conducted approximately 75 interviews and held countless informal conversations with people regarding the work of the TRC.

Faith-based advocacy for a truth and reconciliation commission

A transitional justice approach was absent from the peacebuilding agenda in Solomon Islands until SICA began to advocate for the establishment of a truth and reconciliation commission in the early 2000s – the same time that the South African Truth and Reconciliation Commission was wrapping up its analysis of the human rights abuses committed under 20 years of apartheid. Some scholars have asserted that previous attempts to achieve justice for crimes committed during the conflict – for example, the RAMSI-led tension trials[7] – fell under the transitional justice umbrella (Jeffery 2017, 113–139). However, these prosecutions drew upon domestic criminal law only, making no mention of international human rights standards. Significantly, the tension trials involved no prosecutions

---

7   During the 'tension trials', hundreds of ex-combatants were arrested by RAMSI police to await trial on charges that included murder, arson, theft, extortion, corruption and embezzlement. Arrests and prosecutions were made in accordance with the Solomon Islands Penal Code. For example, 'big fish' Harold Keke, Ronnie Cawa and Francis Lela were charged with the murder of Fr Augustine Geve and sentenced to mandatory life imprisonment in accordance with section 202(a) of the Penal Code.

for rape – one of the most prevalent human rights violations committed during the conflict – demonstrating a lack of concern for prosecuting criminals as human rights offenders. As well as lacking a human rights focus, previous government-led initiatives overlooked the rehabilitation needs of victims, instead focusing on appeasing ex-combatants. For example, in 2000/2001 the Solomon Islands Government oversaw a large-scale compensation scheme with funds from a Taiwanese loan. Those who felt that had a legitimate claim to government compensation registered to be beneficiaries of the EXIM (Export-Import) loan with the Ministry for National Unity, Reconciliation and Peace (MNURP). Yet most of the successful applicants were ex-combatants rather than victims of abuse. The compensation process was widely perceived as corrupt – a commercialisation of traditional *kastom* compensation wherein financial gifts would only be token, preceded by acknowledgement of wrongs and reconciliation between parties (Braithwaite et al. 2010, 46).[8]

SICA proposed that victims of violence needed an opportunity to share their stories in order to heal and move on from their traumatic pasts. In an effort to garner support from other members of Solomon Islands' civil society, SICA was instrumental in forming the Civil Society Network – a collaboration of women's groups, church groups, trade unions, other non-governmental organisations and the Chamber of Commerce. In spite of SICA and the Civil Society Network's efforts, a succession of national governments overlooked their demands, and although attempts were made to garner support from foreign advisers during peacebuilding talks, the notion was dismissed on the grounds that 'you [Solomon Islands] don't have a Mandela' (interview with Matthew Wale, 5 July 2012).

Influential within SICA were a small group of progressive Christians with close connections to international civil society – for example, politician and women's rights campaigner Alice Pollard, and her husband Bob Pollard, the head of Transparency International Solomon Islands (TISI). Most of this small group were members of the Kukum Campus of the South Seas Evangelical Church in Honiara – a parish well known for its political activism and commitment to social justice. Although he himself asserts that TRC advocacy was very much a joint effort of this group,

---

8   After the Solomon Islands Government threatened to switch loyalties to China, Taiwan's EXIM (Export-Import) Bank agreed to a loan of US$25 million, most of which made its way into the pockets of politicians and ex-combatants. Allan Kemakeza who was initially the Minister for National Unity, Reconciliation and Peace during this time, later prime minister, awarded himself US$164,754 and was dismissed for embezzlement (Brady 2010, 166; Fraenkel in Dinnen and Firth 2008, 153).

most people I interviewed during my fieldwork insisted that the TRC was the brainchild of Matthew Wale – then director of the SICA Peace Office, now MP for the Aoke/Langalanga constituency and briefly deputy prime minister in 2015. Wale states that the Peace Office 'tried to harness the *immense* amount of goodwill that rested with the churches, lots of social capital which was not being brought to bear on the conflict; well it was being brought to bear but in [an] anecdotal and a not very well organised fashion' (interview, 5 July 2012). Wale, a half-Canadian, half–Solomon Islander politician, is an example of someone Merry might refer to as a 'translator'. Brought up in Melanesia and educated overseas, he has one foot in the 'local' arena and one in the 'global', fluent in the justice vocabularies of both.[9] In our interview, Wale's rationale for proposing a TRC was overwhelmingly framed in terms of concern for human rights protections in the country. He told me:

> [I]n my mind there were ... themes that were coming out very clearly. One is the general lack of respect for human rights, and understanding human rights ... two, what I really wanted to see was a standing human rights commission, a constitutional human rights commission (Interview, 5 July 2012).

In 2002, Wale visited South Africa to consult with the TRC's principle legal counsel and its chair, the Archbishop Desmond Tutu. Tutu had famously woven overtly Christian theology and symbolism into the truth commission model, overlaying the international human rights norms integral to a transitional justice approach with Christian notions of confession, forgiveness and interpersonal reconciliation grounded in biblical teaching. Although the church had played a role in previous truth commissions (for example, the Catholic Church was a key advocate for Chile's truth commission), it was the South African experience that truly brought Christian theology to the forefront of the TRC's moral philosophy (Cronin 2017, 41). For Solomon Islands' civil society, the South African commission appeared to be a ready-made hybrid, well suited to their pluralistic and strongly Christian society and promising to offer something to everybody.

---

9   This was evident in our initial conversation, which I later noted had tended to flow between the vernaculars of *kastom* and Christianity, and the international human rights lexicon.

Community-based advocacy

As government-level advocacy was falling on deaf ears, SICA turned their attention instead to gathering grassroots support for their cause. Between November 2002 and August 2003, the SICA Peace Committee travelled around the country to engage in community dialogue and gauge levels of public support for a truth and reconciliation commission. With assistance from an international non-government organisation, the International Center for Transitional Justice (ICTJ), SICA relied on its church networks to assist with awareness-raising, the recruitment of participants and setting up of focus group meetings. The whole effort was perceived by the public to be very much a faith-based initiative; as such, the proposed truth commission came to be seen as faith-based as well (interview with Joseph Foukona, former SICA Peace Office employee, 2013).

The outcome of the dialogue suggested that the public overwhelmingly favoured establishing a South African–style truth commission. However, my interviews with both SICA and TRC staff, and with community members, suggest that this groundswell of public support may have been due to a misrepresentation of the ideologies intrinsic to the TRC model. It seems that SICA staff marketed the idea of a truth commission to the Solomon Islands public by underplaying the role that the international legal framework (international human rights, criminal and humanitarian law) would play in the workings of a commission. They instead overemphasised the role that Christianity, theological understandings of and responses to suffering, and the church might play. For example, a 2002 pamphlet reads:

> For SICA, the importance of truth, justice and reconciliation are central themes of scripture, drawing from the very nature of God … Christians are being shaken awake to have concern for justice, by the evidence of frightening injustice in the world in which we live… social justice is at the heart of the gospel, for it reflects the heart of God (SICA pamphlet 2002).

I am in no way suggesting that there was a wilful misleading of the Solomon Islands public. Rather, at this early stage of advocacy, it was envisaged that a truth commission would function as an indigenous initiative in which both spiritual and *kastom* leaders would play central roles. This perspective persisted through the early days of the TRC's implementation, with RAMSI adamantly stating that it would play no role in the truth-seeking process, leaving this to Solomon Islanders to both own and implement (Braithwaite et al. 2010, 81). It was envisioned that a truth-telling process in which both victims and perpetrators were able to tell their stories would lead to both interpersonal and interethnic reconciliation – ultimately contributing to the broader goal of achieving 'national unity'. The concept of reconciliation has particular pertinence in Solomon Islands as it forms as an area of key conceptual overlap between *kastom* and Christianity (Allen et al. 2013). For Solomon Islands *kastom*, reconciliation practices have long been used to maintain social stability following conflict. With the Christianisation of the country, prayers and practices of public confession and forgiveness have been incorporated into *kastom* reconciliation ceremonies in addition to the traditional exchange of pigs, shell money and food. Today, these ceremonies are equally likely to be overseen by a priest as by a chief, and in many communities this may actually be the same person.

Once the TRC was eventually established in 2008, it had a mandate to 'examin[e] the nature, antecedents, root causes, accountability or responsibility for and the extent of the impact on human rights violations or abuses which occurred between 1st January 1998 and 23rd July 2003' and, vaguely, 'engag[e] all stakeholders in the reconciliation process' (Solomon Islands Truth and Reconciliation Act 2008, sections 5(b) and 5(a)). Over a period of five years (the TRC's work was extended due to problems with funding and human resources, as well as the untimely passing away of Commissioner George Kejoa in 2011), the TRC conducted public and private hearings, took statements from victims and perpetrators of rights violations, investigated the location of graves and conducted exhumations, and compiled a Final Report that was handed to parliament in April 2012.

Mis-selling truth and reconciliation

The key problem with SICA's representation of the balance of ideologies intrinsic to the transitional justice approach lies in the contested nature of using the human rights discourse as a means of framing violence and injustice in Solomon Islands. Unlike in many other countries, this discourse did not develop as a language of political resistance against an oppressive state,[10] but, rather, has been promoted post-independence by international and intergovernmental agencies such as the United Nations and international secular NGOs such as Oxfam and Save the Children.

Indeed, it is only really in the conflict and post-conflict years that the human rights vocabulary has begun to flourish. Instead, historically, *kastom* could be argued to have been the primary language of political resistance. Both Akin and Keesing have documented how anti-colonial movements such as Maasina Rule in Malaita and the Moro Movement in Southern Guadalcanal appropriated *kastom* as a political ideology to distinguish the values and norms of Solomons society from those of the colonial government (Akin 2013; Keesing 1982). Akin writes that the term *kastom*:

> labelled a political ideology and actions founded on Malaitans' determination to pursue change on their own terms, according to their own sensibilities … [*kastom* demarcated] a realm that the government was to leave fully to Malaitans and that furthermore would include almost everything. *Kastom* became a voracious category, encompassing all things over which Malaitans now claimed authority … eventually including people's refusal of European rule … (Akin 2013, 7).

Contemporary faith-based organisations tend to view their mandates as morally rather than politically motivated, and today *kastom* has taken a backseat to theological values in their work. Despite *kastom* having its own moral underpinnings (Stritecky 2002), Christianity is generally favoured as the higher authority with regards to questions of morality. In addition, the growth in faith-based civil society in Solomon Islands can be partially attributed to links with global church networks that provide support, ideological motivation for engaging in social justice work, and funding from international faith-based NGOs.

Having said this, in forming the Civil Society Network, SICA demonstrated its willingness to engage with more secular-minded CSOs and non-profit organisations in order to achieve its objectives – which were both moral *and* political in nature. Morgan Wairiu suggests that the formation of the Civil Society Network demonstrated the determination of civil society

---

10   Skinner, for example, has traced the development of the human rights movement in South Africa in resistance to apartheid. Human rights was a popular political resistance discourse at the time when South Africa established its Truth and Reconciliation Commission (Skinner 2010).

'to bring about a new political order' in the face of government inaction over the ethnic tensions (Wairiu 2006). My interview with Matthew Wale suggests a willingness on the part of faith-based organisations in Solomon Islands to adopt a human rights framework where it was expedient and convincing to do so. SICA, as 'intermediaries' or 'translators' of transnational justice discourses, 'danced'[11] between justice lexicons depending on their advocacy audience, translating human rights ideas 'down', and translating customary and religious ideas 'up'. As Merry states:

> Translators negotiate the middle field of power and opportunity … These people translate up and down. They reframe local grievances up by portraying them as human rights violations. They translate transnational ideas and practices down as ways of grappling with particular local problems. In other words, they remake transnational ideas in local terms. At the same time, they reinterpret local ideas and grievances in the language of national and international human rights (Merry 2006, 42).

Human rights activism – a limited trajectory

However, it is important to recognise the fact that in Solomon Islands, as in the broader Pacific Islands region more generally, the human rights discourse has developed along a very specific trajectory – a limited one, concerned on the one hand with the protection of perceived vulnerable groups (women, children and, more recently, people with disabilities), and on the other hand with the promotion of gender equality, and as such it has come to be seen as synonymous with these particular issues. Only a limited number of civil society organisations have adopted a rights-based approach to advocacy – primarily women's and children's rights organisations. This trend is also reflected in Solomon Islands' international human rights treaty ratification. The country is a State Party to only four of the nine major international human rights treaties, including the United Nations Convention on the Rights of the Child (UNCRC) and the Convention on the Elimination of All Forms of Discrimination Against Women (CEDAW).

---

11   The idea of 'dancing' between vernaculars depending on the audience you are presenting an idea to was given to me by an interview with a World Vision staff member in Honiara. She suggested that in advocating for human rights protections, different terminology was thrown back and forth between herself and her audience, like a dance, until eventually they found middle ground and a common understanding.

The tendency to conflate human rights with a limited notion of women's rights or children's rights, rather than understanding the discourse as a universal system of protection that applies equally to the whole population, means that for some people I interviewed during my fieldwork, particularly men in rural communities, approaching the topic was fraught with emotional sensitivities. The concept of human rights was described to me as dangerous and subversive: its association with individual agency, freedom of choice and the redistribution of power between men and women was seen to threaten family and community cohesion, and contribute to the dissolution of traditional authority. Although rights advocates insist that gender inequality was never intrinsic to Solomon Islands *kastom*; nevertheless, *kastom* is often invoked as a justification for women's subordination in the home and public life (Cox 2017). One interviewee told me that women's awareness of human rights was the reason for increasing levels of family violence, as men found it necessary to try to re-establish the gender hierarchy that was being destabilised (interview with anonymous ex-combatant, 2013). For many, this challenge to traditional authority was synonymous with the 'dark side' of human rights – children and young people were increasingly 'aware of their rights' and were challenging the traditionally unchallenged authority of their chiefs and elders. This new awareness of 'rights' and alternative ways of living was described as being made visible through the clothing young people chose to wear. Older Solomon Islanders in particular, when asked about their views on human rights, would often describe how young women were starting to wear shorts and trousers, or boys were wearing messy clothing. This change in dress and the emphasis it expressed on individual choice or an allegiance to an urban or external group, as opposed to prescribed traditional authority, was seen as a threat to the moral fabric of village life and disrespectful to *kastom*.[12] For some, human rights awareness and its individualistic mentality was perceived as anarchic, subversive and chaotic.

This anxiety over human rights may be linked to the rapid modernisation and urbanisation that the conflict has catalysed. As the country's young population has migrated from rural to urban centres in search of work, adventure and the camaraderie of friends, they have experienced greater

---

12   In rural areas of Solomon Islands, 'modern' or non-traditional clothing is associated with Honiara and Auki – urban centres where young people have greater exposure to foreigners and foreign influences such as rock and rap music. Band T-shirts, for example, have become increasingly popular – demonstrating allegiance with a particular music group or style of music, usually from overseas.

exposure to foreigners and new forms of knowledge through affordable and accessible communications, as well as access to 'Western' ideologies such as human rights. This is creating a crisis of authority, as young people increasingly use new information to challenge the traditional authority of their elders and chiefs (and women challenge the authority of men).

The degree to which the Solomon Islands Government has been willing to embrace campaigns that have focused on ending 'family' violence, while simultaneously resisting calls for increased gender equality in public institutions such as parliament, should also be noted. When human rights have been promoted in terms of their capacity to protect, they have been embraced; however, when rights have been promoted in terms of their capacity to empower, they have been resisted. According to an understanding of rights as protection, certain groups of people who are perceived as less able to defend themselves are offered protection from a benevolent state, partner or family, against something that can generally (or outwardly) be agreed upon as morally abhorrent – for example, rape or domestic violence.[13] Alternatively, rights as empowerment is less easy to universally accept as this requires a redistribution of power (for example, from men to women, from adults to children) and an unsettling of the protector/protected dichotomy.

It is within this context that SICA attempted to sell the truth commission model to the Solomon Islands public. With the knowledge of how a human rights approach might ostracise many and discourage certain members of the community from taking part in a truth commission, the language of human rights violations was not a key part of SICA's advocacy to the population at large. Just as SICA had carefully switched between justice discourses depending on their intended audience, so too did the TRC once it was established. A TRC researcher I interviewed told me that he could never use rights vocabulary collecting people's statements because 'human rights is a concept you talk about in English, it just wouldn't make any sense to people if I tried to talk about it in my own language' (interview with TRC researcher, 2014).

---

13   Although most people I have spoken to in Solomon Islands would never outwardly say that domestic violence is acceptable, research conducted in the 2007 Family Health and Safety Study suggests that both men and women believe that there are circumstances in which a man is justified in hitting his wife.

Amnesty – bridging human rights and theology

As human rights is also widely perceived as a legal justice discourse, its use might have discouraged people further, for fear that the truth-telling process would lead to arrests. When the TRC was officially launched in 2008, the shadow of RAMSI's tension trials, still ongoing at the time, meant that very few ex-combatants agreed to take part. The unwillingness of ex-combatants to engage with the TRC may also be related to the Solomon Islands' decision not to offer amnesty in exchange for testimony regarding politically motivated crimes. The promise of amnesties in South Africa's truth-telling process was at least partially responsible for its success in blending the legally based human rights approach with theological notions of confession and forgiveness. Like sinners confessing to a priest, perpetrators were offered legal absolution by the commission's lawyers if they were able to convince them that their crimes had been politically motivated. It was a true mix of judicial and theological approaches to establishing and absolving (criminal and personal) responsibility. This practice also succeeded in bringing both victims and perpetrators together in one, mediated, space allowing the commission to fulfil its mandate of promoting interpersonal reconciliation – an area in which the Solomon Islands TRC fell short.

Solomon Islands chose not to offer amnesty in exchange for testimony partially because of its previous, unsuccessful attempt to offer amnesty through the Amnesty Acts of 2000 and 2001. These laws legislated a key provision of the Townsville Peace Agreement (TPA) that specified two types of amnesty to be offered to ex-combatants. First, members of the two primary militia groups, the Isatabu Freedom Movement (IFM) and the Malaitan Eagle Force (MEF), would be given immunity from prosecution for stealing and possessing weapons if those weapons were surrendered. Second, a general amnesty offered immunity for all who took part in conflict-related crimes (including members of the Solomon Islands Police Force and Prison Service). When RAMSI took control of law and order in 2003, they paid little heed to these amnesty provisions in their arrests and prosecutions. According to Fraenkel, 'There are only two reported cases in which amnesty was granted by the courts *Nokia v Regina* (on appeal it was *Regina v* Maga and Rv Lusibaea, Bartlett, Kili and Fioga). There is no record of the latter in the High Court registry' (Fraenkel, Madraiwiwi and Okole 2014, 4).

Rather than specifically offering amnesty in exchange for testimony, the Truth and Reconciliation Commission Act contained a clause that guaranteed that no information provided through TRC testimony would be admissible as evidence in a court of law (Solomon Islands Truth and Reconciliation Commission Act 2008, Part VI, section 20(f)). The spirit of this provision was undermined, however, when RAMSI police arrested ex-combatants as they testified. Guthrey documents how RAMSI officers arrested a member of the Black Sharks militia group in Western Province as they were testifying to the TRC. This arrest undermined any attempts made by the Commission to convince ex-combatants of its independence from RAMSI, and of their of safety in sharing their stories (Guthrey 2015, 36).

The Forgiveness Bill

Many government leaders and ex-combatants were unhappy with the TRC's unwillingness to offer amnesty and, in 2009, Sam Iduri, then Minister for National Unity, Reconciliation and Peace, proposed a 'Forgiveness Bill'. With heavily theological overtones, the proposed Bill mimicked the amnesty provisions of the South African TRC, offering amnesty to ex-combatants including those who were already in prison. This Bill was a more overt example of selling a political product to the Solomon Islands people through appealing to Christian values. In July 2009, Iduri told the media that a Forgiveness Bill Steering Committee had been established and was in discussion with the churches before the conversation would be rolled out to the public through a national consultation (Jeffery 2017, 130). TRC commissioners strongly objected to the Bill, however, on both human rights and spiritual grounds, and the consultation fell flat before it started. On the one hand, commissioners felt that offering amnesty to people responsible for human rights abuses would not assist the reconciliation process, arguing that the idea would amount to 'some kind of process to remove the responsibility for crimes committed during conflict from former militants and perpetrators … without conceding justice to the victims. Impunity is not helpful for reconciliation' (TRC 2012, 746). On the other hand, commissioners reasoned that forgiveness is a deeply personal process that must remain the 'sole prerogative and domain of the victims' (TRC 2012, 746). This prerogative should not be politicised or legislated for the benefit of ex-militia and should not become seen as a necessary prerequisite to reconciliation and healing. Christianity, therefore, and the prerogative to forgive associated with a Christian subjectivity, was understood as having moral pre-eminence in the *personal* realm, whereas human rights was to take moral pre-eminence in the *political* realm. One (the political morality of human rights) could be legislated, the other (the personal morality of Christianity) could and should not be.

Ostracisation of faith-based organisations and the church

Despite initial attempts to replicate the theological tone of the South African Truth and Reconciliation Commission, church leaders eventually came to feel ostracised by the truth-seeking process. The public face of the commission, particularly at its inception, was Christian. For example, Archbishop Desmond Tutu was invited to Solomon Islands to oversee the TRC's inauguration. Following a grand opening ceremony in Honiara on 29 April 2009, Tutu told an interviewer that peace 'will happen here because God wants to give you the gift called peace and secondly prosperity, such a beautiful place, it looks like the Garden of Eden' (Tutu on Radio Australia 2009). Following in the footsteps of South Africa, the Chair of the Commission was a member of the clergy – Anglican priest Father Sam Ata. Public hearings were also regularly held at churches, and church staff assisted with the overall logistics of the hearings.

Partially, the feeling of ostracisation that eventuated was a result of administrative issues: the United Nations Development Program (UNDP) took on board the financial management of the TRC, and it came to be viewed as marred by UN bureaucracy, delays and mismanagement. There were disagreements between the MNURP and UNDP over ownership and management, including the extent to which the commission should remain free from government interference. This was complicated further by the fact that many of the TRC staff were seconded from government departments, in particular the MNURP, so it was difficult for secondees to know where their allegiances should lie. Among the internal politics, UNDP took control of the financial and logistical management of the commission, further neutralising any ideological influence that the church and civil society might have had. An anonymous interviewee told me that the TRC never really reached out to the church, which was unfortunate considering the influence of faith-based organisations in its establishment.

'It was the TRC's role, to really bring the church in', the interviewee told me, 'and they just never really did it effectively' (anonymous interview, 2012). The ICTJ attempted to bring the church and the TRC together, holding workshops for church leaders in an effort to make them vehicles for awareness raising, but they were largely unsuccessful.

However, this ostracisation was also due to the fact that the TRC's analysis of the violence experienced during the tensions was firmly grounded in international human rights, international humanitarian and international criminal justice norms: Christianity played no official role. For example, TRC staff collected statements from individuals based on a list of predetermined categories of rights violations grounded in definitions of crimes against humanity in the Rome Statute of the International Criminal Court. Despite having no legal ramifications (as the TRC had no judicial powers and Solomon Islands had not ratified the Rome Statute):

> the concern was to have some internationally-recognized benchmark as a guide to assessing the violations of human rights and international humanitarian law which occurred during the armed conflict … in present circumstances, it is being referred to as a reference point in which to contextualize the violations and criminal acts that were committed during the period (TRC 2012, 356).

One interviewee described the statement-taking process as 'majorly problematic', saying 'there wasn't a great opportunity for stream of thought responses, it was a questionnaire – were you sexually abused, yes or no … it was highly problematic' (anonymous interview, 2013). The TRC also failed to incorporate reconciliation in any immediate way into its work, as had been originally envisioned. Instead – truth seeking through statement taking, interviews and public hearings was portrayed as an essential prerequisite to the achievement of national unity – an elusive concept that might happen at a much later date.

Interestingly, following the unofficial release of the report by editor Terry Brown,[14] Wale expressed disappointment that the TRC would be unlikely to lead to the establishment of a war crimes tribunal. As Solomon Islands is a signatory, but not yet a full State Party, to the Rome Statute, even if it were to ratify the Statute now (as per the TRC's recommendations), its provisions are not retrospectively applicable. The most that can be hoped for is that future membership of the ICC (and the threat of prosecution for war crimes and crimes against humanity this brings) might deter individuals from committing crimes against international law in the future. This demonstrates that international human rights and humanitarian standards were extremely important in SICA's expectations of the TRC's function – even if this was not articulated to the public during the initial public consultations.

Spiritual counselling in the TRC process

On an unofficial level, however, Christianity continued to play a subtle yet powerful role in the functioning of the TRC, and this was at the coalface of interaction between staff and the people who testified. Limited human resources in Solomon Islands mean that different sectors of society are relatively porous, and skilled individuals tend to move between civil society, state and intergovernmental sectors as opportunities present themselves. In the case of the TRC, Caritas-trained counsellors were commissioned to provide psychological support to victims and perpetrators the evening before they provided their testimonies. Psychological and psychiatric services in Solomon Islands are extremely limited and most trauma counselling in the post-conflict period has been conducted by the church. As such, counselling tends to have deeply spiritual overtones, and places great emphasis on interpersonal forgiveness and reconciliation.

Counsellors had a very limited amount of time with each person on the evening before they gave their testimony, and tried to utilise their time in the most efficient way possible. Most people who testified had never shared their story in public before, and were extremely nervous about

---

14   In 2014, the TRC Report's editor released the report unofficially via his email networks as a result of his frustration with parliament's refusal to release the report to the public. Despite clauses in the TRC Act that obligate parliament to make the report available to the public immediately after its receipt, parliament and the Prime Minister's Office have repeatedly refused to do so. Reasons cited for this refusal include the report's apparent 'sensitivity', its likelihood to incite further violence, and the cost burden that implementing the TRC's recommendations will put on the government.

what they would say once on stage before a group of TRC commissioners, an audience and a television camera. As such, counselling sessions tended to evolve into coaching sessions in which people were advised how their testimony should be structured and delivered. As a result, although each person's personal story remained unique, the formula of the testimonies was surprisingly homogenous. Individuals would thank God for the opportunity to speak and potentially reconcile with their enemies, then tell their story, before either seeking, or offering, forgiveness for the crimes that had been committed (interview with TRC counsellor, 2014).

As a result of this, two distinct narratives became apparent in the final TRC Report. On the one hand was a narrative that reflected the voices of those who testified – spiritual in tone and reflective of the Christian ideologies on which the idea of a truth commission was initially 'sold' to the Solomon Islands public. On the other, was an official narrative grounded in international legal norms that had seemingly little in common, ideologically, with the first.

Conclusion

Ultimately, neither of these two narratives, grounded in different justice discourses and their related subjectivities, 'touched the heart' of the Solomon Islands people. True resonance seemed to get swallowed in the institutional machinery of the TRC. The counselling process, for example, was described to me as impersonal and dehumanising – 'like a conveyor belt' – as counsellors had such little time with each individual. The spirit of people's individual stories became reduced to cold statistics in the quest for big data to scrutinise for patterns of predefined human rights violations. Merry and Coutin have described human rights reporting with the term 'technologies of truth' claiming that '[a]ssumptions about evidence, categorization, adjudication and measurement privilege certain forms of suffering over others, even as they omit phenomena that defy categorization' (Merry and Coutin 2014, 1). The technology of the TRC as an institutional truth-telling machine generated a particular kind of knowledge, targeted at an international audience fluent in the legal discourse of human rights protections.

To return to the question of vernacularisation, it is possible to argue that the Solomon Islands TRC achieved neither replication nor hybridisation of discourses, but fell somewhere in the middle. Neither the official human rights discourse nor the unofficial theological discourse was 'merely superficial' – each having a level of meaning to a particular audience. However, no substantial attempt was made by TRC staff to address inconsistencies between, or amalgamate, the two discourses. Ultimately, they weave alongside each other, telling two different but interconnected stories throughout the TRC Report.

Bibliography

Akin, David. 2013. *Colonialism, Maasina Rule, and the Origins of Malaitan Kastom*. Honolulu: University of Hawai'i Press. doi.org/10.21313/hawaii/9780824838140.001.0001.

Allen, Matthew, Sinclair Dinnen, Daniel Evans and Rebecca Monson. 2013. *Justice Delivered Locally: Systems, Challenges and Innovations in the Solomon Islands*. Washington DC: The World Bank.

Brady, Anne-Marie, ed. 2010. *Looking North, Looking South: China, Taiwan and South Pacific*. Singapore: World Scientific Publishing. doi.org/10.1142/7718.

Braithwaite, John, Sinclair Dinnen, Matthew Allen, Valerie Braithwaite and Hilary Charlesworth. 2010. *Pillars and Shadows: Statebuilding as Peacebuilding in Solomon Islands*. Canberra: ANU E Press. doi.org/10.22459/PS.11.2010.

Cox, Jon. 2017. 'Kindy and Grassroots Gender Transformations in Solomon Islands'. In *Transformations of Gender in Melanesia*, edited by Martha Macintyre and Ceridwen Spark, 69–94. Canberra: ANU Press. doi.org/10.22459/TGM.02.2017.03.

Cronin, Claire. 2017. 'Subjectivities of Suffering: Human Rights in the Solomon Islands Truth and Reconciliation Commission'. In *Conflict, Justice, and Reconciliation in the Solomon Islands*, edited by Renée Jeffery, 37–62. New York: Palgrave Macmillian. doi.org/10.1057/978-1-137-59695-6_2.

Dinnen, Sinclair and Stewart Firth, eds. 2008. *Politics and State Building in Solomon Islands*. Canberra: ANU E Press. doi.org/10.22459/PSBS.05.2008.

Fraenkel, Jon, Joni Madraiwiwi and Henry Okole. 2014. *The RAMSI Decade: A Review of the Regional Assistance Mission to Solomon Islands, 2003–2013*. Washington DC: East-West Center.

Guthrey, Holly L. 2015. *Victim Healing and Truth Commissions: Transforming Pain Through Voice in Solomon Islands and Timor-Leste*. New York: Springer, Epub. doi.org/10.1007/978-3-319-12487-2.

Hayner, Priscilla B. 2010. *Unspeakable Truths: Transitional Justice and the Challenge of Truth Commissions*. New York: Routledge. doi.org/10.4324/9780203867822.

Jeffery, Renée. 2017. 'The Solomon Islands Truth and Reconciliation Commission Report: Forgiving the Perpetrators, Forgetting the Victims?'. In *Conflict, Justice, and Reconciliation in the Solomon Islands*, edited by Renée Jeffery, 113–139. New York: Palgrave Macmillan. doi.org/10.1057/978-1-137-59695-6_5.

Keesing, Roger. 1982. 'Kastom and Anticolonialism on Malaita: "Culture" as Political Symbol'. *Mankind* 13 (4): 357–373. doi.org/10.1111/j.1835-9310.1982.tb01000.x.

Merry, Sally Engle. 2006. *Human Rights and Gender Violence: Translating International Law into Local Justice*. Chicago: University of Chicago Press. doi.org/10.7208/chicago/9780226520759.001.0001.

Merry, Sally Engle and Susan Bieber Coutin. 2014. 'Technologies of Truth in the Anthropology of Conflict'. *American Ethnologist* 41 (1): 1–16. doi.org/10.1111/amet.12055.

Moyn, Samuel. 2015. *Christianity and Human Rights*. Philadelphia: University of Pennsylvania Press.

Radio Australia. 2009. 'Archbishop Desmond Tutu Says Solomon Islands Can Achieve Reconciliation'. Updated 15 February 2012. www.radioaustralia.net.au/international/radio/onairhighlights/archbishop-desmond-tutu-says-solomon-is-can-achieve-reconciliation (accessed 22 October 2017, site discontinued).

Robertson, Geoffrey. 2012. *Crimes Against Humanity: The Struggle for Global Justice*. New York: Penguin.

Shore, Megan. 2008. 'Christianity and Justice in the South African Truth and Reconciliation Commission: A Case Study in Religious Conflict Resolution'. *Political Theology* 9 (2): 161–178. doi.org/10.1558/poth.v9i2.161.

Skinner, Rob. 2010. *The Foundations of Anti-Apartheid: Liberal Humanitarians and Transnational Activists in Britain and the United States, c.1919–64*. Hampshire, UK: Palgrave Macmillan.

Stritecky, J. M. 2002. 'Looking Through a Moral Lens: Morality, Violence and Empathy in Solomon Islands'. PhD thesis, University of Iowa.

Teitel, Ruti. 2002. *Transitional Justice*. New York: Oxford University Press.

TRC (Truth and Reconciliation Commission). 2012. *Solomon Islands Truth and Reconciliation Commission: Final Report.* Honiara, Solomon Islands: Truth and Reconciliation Commission.

Tutu, Desmond. 2000. *No Future Without Forgiveness.* New York: Image.

Wairiu, Morgan. 2006. 'Governance and Livelihood Realities in Solomon Islands'. In *Globalisation and Governance in the Pacific Islands*, edited by Stewart Firth, 409–416. State, Society and Governance in Melanesia Studies in State and Society in the Pacific, No. 1. Canberra: ANU E Press. doi.org/10.22459/GGPI.12.2006.

Contributors

Volker Boege is an Honorary Research Fellow in the School of Political Science and International Studies at the University of Queensland.

Claire Cronin is a Sessional Lecturer in the Department of International Relations at the Coral Bell School of Asia Pacific Affairs, College of Asia and the Pacific at The Australian National University.

Damian Grenfell is an Associate Professor in the School of Global, Urban and Social Studies at RMIT University.

Rachel Hughes is a Senior Lecturer in Human Geography at the University of Melbourne.

Lia Kent is a Fellow in the School of Regulation and Global Governance (RegNet), College of Asia and the Pacific at The Australian National University.

David Oakeshott is a PhD candidate in the Department of Pacific Affairs, College of Asia and the Pacific at The Australian National University.

Jeudy Oeung is a lawyer working at SNB Law Office in Phnom Penh, Cambodia.

Catherine Renshaw is a Professor in the School of Law at Western Sydney University.

Ken Setiawan is a McKenzie Research Fellow in Asia Institute at the University of Melbourne.

Christoph Sperfeldt is a Senior Research Fellow at the Peter McMullin Centre on Statelessness at the University of Melbourne.

Joanne Wallis is an Associate Professor in the Coral Bell School of Asia Pacific Affairs, College of Asia and the Pacific at The Australian National University.

www.ingramcontent.com/pod-product-compliance
Lightning Source LLC
Chambersburg PA
CBHW050808270326
41926CB00026B/4627